Marx for Today

Edited by

Marcello Musto

AAKAR

Marx for Today
Edited by Marcello Musto

First Published in India 2018
Reprinted 2022

ISBN 978-93-5002-568-0

This book was originally published as a special issue of *Socialism and Democracy* (2010) Vol. 24:3.

Reprinted by permission of Taylor & Francis Ltd. on behalf of The Research Group on Socialism and Democracy for South Asia.

Published by
AAKAR BOOKS
28 E Pocket IV, Mayur Vihar Phase I
Delhi 110 091, India
www.aakarbooks.com

Printed at
Sapra Brothers, Noida

Contents

Preface

Two decades after 1989, when he was too hastily consigned to oblivion, Karl Marx has returned to the limelight. In the last few years he has not only received the attention of intellectuals, but has also been the focus of widespread interest prompted by the international financial crisis, as leading daily and weekly papers throughout the world have been discussing the contemporary relevance of his thought.

In this context of what has been called a 'Marx renaissance,' the present collection has two aims, reflected in corresponding sets of essays. The first is to offer new interpretations of some of Marx's writings, showing his distance from certain dogmatic and economistic Marxisms of the 20th century, and suggesting the usefulness of his theories for analysis and critique of the contemporary world.

The second aim of this publication is to give scholars and political activists a global account of research on Marx during the last decade. Thanks to the rigorous work of ten authoritative international scholars of Marx, whom I thank for having patiently met my guidelines aimed at consistency of presentation, this special issue of *Socialism and Democracy* provides a unique survey of the reception of Marx's work today – from Hispanic America to the Anglophone World and from Europe to Asia – based on the review of about 200 books on Marx; editions of the writings of Marx (and Engels); Marxist journals; university conferences and seminars; and political parties and social movements. What emerges is a fascinating picture of the different ways in which Marx is received, used, criticized, and, in some instances, misinterpreted.

I would like to thank Leo Panitch and George Comninel for the support they gave to the research underpinning this work. My special gratitude goes to Victor Wallis, the managing editor of *Socialism and Democracy*. Victor has participated not only as an author and sometime translator; he has given me valuable suggestions throughout the work; has helped me to revise all the texts; and has been a permanent source of 'militant support' during the eight months in which I've been working on this project. Thanks are due to him both from myself and from all the authors.

Finally, I dedicate this work to my friends Ernst Theodor Mohl and Patrick Camiller, masters of rigor and modesty.

Marcello Musto

Socialism and Democracy, Vol.24, No.3, November 2010, p.iv
ISSN 0885-4300 print/ISSN 1745-2635 online
DOI: 10.1080/08854300.2010.527554

Introduction

Marcello Musto

Returns to Marx

Owing to theoretical disputes or political events, interest in Marx's work has fluctuated over time and has gone through indisputable periods of decline. From the early twentieth century "crisis of Marxism" in Italy and France to the dissolution of the Second International; from debates over the contradictions of Marx's economic theory to the tragedy of Soviet communism, criticism of the ideas of Marx seemed persistently to point beyond the conceptual horizon of Marxism. Yet there has always been a "return to Marx." A new need develops to refer to his work – whether the critique of political economy, the formulations on alienation, or the brilliant pages of political polemic – and it has continued to exercise an irresistible fascination to both followers and opponents. Pronounced dead at the end of the twentieth century, Marx has now suddenly reappeared on the stage of history: there is a rekindling of interest in his thought, and the dust is ever more frequently brushed off his books in the libraries of Europe, America and Asia.

The rediscovery of Marx is based on his continuing capacity to explain the present; indeed, his thought remains an indispensable instrument with which to understand and transform it. In face of the crisis of capitalist society and the profound contradictions that traverse it, this author who was hastily dismissed after 1989 is once more being taken up and interrogated. Thus, Jacques Derrida's assertion that "it will always be a mistake not to read and reread and discuss Marx"[1] – which only a few years ago seemed an isolated provocation – has found increasing approval. Since the late 1990s, newspapers, periodicals and TV or radio programs have repeatedly discussed Marx as being the most relevant thinker for our times. The first article of this kind that had a certain resonance was "The Return of Karl Marx,"

1. Jacques Derrida, *Specters of Marx*, London: Routledge, 1994, 13.

Socialism and Democracy, Vol.24, No.3, November 2010, pp.1–5
ISSN 0885-4300 print/ISSN 1745-2635 online
DOI: 10.1080/08854300.2010.543500

published in *The New Yorker*.[2] Then it was the turn of the BBC, which cited Marx as the greatest thinker of the millennium. A few years later, the weekly *Nouvel Observateur* devoted a whole issue to the theme *Karl Marx – le penseur du troisième millénaire?* (thinker of the third millennium?).[3] Soon after, Germany paid its tribute to the man it once forced into a 40-year exile: in 2004, more than 500,000 viewers of the national television station ZDF voted Marx the third most important German personality of all time (he was first in the category of "contemporary relevance"), and during the national elections of 2005 the mass-circulation magazine *Der Spiegel* carried his image on the cover, giving the victory sign, under the title *Ein Gespenst kehrt zurück* (A spectre is back).[4] Completing this curious collection, a poll conducted in 2005 by the radio station BBC4 gave Marx the accolade of the philosopher most admired by its listeners.

Furthermore, the literature dealing with Marx, which all but dried up 15 years ago, is showing signs of revival in many countries, both in the form of new studies and in booklets in various languages with titles such as *Why Read Marx Today?*[5] Journals are increasingly open to contributions on Marx and Marxism, just as there are now many international conferences, university courses and seminars on the theme. Finally, although timid and often confused in form, a new demand for Marx is also making itself felt in politics – from Latin America to Europe, passing through the alternative globalization movement. In particular, since the onset of the international economic crisis in mid-2007, academics and economic theorists from various political and cultural backgrounds have again been drawn to Marx's analysis of the inherent instability of capitalism, whose self-generated cyclical crises have grave effects on political and social life. In all parts of the world leading daily and weekly papers have been discussing the contemporary relevance of Marx's thought.

In this context of what some commentators have described as a "Marx renaissance," the aim of the present special issue of *Socialism and Democracy* is to make a close study of Marx's principal writings

---

2. John Cassidy, "The Return of Karl Marx," *The New Yorker*, October 20/27 1997, 248–59.
3. *Le Nouvel Observateur*, October/November 2003.
4. *Der Spiegel*, 22 August 2005.
5. One of the most significant examples of this new interest in Marx's writings is the continuation of the *Marx-Engels-Gesamtausgabe* (MEGA^2), the historico-critical edition of his complete works, which resumed in 1998 after the interruption that followed the collapse of the socialist countries. See Marcello Musto, "The rediscovery of Karl Marx," *International Review of Social History*, 2007, no. 52/3, 477–98.

in relation to some of the major problems of our own time, and to show how and why some of his theories constitute a precious tool for the understanding and critique of the twenty-first century world.

Marx and the analysis of contemporary capitalism

Of course, the writings that Marx composed a century and a half ago do not contain a precise description of the world today. It should be stressed, however, that the focus of *Capital* was not on nineteenth century capitalism either, but rather – as he put it in the third volume of this work, his *magnum opus* – on the "organization of the capitalist mode of production, in its ideal average," and hence in its most complete and most general form. When he was writing *Capital*, capitalism had developed only in England and a few other European industrial centres. Yet he foresaw that it would expand on a global scale, and formulated his theories on that basis. This is why *Capital* is not only a great classic of economic and political thought, but still provides today – despite all the profound transformations that have intervened – a rich array of tools with which to understand the nature of capitalist development.

The truth of this has been all the more apparent since the collapse of the Soviet Union and the spread of the capitalist mode of production to new areas of the planet like China. Capitalism has become a truly worldwide system, and some of Marx's analyses – not others, of course, which gave rise to mistaken predictions – have revealed their significance even more clearly than in his own time.[6] As this geographical expansion has taken place, the internal contradictions of capitalism have asserted themselves with greater stringency. Marx has probed the logic of the system more deeply than any other modern political thinker. If his analysis is updated and applied to the most recent developments, it can help explain many problems that did not manifest themselves fully until the twentieth century. One thinks, for instance, of the role of finance in capitalist accumulation – a widely debated issue today, which Marx already made the object of a penetrating analysis.

Themes and objectives of this issue

Despite the new interest in Marx, few recent studies of his ideas have gone beyond generic formulas – such as "Marx, the prophet of

6. See Ellen Meiksins Wood, *Democracy Against Capitalism*, London: Cambridge University Press, 1995.

capitalist globalization" – to discuss in a theoretically effective, textually rigorous manner the ways in which a rereading of his work can help to explain the political, economic and social phenomena of today. The present collection attempts to address this task, without adopting an apologetic approach to Marx's work or indeed neglecting to demonstrate some of its contradictions. The aim is to bring together varied reflections on the Marxian *oeuvre*, drawing on different perspectives and fields.

Marx's analysis of capitalism was not merely an economic investigation but was also relevant to the understanding of power structures and social relations. With the extension of capitalism into most aspects of human life, Marx's thought turns out to have been extraordinarily prescient in many fields not addressed by twentieth century orthodox Marxism. One of these is certainly the transformations brought about by so-called economic globalization; others that we address in this collection encompass the full complexity of present-day politics, including issues of ethnicity, nationalism, freedom and democracy. In each dimension, we see how Marx even today has an invaluable contribution to make. The essays in the second part of this collection show how these varying insights have emerged in a wide range of national settings.

Why Marx again?

After years of postmodern manifestos, solemn talk of the "end of history" and infatuation with vacuous "biopolitical" ideas, the value of Marx's theories is again becoming more and more widely recognized.

What remains of Marx today? How useful is his thought to the workers' struggle for freedom? What part of his work is most fertile for stimulating the critique of our times? These are some of the questions that receive widely varying answers. If the contemporary Marx renaissance has a certainty, it lies in a rejection of the orthodoxies that have dominated and profoundly conditioned the interpretation of this philosopher. Even though marked by evident limits and the risk of syncretism, a period has arrived that is characterized by many theoretical incarnations of Marx. After the age of dogmatisms, perhaps it could not have happened in any other way. The task of responding to this new situation is therefore up to the research, theoretical and practical, of an emerging generation of scholars and political activists.

Among the "Marxes" that remain indispensable, at least two can be identified. One is the critic of the capitalist mode of production: the tireless researcher who intuited and analysed this development on a global scale and described bourgeois society better than anyone else. This is the thinker who refused to conceive of capitalism and the regime of private property as immutable scenarios intrinsic to human nature and who still offers crucial suggestions to those who want to realize alternatives to capitalism. The other Marx to whom great attention should be paid, is the theoretician of socialism: the author who repudiated the idea of state socialism, already propagated in his time by Lassalle and Rodbertus; the thinker who understood socialism as the possible complete transformation of productive and social relations, and not as a set of bland palliatives for the problems of capitalist society.

Without Marx we will be condemned to a critical aphasia. The cause of human emancipation will therefore continue to need him. His "spectre" is destined to haunt the world and shake humanity for a good while to come.

Not Just Capital and Class: Marx on Non-Western Societies, Nationalism and Ethnicity

Kevin B. Anderson

Despite the revival of interest in Marx since the economic crisis hit, some important ideological and conceptual barriers continue to block what would be a very positive step, returning to Marx as the primary source of leftist critique of capitalist modernity as a whole, and as providing the theoretical ground for its overcoming [*Aufhebung*].

In recent decades, Marx's critics have fallen into two large groups, sometimes overlapping of course. In neoliberal ideology, Marx is considered a dead dog because he tried to take us beyond capitalism, to which there is supposedly no alternative. Along similar lines, it is also claimed the Soviet collapse invalidates empirically Marx's allegedly impractical and utopian schemes.

In left and progressive academic circles, however, the critique of Marx has usually taken a different direction. In these quarters it is often said that the problem with Marx is not that he was too radical, as the neoliberals say, but that he was not radical enough. Some add that the truly radical thinkers are people like Foucault, Deleuze, even Nietzsche. These critics – most famously Edward Said – attack Marx for adopting what they see as a unilinear model of development in the modernist mode. (Postmodernists term this a "grand narrative".) Here, much of the debate has revolved around Marx's 1853 articles on India and a passage in the *Communist Manifesto* (1848) on China. At a more general level, it is said even more often among progressives that Marx informs us on class and economic structures but that his theoretical model does not incorporate race, ethnicity, gender, or nationalism at all, or at least not very much.

I think responding to these critiques – especially the ones from the progressive left – is as important as the earlier effort to separate Marx's original vision from Stalinism and totalitarianism, an effort that still remains necessary today. That link of Marx to Stalinism – although

Socialism and Democracy, Vol.24, No.3, November 2010, pp.7–22
ISSN 0885-4300 print/ISSN 1745-2635 online
DOI: 10.1080/08854300.2010.513606

in my view invalid – is part of what has fostered the growth of anarchism among so many younger radicals today.

In this article, I will respond to the kinds of criticisms of Marx that have been coming from parts of the progressive left and which center on charges of unilinearism and grand narrative, ethnocentrism, and lack of concern with race, ethnicity, gender, and nationalism.[1] At the outset, it should be noted that Marx himself lived at the margins, where his thought is still relegated to this day. The deconstructionist philosopher Jacques Derrida captures well Marx's marginality as a political refugee in Victorian London, linking it to his equally marginal position within the Western intellectual tradition: "Marx remains an immigrant among us, a glorious, sacred, accursed but still clandestine immigrant as he was all his life" (1994: 174).

I. The non-Western "other": India, China, Russia

Some of Marx's critics have a point in terms of his early writings on India and China. Marx begins with a somewhat modernist and unilinear perspective toward those countries, but moves gradually toward a more multilinear and multicultural approach toward India and other non-Western societies.

As noted by Edward Said in his *Orientalism* (1978) and by other critics, Marx's 1848–53 writings on India and China exhibit Orientalist notions of modernity, occasionally accompanied by ethnocentric ones, in which European colonialism is portrayed as a necessary stage on the road toward social development for societies trapped in an unchanging traditionalism. He begins to alter this perspective in the late 1850s, particularly in the *Grundrisse* and in his writings on anti-colonial resistance in India and China. By the time of his late writings of 1879–82 (some of which are still unpublished), Marx has moved toward a more anti-colonialist position and a more multilinear approach to social development in which certain premodern social forms, especially communal property, are seen as building blocks for an alternative, socialist form of modernity. Let us trace some of this evolution in his thought.

In the *Communist Manifesto,* Marx and Engels write famously in praise of Western capital's penetration of Asia, of its "battering down of all Chinese walls" and of its drawing "even the most barbarian nations into civilization" (MECW 6: 488). Here they seem (1) to view

1. For reasons of space, I have largely eschewed references to the wide-ranging commentaries on Marx on the issues under discussion here. These and other related issues are discussed in my *Marx at the Margins* (2010).

Western colonial incursions into Asia, including England's notorious First Opium War against China of 1839–42, as on the whole a progressive and beneficial undermining of Oriental "barbarism" and (2) to assume that the rest of the world would sooner or later follow in the footsteps of the more technologically advanced Western European nations. Marx and Engels' praise for this early stage of capitalist globalization can be seen as part of their overall sketch (in the *Communist Manifesto*) of the achievements of capitalism in Western Europe and North America, a sketch that is followed by a withering critique of capitalist exploitation. However, they do not follow their praise of Western colonialism in Asia with a similar critique. Instead, Marx held in 1848 to an implicitly unilinear model of development in which India and China would, as they were swept more deeply into the world capitalist system, over time develop similar contradictions to those of the already industrializing countries of Western Europe and North America.

These themes are developed further in Marx's 1853 writings on India for the *New York Tribune*. It is true that in one passage Marx evokes notions of an independent India shaking off the chains of British colonialism (MECW 12: 221), something not mentioned by Said. But it should be noted that even in his evocation of an independent India, he implies that this is to be an India that has first modernized along Western European lines.

Moreover, Marx's portrait of Indian culture and society in 1853 is often condescending. Here following Hegel, he describes India as a static society that lacks any real historical development, except that introduced by its conquerors, from the Arabs and the Mughals to the British (MECW 12: 217). The British represent a "superior" civilization, he concludes (218). In the face of these conquerors over the centuries, he writes, India proved to be "an unresisting and unchanging society" (217). The roots of this are said to lie in India's economically self-contained villages, which stifled individual development and social progress. In fact, Marx portrays the communal structures of these villages, which he erroneously sees as precluding the development of private property in land, as "the solid foundation of Oriental despotism" (MECW 12: 132). While he also begins to attack the "barbarism" of British colonialism, he still views that colonialism, in a rather unilinear fashion, as bringing about necessary if painful progress through modernization (MECW 12: 221).

Four years later, Marx begins to shift his position on India. In 1857, the anti-British Sepoy Uprising broke out, which led to two years of conflict in which the British almost lost control of the Indian subcontinent. Marx enthusiastically supports the uprising, noting in dialectical fashion that the rebellious this time sepoy troops (British-trained Indian soldiers) were themselves a product of British colonialism: "There is something in human history like retribution; and it is a rule of historical retribution that its instrument be forged not by the offended, but by the offender himself" (MECW 15: 353). For the next two years, also in the *New York Tribune*, he and Engels describe the Sepoy Uprising and its brutal suppression by the British. Contrasting the uprising in India to the relative quiescence of European labor at that time, Marx declares tellingly in an 1858 letter to Engels: "India is now our best ally" (MECW 40: 249). By this time, he has assumed a more anti-colonialist position.

By the late 1850s, Marx also shifts his attitude toward China, now strongly supporting the Chinese during the Second Opium War (1856–60). Referring to the shelling of Canton [Guangzhou] harbor, he writes:

> The unoffending citizens and peaceful tradesmen of Canton have been slaughtered, their habitations battered to the ground, and the claims of humanity violated, on the flimsy pretence that "English life and property are endangered by the aggressive acts of the Chinese!" ...These sweeping assertions are baseless. The Chinese have at least ninety-nine injuries to complain of to one on the part of the English. (MECW 15: 234)

As with India, Marx has moved toward a more anti-colonialist position.

In 1857–59, during the period of these events in India and China, Marx also elaborates a multilinear theory of history in the *Grundrisse* and the *Contribution to a Critique of Political Economy*. This constituted a revision of his earlier conceptualization of three successive modes of production: (1) the Greco-Roman slave-based "ancient" mode of production, (2) the medieval European serf-based "feudal" mode of production, and (3) the modern "bourgeois" mode of production, based on formally free wage labor. Referring mainly to India, Marx inserts alongside this Europe-based model an "Asiatic" mode of production, suggesting that pre-capitalist Asian societies had been on a different historical trajectory. Moreover, although the "Asiatic" mode of production was said to be based on a rather static form of communal property, Marx now no longer saw it as necessarily despotic, referring also to "democratic" forms of communal governance in pre-colonial societies (1973: 473).[2]

2. Although this was a multilinear theory of history, it did not directly address contemporary societies like India and China under the impact of capitalism and colonialism.

Marx picks up and develops these multilinear threads of argument in new ways during his last decade, 1872–83. Three strands of his late writings are important here. The first of these strands is found in the changes he introduced into the 1872–75 French edition of *Capital*. I confine myself here to one passage that bears on the issue of multilinearism and which cannot be found in standard English or German editions, this one from the section on primitive accumulation, where he discussed the origin of capitalism in the expropriation of the peasantry. In the standard English and German editions, Marx writes: "The expropriation of the agricultural producer, of the peasant, from the soil, is the basis of the whole process.... *Only in England, which we therefore take as our example, has it the classic form*" (Marx 1976: 876; emphasis added). However, in the later French edition, this passage reads: "But the basis of this whole development is the expropriation of the peasants. *So far, it has been carried out in a radical manner only in England.... But all the countries of Western Europe are going through the same development*" (Marx 1963: 1170–71; emphasis added). Here, he left room for an alternative development for societies outside Western Europe, including India, China, and Russia.[3]

The second strand in Marx's late writings on non-Western and precapitalist societies concerns Russia. In several texts, Marx examined anew the issue of whether Russia and the other agrarian empires of Asia were inevitably destined to modernize in the Western capitalist manner. In an 1877 letter responding to a discussion of *Capital* by the Russian writer N.K. Mikhailovsky, Marx defended himself from the charge of unilinearism, in part by citing the French edition of *Capital*. He denied strongly that he had developed "a historico-philosophical theory of the general course fatally imposed on all peoples" (Shanin 1983: 136). In his well-known 1881 letter to the Russian revolutionary Vera Zasulich, the topic was again whether Russia was destined to be swept into the pathway of capitalist development that was already taking place in Western Europe. Again, he concluded that alternate pathways of development might be possible. He based his judgment in large part upon the marked differences between the social structure of the Russian village, with its communal property, and the village under Western European feudalism's somewhat more

3. Few editions of *Capital* – and none in English – take these textual variants seriously. One exception is the recent Persian translation, which carries the alternate texts from the French edition as marginal notes (Marx 2008). Primary translator Hassan Mortazavi's introduction is available in English: http://iranianvoicesintranslation.blogspot.com/2009/07/translators-preface-to-new-persian.html

individualized property relations. He added that his recent studies of Russian society "convinced me that the commune is the fulcrum for a social regeneration in Russia" (Shanin 1983: 124). In his far lengthier drafts for the letter to Zasulich, Marx indicated that versions of the communal social relations he was discussing in Russia could also be found in other non-Western societies such as India, but were not common in pre-capitalist Western Europe. In the 1882 preface to the Russian edition of the *Communist Manifesto,* Marx and Engels suggested that these communal social formations in Russia could form the starting point for a communist revolution, if they could link up with the revolutionary labor movement in the Western capitalist lands.

The third strand in Marx's late writings on non-Western societies lies in his 1879–82 notebooks on colonialism, indigenous communal property, and gender in India, Indonesia, Algeria, Latin America, Egypt, and other non-Western and pre-capitalist societies, some of which have yet to be published but which I am helping to edit for the *Marx-Engels Gesamtausgabe* [Complete Writings or MEGA]. Marx took extensive notes on the young Russian anthropologist Maxim Kovalevsky's *Communal Landownership*, published in Russian in 1879, most of which is devoted to India. He also annotated the young British historian Robert Sewell's *Analytical History of India* (1870). Marx's notes on the Indian subcontinent from this period comprise nearly 90,000 words.

In his 1879 notes on Kovalevsky (Marx in Krader 1975: 343–412), Marx examines social relations, especially in terms of changes in the forms of communal property, across the entirety of Indian history, from (1) the period before the Muslim conquests, to (2) that of Muslim domination, and (3) that of British colonialism. Marx closely follows Kovalevsky's historical typology of communal forms in rural India, which consisted of several stages, moving from clan or kin-based communities to village communities not organized around kinship that periodically re-divided the common land on an equal basis. Marx also writes of social antagonisms, especially within the non-kinship based rural commune. Given this focus on broad changes in India's communal forms, it would appear that pre-colonial India was for Marx no longer an "unchanging" society without any real history, as in 1853. The second part of Marx's notes on Kovalevsky on India, which deals with the impact of Muslim rule on these earlier social relationships, calls forth a strong attack on the notion that pre-colonial India was feudal: Not only was he keeping away from such unilinear notions, as he had in the *Grundrisse* two decades earlier, but he was also explicitly attacking those like Kovalevsky who maintained the "feudal" interpretation.

On the other hand, Kovalevsky shared much of Marx's hostility to colonialism, which became clear in the third section of Marx's notes on Kovalevsky on India, where Marx focused on the rise of British colonial domination, up through the 1857–58 Sepoy Uprising. Marx strenuously attacks the "scoundrel" Cornwallis's "permanent settlement" of 1793, which created capitalist-style landed property in Indian villages, at tremendous cost to the peasants (Marx in Krader 1975: 385). Calling the British colonialists "dogs," "asses," "oxen," "blockheads," and the like, Marx alludes to a "general hatred of the English government" (390–92, passim). Marx also celebrates the Sepoy Uprising once again. Finally, here following Kovalevsky's data, Marx discerns the continuation of communal forms in the villages, underneath the more atomized capitalist structures introduced by the British: "Nevertheless *between these atoms certain connections continue to exist,* distantly reminiscent of the earlier communal village landowning groups" (388; emphasis in original). This suggests a link between Marx's notes on India and his late writings on Russia, discussed above. If these communal relationships endured in India, might they not also, as in Russia, serve as points of resistance to capital? Marx answers this implicit query by indicating that it was not so much the preservation of these forms as their forceful dissolution in the name of "economic progress" that could unleash new social forces dangerous to British rule. The older communal forms may not have been revolutionary in and of themselves, but they could become a "danger" to the social order as they collided with capitalist modernity (394).

Marx supplements these anthropological studies with one on Indian political and military history in his notes on Sewell's *Analytical History of India.* If the Kovalevsky notes suggest that Marx no longer saw India as a society without a history, those on Sewell suggest that a second problematic feature of the 1853 India writings was falling aside: the notion that India had responded passively to outside conquest. Again and again, Marx's notes emphasize the contingent character of the Muslim and British conquests, rather than, as in 1853, the ineluctable march of large historical forces. At every stage, he now highlights indigenous Indian resistance to foreign conquest. For example, Marx records passages such as the following from Sewell, emphasizing how in 1704 the Hindu Maratha forces - based near present-day Mumbai (Bombay) - had put Mughal Emperor Aurangzeb on the defensive, this before the British had gained much of a foothold in India:

> 1704.... In the last four years of his life whole government disorganized; *Marathas* began to recover their forts and gather strength; a terrible famine exhausted the provisions for troops and drained the treasury; soldiers mutinous over want of pay; hard pressed by the Marathas [Mughal Emperor] *Aurangzeb* retreated in great confusion *to Ahmadnagar*. (Marx 1960: 43; emphasis in original; see also Sewell 1870: 66)

In another reference to the Marathas, Marx uses the word "clan ancestor [*Stammvater*]" in describing the Maratha leadership, thus highlighting the notion that the Marathas, who formed the most important locus of Indian resistance to both the Mughals and the British, were organized on a clan basis. None of the above is meant to suggest that Marx's notes on India are anti-Muslim, for on numerous occasions, he notes the considerable contributions of Muslims to Indian culture and society. At one point, he writes that Mughal Emperor Akbar "made *Delhi* into the greatest and finest city then existing in the world" (Marx 1960: 33; emphasis in original). Marx portrays Akbar in a relatively secular light, characterizing him as "indifferent in religious matters, therefore tolerant" (32).

Marx devotes the bulk of the notes on Sewell to the period of British ascendancy, where he stresses the contingent character of Britain's conquests, and the many instances in which its power in India hung by a thread. He frequently terms the British "blockheads" or "dogs," whom he sometimes describes as terribly frightened in the face of Indian resistance. Throughout these notes, Marx shows a pronounced sympathy for the Marathas, while occasionally expressing disdain for their warlordism. The notes on Sewell suggest that Marx's sympathy for the Sepoy Uprising had only increased since his *New York Tribune* articles on these same events during the late 1850s.

II. Race, ethnicity, and nationalism: Poland, the US, and Ireland

In another set of writings spanning four decades, Marx examined the relationship of race, ethnicity, and nationalism to revolution, particularly in Poland, the US during the Civil War, and Ireland. These writings belie the notion that Marx's conceptualization of capitalist modernity constitutes a "totalizing" grand narrative under which the particulars of race, ethnicity, and nation are subsumed.

Marx and Engels were always concerned with Polish national liberation, a cause warmly adopted by most of their generation of revolutionaries, who were outraged at the eighteenth-century partition of Poland by Russia, Prussia, and Austria, and who stood for Poland's restoration as an independent nation. In the programmatic conclusion to the *Communist*

Manifesto (1848), Marx and Engels specifically supported the left wing of the Polish national movement: "In Poland [the communists] support the party that insists on an agrarian revolution as the prime condition for national emancipation, that party which fomented the insurrection in Cracow in 1846" (MECW 6: 518). In February 1848, when revolution broke out in France once again, "Vive la Pologne" was a prominent slogan of the revolutionary movement, which saw Tsarist Russia as the most reactionary force in European politics, and Poland as a key ally.

Eight years later, in a letter to Engels of December 2, 1856, Marx calls support for Poland the "'external' thermometer" by which one could measure "the intensity and viability of all revolutions since 1789." He adds: "This is demonstrable in detail from French history. It is conspicuous in our brief German revolutionary period, likewise in the Hungarian" (MECW 40: 85). Marx considered Poland to be a major positive factor in the international revolutionary movement, as seen in an 1875 speech, where he stressed the "cosmopolitan" character of Polish revolutionaries, by now including a reference to the Paris Commune. The Poles, he declared, are

> the only European people that has fought and is fighting as the *cosmopolitan soldier of the revolution*. Poland shed its blood during the American War of Independence; its legions fought under the banner of the first French Republic; by its revolution of 1830 it prevented the invasion of France that had been decided by the partitioners of Poland; in 1846 in Cracow it was the first in Europe to plant the banner of social revolution; in 1848 it played an outstanding part in the revolutionary struggle in Hungary, Germany, and Italy; finally, in 1871 it supplied the Paris Commune with its best generals and most heroic soldiers. (MECW 24: 57–58; emphasis in original)

The above passages suggest that support for Poland was one of the political passions of Marx's life.

Poland was also a major factor in the establishment of the First International in 1864. European labor networks supporting the 1863 Polish uprising against Russian occupation often intersected with those defending the US against the threat of a British intervention on the side of the South during the Civil War. Marx summed this up in a letter to a family member of November 29, 1864 recounting the founding of the International:

> In September the Parisian workers sent a delegation to the London workers to demonstrate support for Poland. On that occasion, an international Workers' Committee was formed. The matter is not without importance because... in London the same people... by their monster meeting... *prevented war with the United States*. (MECW 42: 47; emphasis in original)

Despite this, debates over Poland soon broke out in the First International between Marx and the Proudhonists – a minority tendency in the socialist movement that sided with Russia and that opposed taking up Polish national emancipation inside the working class and socialist movement.

Marx's discussions of Poland inside the International also addressed larger issues concerning the relationship of national liberation to social revolution. He argued that in three key periods – the French Revolution of 1789–94, the Napoleonic era, and the Revolution of 1830 – France had betrayed Poland. This was connected to a broader point, one aimed at future revolutionary movements in Europe. He argued that in betraying Poland, the French revolutionaries constricted or even destroyed themselves, leading to defeat by external enemies or to a too limited revolution at home, one that did not really uproot the old system. In short, he was suggesting that unless democratic and class struggles could link up with those of oppressed nationalities, both would fail to realize fully their aims, if not go down to defeat.

Marx's writings on Poland are little known today, in no small part because the Stalinist apparatus never produced popular editions of these writings, as they did with those on the US Civil War and on Ireland.

Although widely available in English through the collection *The Civil War in the United States* (Marx and Engels 1937),[4] Marx's Civil War writings have not received much discussion recently, despite his treatment in them of a hotly debated topic, the intersections of class and race. On the one hand, earlier Marxist thinkers like W.E.B. Du Bois, C.L.R. James, and Raya Dunayevskaya stressed these writings' originality and their pertinence in intertwining the issues of race and class in American society. On the other hand, some like the erstwhile Marxist historian Eugene Genovese chided "the retreat of Marx, Engels, and too many Marxists into liberalism" when it came to the Civil War (1971: 327). In Genovese's view, Marx's "burning hatred of slavery and commitment to the Union cause interfered with his judgment" (1971: 321). In short, the Civil War writings did not conform to Genovese's reductionist notions of Marxism and therefore were not Marxist!

Looking at these writings directly, one finds a wealth of insights into the dialectics of race and class. As early as a letter of December

4. See also the non-Marxist Saul Padover's collection, often translated with greater fluidity (Marx 1972).

28, 1846, Marx writes of the intimate connection between slavery and capitalism:

> Direct slavery is as much the pivot upon which our present-day industrialism turns as are machinery, credit, etc. Without slavery there would be no cotton, without cotton there would be no modern industry. It is slavery which has given value to the colonies, it is the colonies which have created world trade, and world trade is the necessary condition for large-scale machine industry.... Slavery is therefore an economic category of paramount importance. (MECW 38: 101–2)

Marx also saw African Americans as important revolutionary subjects. On January 11, 1860, in the aftermath of John Brown's raid on Harper's Ferry, he writes to Engels concerning this and the emancipation of the Russian serfs:

> In my view, the most momentous thing happening in the world today is, on the one hand, the movement among the slaves in America, started by the death of Brown, and the movement among the slaves in Russia, on the other.... I have just seen in the *Tribune* that there was a new slave uprising in Missouri, naturally suppressed. But the signal has now been given. (MECW 41: 4)[5]

The following year, he begins to cover the US Civil War, which he sees as carrying the potential of a continuation of these slave insurrections.

Overall, Marx held to the view that poor and working-class whites had their class consciousness distorted by slavery and racism. After the war ended, Marx argued that the abolition of slavery had destroyed a major barrier to the development of class consciousness within the US working class, reporting in *Capital*, Vol. I:

> In the United States of America, every independent workers' movement was paralyzed as long as slavery disfigured a part of the republic. Labor in a white skin cannot emancipate itself where it is branded in a black skin. However, a new life immediately arose from the death of slavery. (1976: 414)

Less known is the September 1865 Address of the First International to the notoriously racist President Andrew Johnson, which contained this prescient warning: "Let your citizens of to-day be declared free and equal, without reserve. If you fail to give them citizens' rights, while you demand citizens' duties, there will yet remain a struggle for the future which may again stain your country with your people's blood" (*General Council of the First International. Minutes. 1864-1866*: 311–12).

---

5. Although I refer to the standard edition of this letter in MECW, I have altered the translation after consulting the German original. I will do so occasionally below with respect to texts originally written in German or French.

Inside Britain, a fierce debate raged during the early years of the Civil War, 1861–62, over whether to side with the South in the name of "freedom of the seas" in response to the Union blockade of southern ports. Sometimes the issue was posed less ideologically and more openly as the need to maintain a supply of cheap cotton for British capital. In 1861–62, the British establishment also charged that the war was not really about slavery, noting that Lincoln had not yet proclaimed abolition as a goal. In response, Marx noted repeatedly that the South had made slavery into a core principle of its constitution.

As Marx reported at great length, large meetings organized by British workers passionately opposed intervention, siding with the North despite the enormous economic hardships inflicted upon them by the layoffs resulting from curtailment of the cotton trade. Such sentiments were echoed throughout Western Europe because, he wrote, the emergent working class saw the US as the most democratic society of the time, virtually the only country where even white male workers enjoyed full suffrage:

> The true people of England, of France, of Germany, of Europe, consider the cause of the United States as their own cause, as the cause of liberty, and ... despite all paid sophistry, they consider the soil of the United States as the free soil of the landless millions of Europe, as their land of promise,[6] now to be defended sword in hand, from the sordid grasp of the slaveholder.... In this contest the highest form of popular self-government till now realized is giving battle to the meanest and most shameless form of man's enslaving recorded in the annals of history. (MECW 19: 29–30)

In evoking this as a key example of proletarian internationalism, Marx at the same time strongly criticized Lincoln for his slowness to act against slavery and his early failure to allow Black troops to fight in the war.[7] At the same time, Marx disagreed with those on the left who saw no real difference between a capitalist North with its exploitation of labor and the slave plantations of the South.

As with their writings on the Civil War, the writings of Marx and Engels on Ireland have long been easily available through the volume

6. Elsewhere, especially in *Capital*, he lashed out against the brutal massacre of the indigenous population by the American colonists, an issue not addressed here.
7. In a letter to Engels of August 7, 1862 that was marred by the use of the n-word (in English in the midst of a German sentence), Marx hit out strongly on this point: "A single nigger-regiment would have a remarkable effect on Southern nerves" (MECW 41: 400). This is an instance of Marx using a racist phrase to make an anti-racist point. This use of the n-word was revealed to readers of English in Padover's edition (Marx 1972) and was subsequently included in MECW; it had been rendered as "Negro" in Marx and Engels (1937).

Ireland and the Irish Question, published in 1972 as a successor to previous less comprehensive editions. As early as *The Condition of the Working Class in England* (1845) (MECW 4), Engels singled out the special oppression of Irish immigrant labor in Britain.

During the 1850s, Marx wrote occasionally on Ireland, but it was soon after the founding of the International that the rise of the insurrectionary Fenian movement brought the issue of Ireland to the fore. In a letter to Engels of December 10, 1869, Marx wrote famously that he had changed his position on Ireland, revising his earlier view that British labor would form the vanguard of social revolution in Britain and Ireland:

> For a long time, I believed it would be possible to overthrow the Irish regime by English working class ascendancy.... Deeper study has now convinced me of the opposite. The English working class will never accomplish anything before it has got rid of Ireland. The lever must be applied in Ireland. This is why the Irish question is so important for the social movement in general. (MECW 43: 398)

Here, Marx's reversal of his earlier positions is made quite explicit, but as I have been arguing, a similar evolution of his thinking was taking place concerning India and other non-Western societies.

During this period, he had been immersing himself in Irish history, writing voluminous notes on Irish-British relations, on the Irish peasantry, and on prehistoric Irish society and its communal social forms. These notebooks will eventually be published in the MEGA. An indication of their content with respect to early Irish communal social forms can be found in a letter to Engels of May 11, 1870, where Marx quoted the German historian Ernst Wachsmuth:

> The community of goods was accompanied by Celtic laxity in the marriage tie, already known in antiquity, at the same time, however, [as] *voting rights for women in the tribal assembly*.... The first chapter of the book on common law deals with women: "If his wife lay with another man and *he beats her*, he sacrifices his claim to indemnification.... *Sufficient grounds for divorce for a wife were* the man's impotence, scabies, and bad breath." (MECW 43: 515; emphasis in original)

Marx adds humorously: "Such gallant youngsters, these Celts!" (MECW 43: 516).

Marx's writings on Ireland, especially those around 1870, constitute his most theoretically developed discussion of the interweaving of class with nationalism, race, and ethnicity – a discussion that began with his writings on Poland and on the American Civil War. Inside the International, Ireland was also a major reason behind his break with the anarchist Mikhail Bakunin, who did not want the International to get involved in non-class issues like defense of Irish political prisoners. For his part, Marx thought that this issue was intimately connected to the class struggle in Britain. All of this led him to some important theoretical reflections.

Marx now saw the Irish independence struggle as deeply linked to the struggles of British workers against capital, as he wrote in a letter of November 29, 1869 to the German socialist Ludwig Kugelmann: "I have become more and more convinced - and the thing now is to drum this conviction into the English working class - that they will never do anything decisive here in England before they separate their attitude towards Ireland quite definitely from that of the ruling classes, and... make common cause with the Irish.... Every movement in England itself is crippled by the dissension with the Irish, who form a very important section of the working class in England itself" (MECW 43: 390).

Marx returned to these issues in the "Confidential Communication" of March 1870, a statement against Bakunin he drafted on behalf of the General Council of the International. English working-class consciousness, he wrote, was attenuated by anti-Irish prejudice, in a dynamic similar to that of white racism in the US: "The common English worker hates the Irish worker as a competitor who lowers wages and the *standard of life*.... He views him similarly to how the poor whites of the Southern states of North America viewed black slaves. This antagonism among the proletarians of England is artificially nourished and kept up by the bourgeoisie. It knows that this split is the true secret of the preservation of its power" (MECW 21: 120; emphasis in original).

Moreover, the Irish independence struggle could be, he wrote in this polemic with Bakunin, the "lever" that could pry apart British and thus global capitalism as part of an international revolutionary struggle:

> Although revolutionary initiative will probably come from France, England alone can serve as the lever for a serious economic Revolution.... It is the only country where *the capitalist form*, that is to say, combined labor on a large scale under the authority of capitalists, has seized hold of almost the whole of production.... The English have all the *material* conditions for social revolution. What they lack is *a sense of generalization and revolutionary passion*. It is only the General Council [of the International] that can provide them with this, that can thus accelerate the truly revolutionary movement in this country, and consequently *everywhere*.... If England is the bulwark of landlordism and European capitalism, the only point where official England can be struck a great blow *is Ireland*. (MECW 21: 118–19; emphasis in original)

The above referred to Ireland's peasantry, whose opposition to the system was enhanced by a national factor, that the landlord class in Ireland was to a great extent British, not Irish. Ireland was also where the landed aristocracy, part of the British ruling class alongside the industrial capitalists, had important holdings.

III. Implications for today

I have argued that Marx's critique of capital was far broader than is usually supposed. To be sure, he concentrated on the labor-capital relation within Western Europe and North America. But at the same time, he expended considerable time and energy on the analysis of non-Western societies, as well as on race, ethnicity, and nationalism in Western Europe and North America. These are problems of our time and it behooves us to stop attacking Marx for allegedly ignoring them. Moreover, it also behooves us to see what we can learn from the ways in which Marx never separated these questions from the critique of capital and at the same time, took each of them seriously as social factors.

Let me conclude with a few general comments on how the writings under consideration here illuminate more general issues in Marx's work. One could say that he began with a somewhat one-sided appreciation of capitalist modernity, of its progressiveness. His writings on non-Western societies, particularly India and China, help us to problematize this aspect of his work. At the same time, these writings help us to discern a larger issue, his growing hostility to capitalist modernity, as he moved from the fulsome praise of capitalist modernity in the opening pages of the *Communist Manifesto,* to an appreciation in the *Grundrisse* of capital's role in building up the productive forces of society, to the much harsher critique of modernity elaborated in *Capital*. This is especially true of the discussion of commodity fetishism in *Capital,* where human relations are seen as relations between things because that is "what they really are" under capitalism (Marx 1976: 166). It is also true of the chapter on machinery, where he argues that the most modern forms of technology (as of the 1870s) only served to deepen the exploitation and alienation of the worker.

Several more specific implications for today of Marx's writings discussed here should also be considered: (1) Marx's general dialectic is not one of abstract universalism but has plenty of room for the specificities of nation, ethnicity, and race, issues on which he makes important and original contributions. (2) Especially in his later writings, Marx theorizes indigenous forms of resistance to capital and their need to connect to the working classes of more technologically developed sectors (and vice versa). The persistence of these issues can be seen most prominently in parts of Latin America today. (3) Marx's theorization of race, ethnicity and nationalism in relation to class and to revolution remains very relevant today, as seen in the struggles inside the urban ghettoes and prisons of the US and Western Europe.

References

Anderson, Kevin B. 2010. *Marx at the Margins: On Nationalism, Ethnicity, and Non-Western Societies*. Chicago: University of Chicago Press.

Derrida, Jacques. 1994. *Specters of Marx*, Trans. Peggy Kamuf. New York: Routledge.

General Council of the First International. Minutes. 1864-1866. 1962. Moscow: Progress Publishers.

Genovese, Eugene. 1971 [1968]. "Marxian Interpretations of the Slave South." In *In Red and Black: Marxian Explorations in Southern and Afro-American History*. New York: Pantheon, 315–53.

Krader, Lawrence. 1975. *The Asiatic Mode of Production: Sources, Development and Critique in the Writings of Karl Marx*. Assen: Van Gorcum.

Marx, Karl. 1960. *Notes on Indian History (664-1858)*. Moscow: Progress Publishers.

Marx, Karl. 1963. *Oeuvres*. Vol. I. Ed. Maximilien Rubel. Paris: Gallimard.

Marx, Karl. 1972. *On America and the Civil War*. Vol. II of the *Karl Marx Library*, ed. and trans. by Saul K. Padover. New York: McGraw-Hill.

Marx, Karl. 1973. *Grundrisse*. Trans. Martin Nicolaus. New York: Penguin.

Marx, Karl. 1976. *Capital*, Vol. I. Trans. Ben Fowkes. London: Penguin.

Marx, Karl. 2008. *Capital*, Vol. 1. Trans. into Persian by Hassan Mortazavi, with Kaveh Boveiri. Tehran, Iran: Agah Publishing.

Marx, Karl and Friedrich Engels. 1937. *The Civil War in the United States*. Edited and introduced by Richard Enmale [Richard Morais]. New York: International Publishers.

Marx, Karl and Friedrich Engels. 1972. *Ireland and the Irish Question*. Moscow: Progress Publishers.

MECW: Marx, Karl and Friedrich Engels. 1975–2004. *Collected Works*. Fifty volumes. New York: International Publishers.

Said, Edward. 1978. *Orientalism*. New York: Vintage.

Sewell, Robert. 1870. *Analytical History of India*. London: W. H. Allen & Co.

Shanin, Teodor, ed. 1983. *Late Marx and the Russian Road: Marx and the "Peripheries" of Capitalism*. New York: Monthly Review Press.

The Myth of Twentieth-Century Socialism and the Continuing Relevance of Karl Marx

Paresh Chattopadhyay

Today there is a curious convergence of views between the Right and the dominant Left on the meaning of socialism. Put more concretely, for both the Right and the dominant Left socialism refers to the system which came into being with the conquest of political power by the Bolsheviks in Russia in 1917, and signifies a society governed by a single political party - basically the Communist Party - and where means of production are owned predominantly by the state, and the economy is directed by central planning. The two most important points stressed by both sides for this socialism are the existence of a single central authority exercising political power and the institution of 'public property' - signifying the replacement of private property in the means of production predominantly by state property. Needless to add, the Right looks at this 'socialism' negatively while the (dominant) Left considers it positively. Both these tendencies, again, find the origin of this socialism in the ideas of Marx.

Now that this socialism has almost evaporated, two kinds of responsibility have been attributed to Marx, involving two kinds of criticism of Marx in regard to this socialism. First, it is held, since the inspiration for this system supposedly came from Marx, and, consequently, since Marx is thought to be responsible for its creation, its disappearance only shows the failure of Marx's ideas. Similarly, under the same assumption that this socialism was Marx's brainchild, a contrary charge is directed against him. Here the point is stressed that the horrible reality of this system, as shown above all in its relation to human individuals, only demonstrates that (Marxian) socialism by nature is repressive, that is, it is an inhuman regime. The second kind of responsibility attributed to Marx and, consequently, the second kind of criticism of Marx is very different. It involves Marx's prognostication of the future after capitalism. The affirmation is made that what Marx had envisaged for the future, that capitalism undermined by its own inner contradictions would go out of existence yielding place to a

Socialism and Democracy, Vol.24, No.3, November 2010, pp.23–45
ISSN 0885-4300 print/ISSN 1745-2635 online
DOI: 10.1080/08854300.2010.513610

new, infinitely more humane society – socialism – has been proved wrong. Capitalism continues to exist in spite of all its ups and downs, and socialism continues to elude us. Marx's vision has simply proved to be unrealizable; at best it is for the "music of the future" (*Zukunftsmusik*).[1]

The present paper aims to demonstrate that socialism in Marx is completely different from, if not opposed to, socialism as we find it in its common theoretical presentation as well as in the practice in its name in the twentieth century, and that what Marx had envisaged as socialism has not yet been tried. Secondly, as regards the alleged failure of Marx's prognostication of society after capital, the advent of socialism in Marx's sense is conditional upon the presence of certain material and subjective conditions which require a prolonged historical period for their fruition within the existing society itself before the new society could appear – for which Marx did not set any calendar. Marx's emancipatory socialist project has lost none of its luster and is still worth striving for.

For a proper perspective we first offer, in what follows, a synoptic overview of socialism as envisaged by Marx. Then we present the specificity of the concept of socialism as it took shape in the last century before proceeding to give a brief account of that socialism in reality. As regards both the concept and the reality of socialism in the last century, we consider socialism in Russia after October 1917 as the prototype of all later socialisms. Hence we first analyze the Russian case at some length, discussing Lenin, then Stalin, and we then offer a shorter account of the next outstanding case, that of China under Mao. We conclude by (re)asserting the relevance of Marx's emancipatory socialism today.

Socialism in Marx

First, a word on the confusion about the term "socialism." There is a widespread idea that socialism and communism are two successive societies, that socialism is the transition to communism and hence precedes communism. Later in this essay we will say more about the origin of this thesis and the consequences of its acceptance. For Marx this distinction is non-existent. For Marx, socialism is neither the transition to communism, nor the lower phase of communism. It *is* communism *tout court.* In fact Marx calls capitalism itself the

1. To use Marx's term having an ironic reference to the composer Richard Wagner (Marx 2008: 794).

"transitional point" or "transitional phase" to communism (Marx 1953: 438; 1962a: 425–26; in Most 1989: 783). For him socialism and communism are simply equivalent and alternative terms for the same society that he envisages for the post-capitalist epoch which he calls, in different texts, equivalently: communism, socialism, Republic of Labour, society of free and associated producers or simply Association, Cooperative Society, (re)union of free individuals. Hence what Marx says in one of his famous texts – *Critique of the Gotha Programme* (Marx 1964c; hereafter *Gothacritique*) – about the two stages of communism[2] could as well apply to socialism having the same two stages.

Socialism or communism appears in two different senses in Marx (and Engels). First, as a theoretical expression. In this sense the term does not mean a state of things which should be established or an ideal to which reality should conform. It is rather the "real movement which abolishes the present state of things. The movement arises from today's (pre)conditions" (Marx & Engels 1973a: 35). Engels says of socialism/communism: "to the extent that it is theoretical, it is the theoretical expression of the place of the proletariat in the class struggle between the proletariat and the bourgeoisie, the résumé of the conditions of the emancipation of the proletariat" (Engels 1972: 322). Again (in the *Communist Manifesto*), "the theoretical principles of the communists...are only the general expressions of the real relations of the existing class struggle, of a historical movement that is going on before our eyes" (Marx & Engels 1966: 70). In the second sense, socialism/communism refers to the society which is envisaged as arising after the demise of capitalism. Now, to drive home our point that socialism and communism in Marx mean the same social formation, and thereby to refute the uncritically accepted idea – a sequel to Bolshevism – of socialism being only the transition to communism, we can mention at least four of Marx's texts where, referring to the future society after capital, Marx speaks exclusively of "socialism" and does not mention "communism." Thus in an 1844 polemic Marx writes: "Generally a revolution – overthrow of the existing power and the dissolution of the old relations – is a political act. Without revolution socialism cannot be viable. It needs this political act to the extent that it needs destruction and dissolution. However, where its organizing activity begins, where its aim and soul stand out, socialism throws away its political cover" (Marx 1976a: 409). The second and the third texts are almost identical, appearing respectively in his 1861–63

2. This text is the only place in Marx's writings where this two-phase temporal division of the future society is found.

notebooks (second notebook) and in the so-called "main manuscript" for *Capital III*. Here is the 1861–63 text, in Marx's own English:

> Capitalist production ...is a greater spendthrift than any other mode of production of man, of living labour, spendthrift not only of flesh and blood and muscles, but of brains and nerves. It is, in fact, at [the cost of] the greatest waste of individual development that the development of general men [the general development of human beings] is secured in those epochs of history which prelude to [which presage] a socialist constitution of mankind. (Marx 1976b: 324–27; our bracketed insertions)

This text is repeated almost word for word in the "main manuscript" for the third volume of *Capital* (Marx 1992: 124–6).[3] Finally, in the course of correcting and improving the text of a book by a worker (Johann Most), meant for popularizing *Capital*, Marx inserted: "The capitalist mode of production is really a transitional form which by its own organism must lead to a higher, to a co-operative mode of production, to socialism" (in Most 1989: 783).

The conditions for the rise of socialism are not given by nature. Socialism is a product of history. "Individuals build a new world from the historical acquisitions of their foundering world. They must themselves in course of their development first produce the *material conditions* of a new society, and no effort of spirit or will can free them from this destiny" (Marx 1972: 339; emphasis in original). It is capital which creates the material conditions and the subjective agents for transforming the present society into a society of free and associated producers. "The material and the spiritual conditions of the negation of wage labor and capital – themselves the negation of the earlier forms of unfree social production – are in turn the result of its [capital's] (own) process of production" (Marx 1953: 635). The material conditions are created by capital's inherent tendency towards universal development of the productive forces and by the socialization of labor and production. As regards the subjective – "spiritual" – condition, it is provided by capital's "grave diggers" – the proletariat – begotten by capital itself. Even with the strongest will and greatest subjective effort, if the material conditions of production and the corresponding relations of circulation for a classless society do not exist in a latent form, "all attempts to explode the society would be Don Quixotism" (Marx 1953: 77).

More than two decades later Marx wrote: "A radical social revolution is bound up with certain historical conditions of economic

---

3. In his edition of the manuscript published as *Capital III* Engels translates this passage into German, but not quite literally (Marx 1964a: 99).

development. The latter are its preconditions. It is therefore only possible where, with capitalist development, the industrial proletariat occupies at least a significant position" (Marx 1973b: 633). It must be stressed that capitalist relations are not revolutionized within capitalism automatically even with all the requisite material conditions prepared by capital itself. It is the working class which is the active agent for eliminating capital and building the socialist society; the proletarian revolution is thus an act of *self-emancipation*: "The emancipation of the working classes must be conquered by the working classes themselves" (Marx 1964b: 288). Marx and Engels equally underline that "consciousness of the necessity of a profound revolution arises from the working class itself" (Marx & Engels 1973a: 69). The starting point of the proletarian revolution is the conquest of political power by the proletariat – the rule of the "immense majority in the interest of the immense majority," the "conquest of democracy" (Marx & Engels 1966: 74, 76). This so-called "seizure of power" by the proletariat does not immediately signify the *victory* of the revolution;[4] it is only the "first step in the worker revolution" (76) which continues through a prolonged "period of revolutionary transformation" required for superseding the bourgeois social order (Marx, in Marx & Engels 1964c: 24). Until capital totally disappears, the workers remain proletarians and the revolution continues, victorious though they are *politically*. "The superseding of the economical conditions of the slavery of labor by the conditions of free and associated labor can only be the progressive work of time," and the "working class will have to pass through long struggles, through a series of historic processes transforming circumstances and men," wrote Marx with reference to the victory of the Commune (Marx 1971: 76, 156–7). Later he reminded Bakunin that even with the installation of proletarian rule "the classes and the old organization of society still do not disappear" (Marx 1973: 630). At the end of the process, with the disappearance of capital, the proletariat along with its "dictatorship" also disappears, leaving individuals as simple producers, and wage labor naturally vanishes. Classes disappear along with the state in its last form as proletarian power and the society of free and associated producers – socialism – is inaugurated.

In all hitherto existing societies – based on class rule – the community has stood as an independent power against individuals and has subjugated them. Thus it has really been a "false" or "illusory" or "apparent" community. The outcome of the workers' self-emancipatory

4. Like the widely used phrase of the Left, "victory of the October 1917 revolution," by which is of course meant the seizure of political power.

revolution is the socialist society, an "association of free individuals" - individuals neither personally dependent as in pre-capitalism nor objectively dependent as in capitalism - and there arises, for the first time, the "true" community where universally developed individuals dominate their own social relations (Marx 1932: 536; 1973a: 136; 1953: 593; 1987: 109). Correspondingly, the capitalist mode of production (CMP) yields place to the "associated mode of production" (AMP). With the disappearance of classes, there is also no state and hence no politics in the new society. We cited Marx above holding that with the victory of the proletarian revolution politics ceases to exist and socialism throws away its political cover. This 1844 position of Marx (1976a) is repeated in his 1847 polemic against Proudhon and (with Engels) in the *Communist Manifesto* (1848). Following the same logic he and Engels affirm that the "organization of communism [socialism] is essentially economic" (Marx & Engels 1973a: 70). Here the appropriation of the conditions of production is no longer private; it is collective, social.

Similarly, with the transformation of society's production relations, its exchange relations - with nature as well as among individuals - are also transformed. Capital, driven by the logic of accumulation, seriously damages the environment and undermines the natural powers of the earth together with those of the human producer, the "twin fountains of all wealth" (Marx 1987: 477). In contrast, in the new society, freed from the mad drive for accumulation and with the unique goal of satisfying human needs, individuals rationally regulate their material exchanges with nature with the "least expenditure of force and carry on these exchanges in the conditions most worthy of and in fullest conformity with their human nature" (Marx 1992: 838). As regards the exchange relations among individuals, the inauguration of collective appropriation of the conditions of production ends the commodity form of products of labor. Here the directly social character of production is presupposed and hence exchange value ceases to exist. "Community" here is "posited before production" (Marx 1980: 113). From the very inception of the new society as it has just come out of the womb of capital - Marx's first phase of socialism - "producers do not exchange their products and as little does labor employed on these products appear as value" (Marx 1964c: 15).

Finally we come to the allocation/distribution of instruments of production - the material means of production and the living labor power - and the consequent distribution of products in the new society. The distribution of the instruments of production boils down really to the allocation of society's total labor time (dead and living). This allocation, effected under capitalism through exchange taking value form, is contrariwise performed in socialism by direct and conscious control of society over its labor time. At the same time, in conformity with the nature of the new society, free time beyond the labor time required for satisfying material needs must be provided by society to the associated individuals for their "all-sided development." Hence the "economy of time is the first economic law on the basis of communitarian production" (Marx 1953: 89). As regards the distribution of the total social product in socialism, it is first divided between the production needs and the consumption needs of society. Production needs here refer to needs of replacement and extension of society's productive apparatus as well as insurance and reserve funds against uncertainty. Consumption is both collective - healthcare, education, provision for those unable to work - and personal. The principle governing personal consumption remains that of commodity exchange: the quantity of labor given to society by the individual is received back from society (after necessary deductions) by the individual. However, the mediating "labor coupons" have no *exchange value.* In fact, in commodity production there is a contradiction between "principle and practice"; equivalence is established *"only on average,"* since the individual share in total social labor is unknowable. Opposite is the case with socialism (Marx 1964c: 16; emphasis in original). Similarly, in his famous discussion of the "association of free individuals" in *Capital I,* Marx posits that under "socialised labor, diametrically opposed to commodity production," the mediating labor certificates are not money, they simply ascertain the share allocated to each laboring individual - "only for the sake of a parallel with commodity production" - according to the individual's labor time (Marx 1987: 109, 122).[5] At the initial phase of the new society this principle of equivalence, in parallel with the principle under commodity production (hence called by Marx "bourgeois right") but without having *value form* assumed by the product, cannot be avoided. This process is wholly overcome only at a higher phase of the society when all the springs of co-operative wealth open up, leading to adoption of the principle "from each according to one's ability, to each according to one's needs" (Marx 1964c: 17).

5. This idea reappears in Marx's second manuscript for *Capital II* (Marx 2008: 347). Interestingly, considering both the texts of the two volumes of *Capital* on allocation-distribution as given here, one sees clearly that they refer not to the higher phase of the socialist society but to its lower phase referred to in the *Gothacritique;* that is, we already have a society of free and associated individuals with neither commodity production nor wage labor.

Anti-emancipatory character of twentieth-century socialism

First, a word on the theoretical categories underlying twentieth-century socialism (hereafter TCS). These categories were shaped originally and principally by Lenin, developed and perfected later by Stalin. The resulting conceptual framework became, broadly speaking, the heritage of TCS. Indeed the theoretical categories of TCS are only footnotes to Lenin (to paraphrase A.N. Whitehead on Western philosophy in relation to Plato). They had little relation with the categories that Marx (and Engels) had put forward in their own presentation of the future society. In fact TCS's theoretical representation of the post-capitalist society shows a near complete *revision* (in Lenin's precise sense of the term) of Marx's ideas.

As regards the conditions for socialist revolution, Lenin advanced two important arguments for socialist revolution in Russia after the February uprising (1917). First, a few months before the seizure of power, he affirmed that as a result of the February revolution state power in Russia had passed into the hands of the bourgeoisie and the landlords turned bourgeois. "*To this extent* the bourgeois revolution is completed" (Lenin 1982b: 19; emphasis in original). Shortly afterwards he asserted, without any qualification this time, "the bourgeois revolution is already completed" (Lenin 1982b: 51). The second argument for a successful socialist revolution in backward Russia – already implicit in Lenin's 1915 declaration on the possibility of socialist revolution outside Europe, given "unequal development of capitalism" (Lenin 1982a: 635–6) – was explicitly made only a few months after the October seizure of power: it was easier for "the [socialist revolutionary] movement to start" in a backward capitalist country like Russia; "things had worked [out] differently from what Marx and Engels had expected" (Lenin 1982b: 509, 510).

To paraphrase Keynes's statement about Ricardo, Lenin conquered not only the revolutionary Left but also some of the lucid minds of the twentieth century as completely as the Inquisition had conquered Spain. They thought without question that a socialist revolution had indeed taken place and been victorious in one of the most backward capitalist countries, thereby disproving Marx's prognostication. Thus E.H. Carr thought that "the Marxist scheme of revolution was bound to break down when the proletarian revolution occurred in the most backward capitalist country" (Carr 1964: 43–4). In his turn Isaac Deutscher wrote that "it was the Russian Marxists, and not Marx and Engels whom [the events in Russia] proved to be right" (Deutscher 1960: 184). In the same way Paul Sweezy opined: "The revolutions that put socialism in history's agenda took place not in economically developed countries, as Marx and Engels thought they would, but in countries where capitalism was still in early stages" (Sweezy 1993: 6). The position of these people confirms what Marx and Engels noted in an early text: "While in daily life every shopkeeper knows very well the distinction between what a person claims to be and what s/he really is, our historiography has not yet come to know this triviality. It takes at its word what each epoch affirms and imagines itself to be" (Marx & Engels 1973a: 49).[6]

Both the arguments of Lenin in favor of socialist revolution in Russia in 1917 were a radical *revision* of the materialist conception of history. As regards the first argument, Lenin predicated the "completion" of the bourgeois democratic revolution simply on the basis of the passage to political power of the bourgeoisie independently of the question of any change in the social relations of production in Russia, whereas for Marx only a radical transformation of these relations, and not a mere change in political power, would signify "completion" of a social (including bourgeois) revolution. As to Lenin's second argument mentioned above, the fundamental question is, even assuming the presence of the revolutionary class (the proletariat), whether it is possible to have a socialist revolution without the presence of adequate material conditions for inaugurating an "association of free individuals," contrary to what Marx had stressed in his different texts including his latter-day anti-Bakunin text given above (Marx 1973b).

Theoretically not inconceivable, Marx's thesis could only be refuted by the reality of a successful socialist revolution under Lenin's conditions (see below). Apart from Lenin's argument about the conditions of socialist revolution, his theoretical position on socialism itself is of enormous importance in view of its lasting effect on the way socialism was conceived and practiced by the regimes which followed worldwide after the Bolshevik victory, calling themselves "socialist". Lenin distinguishes between socialism and communism, equating them, respectively, with Marx's lower and higher phase of communism. He also speaks of two transitions, one from capitalism to socialism, another from socialism to communism (Lenin 1982b: 42, 301–2, 305; 1982c: 530, 541–2). We already saw above that for Marx socialism and communism are equivalent terms. In this light one could also speak of a lower and a higher phase of socialism. The Leninist distinction in question, although apparently merely

6. The term "shopkeeper" is in English in the text.

terminological and innocent-looking, had far-reaching consequences which were far from innocent and far from what Lenin himself presumably might have expected. It became a convenient instrument for legitimizing and justifying every oppressive act of the party-states from 1917 onward in the name of socialism, which, it was maintained, was only a *transitional* phase toward communism, thus shelving all the vital aspects of Marx's immense emancipatory project and metamorphosing Marx's project of communism into an unalloyed utopia.

The Russian case: concept and reality

Lenin

Lenin speaks of socialism basically in *juridical* terms, not in terms of a complex of *social relations of production*. For him socialism is "social ownership" of the means of production, which he further specifies as "ownership by the working class state" (Lenin 1982b: 300, 302, 669; 1982c: 711, 712, 714). Of course Marx also speaks of the ownership of the means of production in the new society as "social" where *society* itself and not the state – which is absent from the new society – is the owner, but for Lenin it is the working class *state* which is the new owner (*sobstvennost' na sredstva proizvodstva v rukakh gosudarstva*) (Lenin 1982c: 711, 712). Here Lenin has successfully stood Marx on his head. For Marx socialism – even in Lenin's *revised* sense of the first phase of communism – is already a *classless* society, a "union of free individuals" coming into existence *after* the working *class* along with the last form of *state* – the dictatorship of the proletariat – has vanished. The proletariat (wage laborers) has been transformed into simple producers as free individuals and it is their society (the collectivity of free individuals) – and not any state – which possesses the means of production.

Lenin speaks not only of the working-class state but also of what he considers to be its equivalent, the "socialist state" (Lenin 1982c: 714). Needless to say, this last expression is nowhere to be found in Marx. Earlier we referred to Marx's texts showing that there can be no state in socialism. Lenin tries to smuggle "state" into Marx's text of the *Gothacritique* by brazenly *revising* it. This he does by connecting two independent ideas in two analytically separate places of the text: Marx's discussion of the continuation of "bourgeois right" in the first phase of communism and Marx's speculation about the future of the "present day functions of the state." Lenin emphasizes the need for the existence of the "bourgeois state" to enforce "bourgeois right" in the first phase of the new society (Lenin 1982b: 304). His logic is baffling. For Marx this first phase is inaugurated *after* the disappearance of proletarian rule – the last form of state.[7] From Lenin's position it follows that in the absence of the bourgeoisie (by assumption), the producers themselves – no longer proletarians – would have to recreate, not even their old state, but the *bourgeois state* to enforce bourgeois right. For Marx, from the start of the new society there are no classes and hence there is no state and no politics. Whatever bourgeois right remains in the area of distribution does not require a particular *political apparatus* to enforce it. It is now *society* itself which is in charge. One can read this textually in Section I of the *Gothacritique* (Marx 1962c: 16). Similarly, for the first phase of communism (Lenin's socialism) Lenin envisages the economy as one "state syndicate" or one "single factory" where "all citizens" are transformed into "*hired employees* of the state" (*sluzhashikh po naymu*) with "equality of labor, equality of *wages* (*zarabotnoyplatyi*)" (1982b: 306, 308; emphasis added). What a contrast with Marx who in his 1864 "Inaugural Address" had clearly distinguished between "hired labor" (of capitalism) and "associated labor" (of socialism)! For Marx what Lenin is talking about is simply the "state itself as capitalist," "in so far as it employs wage labour" (1962b: 370; 2008: 636). So, what Lenin presents as socialism is really *state capitalism* which with a "single state syndicate" or a "single factory," as Lenin puts it, will be – in Marx's terms, as we find in *Capital*'s French version – the "total national capital constituting a single capital in the hands of a single capitalist" (Marx 1965: 1139).

Let us now try to see this socialism, the prototype for the twentieth century, in reality. The problematic begins right at the start. There is no evidence that the accession to political power by the Bolsheviks signaled a proletarian or socialist revolution (or at least its beginning) in Russia in the sense of Marx, that is, a revolution which is the outcome of the "autonomous movement of the immense majority in the interest of the immense majority," as the 1848 *Manifesto* affirms (Marx & Engels 1966: 68). The so-called October revolution was neither initiated nor led by the proletariat. The same goes for the subsequent installation of single-party rule. In October 1917, the fate of over 170 million people was decided by a handful of non-proletarian radicalized intelligentsia – far removed from the site of the real process of production and exploitation, unelected and irrevocable by and totally unaccountable to the laboring people. Through the substitution of a whole class by a single party, power was seized under the

7. Although Marx considered the 1871 Commune as proletarian rule, he never connected the Commune with the first phase of communism.

slogan "all power to the soviets" not from the Provisional Government but really from the *soviets themselves,* the authentic organs of laboring people's self rule created by the self-emancipatory country-wide spontaneous popular uprising in February. This pre-emptive strike was perpetrated independently of and behind the back of the Congress of Soviets depriving, it of the right of maternity regarding the founding act of the new order. Revealing in this regard is Lenin's secret correspondence (September-October 1917) expressing to his comrades in the party leadership his utter distrust and disdain of the soviets: "To wait for the Congress [to meet] is complete idiocy and total treachery (*polnaya izmena*). The Congress will give nothing and *can give nothing* (*nichevo ni mozhet dat'*)" (Lenin 1982b: 345, 346; emphasis in original).

Undergoing a virtual radioactive decay, the soviets as independent self-governing organs of laborers evaporated as early as summer 1918. "Soviet democracy lasted from October 1917 to the summer of 1918"; "beginning with 1919 Bolshevism started to deny all the dissidents of the revolution the right to political existence" (Serge 2001: 832). " 'All power to the soviets' appeared to be a reality on the 26th of October, 1917," wrote an eminent historian, "but it was mostly power to the Bolsheviks in those soviets.... The whole system of soviets and executive committees was reduced to an administrative and propaganda auxiliary of the party.... Deprived of power in the soviets and in the factories, the Russian proletariat...found that the triumph of the dictatorship in its name was a very hollow victory" (Daniels 1967: 223–4). The masses and the majority of soviets representing them certainly greeted the fall of the hated old regime, but refused to have a Bolshevik hegemony. Alexander Rabinowitch in his blow-by-blow account of the events wrote, "The mass mood was not specifically Bolshevik in the sense of reflecting a desire for a Bolshevik government. As the flood of post-Kornilov political resolutions revealed, Petrograd soldiers, sailors, and workers were attracted more than ever by the goal of creating a soviet government *uniting all socialist elements.* And *in their eyes* the Bolsheviks stood for *soviet power – for soviet democracy*" (2004: 139, 167; our emphasis).

There was also another important set of workers' self-governing organs created in workplaces before October 1917: factory committees with their own soviets (Ferro 1980: 20). After having seized power from the Congress of Soviets, the Bolsheviks turned their eyes on the factory committees who were exercising workers' democracy in their workplaces and asserting control over the management. "The Bolsheviks saw for the first time the danger of radical democracy confronting them, following literally Lenin's words on the sovereignty of the soviets" (Anweiler 1958: 277). The Bolsheviks now asked the trade unions where they had a majority to help them to subdue these self-governing organs of the workers. The trade unions obliged by simply annexing them as their lowest level (Bunyan & Fisher 1934: 639–41). It should be clear that far from itself conquering political power as an act of *self-emancipation* (in Marx's 1864 sense), the Russian proletariat participated in the seizure of power - effected in the name of the proletariat by a party completely substituting itself for the proletariat - only as *followers*. It must be underlined that by their pre-emptive strike against the soviets, the Bolsheviks successfully destroyed any possibility that the unfurling (bourgeois) democratic revolution - so magnificently started by the quasi-totality of the country's laboring people in February - would develop over time into a genuine proletarian revolution as a process of "revolution in permanence," to use the 1850 "battle cry" of Marx and Engels.

Before the seizure of power Lenin had stressed the need to destroy the old state apparatus and to replace it with a "commune-state" with freely elected and revocable officials, and to replace the police and the standing army with the armed workers. Later he had to admit that the Bolsheviks "effectively took over the old apparatus of the tsar and the bourgeoisie" (Lenin 1982c: 695). Instead of officials being elected and subject to recall, there appeared bureaucrats, all party nominees and hierarchically organized from top downward. Similarly there appeared a special police apparatus, particularly the dreaded secret police, before the end of 1917. In the same way the "Red" army was fashioned, beginning in early 1918, not very differently from the professional army of a class society with ex-tsarist officers in higher positions in increasing numbers. As regards industry, with the virtual liquidation of the self-managed factory committees, the principle of direction from above was imposed. Lenin now discovered that "the Russian is a bad worker in comparison with the worker of the advanced nations," hence the workers must show "*unquestioning obedience* to the *single will* of the leaders of the labor process ... to the one-person decision of the soviet directors" (Lenin 1982b: 610, 618, 630; emphasis in text). One year later he added: "Till now we have not reached the stage where the labouring masses could participate in administration" (Lenin 1982c: 115).

We thus see that the regime created by October was anything but a proletarian regime. It was the party's dictatorship over the proletariat. Naturally workers' opposition to the regime became more and more widespread, and was increasingly suppressed by force. The climax was reached with the mass massacre of the Kronstadt sailors and toilers in early 1921 on the totally false charge of their collaboration with the Whites, on Lenin's own testimony at the tenth congress of the party in 1921. Isaac Deutscher writes that by 1921–22 for the first time since 1917 "the bulk of the working class unmistakably turned against the Bolsheviks.... If the Bolsheviks had now permitted free elections to the soviets they would almost certainly have been swept from power" (Deutscher 1963: 504).

Stalin

It was Stalin who, following Lenin's lead on the concept of socialism, gave it the finished form on which the whole rationale of TCS was founded. Needless to add, Stalin totally subscribes to the Leninist identity of socialism with Marx's "first phase of communism" and the Leninist idea of socialism as the transition to (full) communism. Stalin's inversion of Marx's materialist position goes even further than Lenin's. Whereas in Lenin socialism is conceived in terms of ownership of means of production, that is, in juridical terms, independently of the real relations of production, Stalin specifically makes "ownership of means of production the basis of production relations" (1980: 505), and state ownership of means of production is again, *à la Lénine*, identified with socialist ownership (Stalin 1970: 383, 386). Lenin's idea of citizens as hired wage laborers of the state in socialism is also taken over by Stalin. Stalin's "improvement" on Lenin's position here lies in his statement that given the absence of private property in the means of production in socialism, labor power has ceased to be a commodity and there are no hired wage laborers (Stalin 1980: 580–1). However the laborers receive their remuneration "in the form of wage" reflecting the material incentive according to the quantity and quality of labor. But this "wage under socialism is fundamentally different from wage under capitalism" because contrary to what happens in capitalism, labor power under socialism is not a commodity (Akademiya Nauk SSSR 1954: 452, 453). In other words, wages exist and labor exists, but wage labor does not.[8] It seems Lenin lacked this "subtle" logic of his follower.

Finally, given the existence of two forms of ownership in the means of production – state ownership and collective farm ownership with exchange of products between them mediated by money – Stalin affirms the necessity of the existence of commodity production and hence of the law of value in socialism. However, in the absence of

8. For Marx wage is simply the value of labor power, which is a commodity (see e.g. Marx 1988: 16).

private ownership, socialist commodity production is totally different from commodity production under capitalism (Akademiya Nauk 1954: 440–1; Stalin 1980: 580–1). So we have socialist commodity and socialist wage as the specific products of *socialism*, completely different from their counterparts in capitalism. It should be stressed that the foundation of the rationale for the existence of socialism in the new regime – underlined by Stalin following Lenin, from which all its other characteristics follow – is the alleged absence of private property in the means of production.[9] Here private property signifies for Lenin "property of separate individuals" (1982b: 300, 302) in the means of production.[10]

We submit that the concept of capitalist private property (in the means of production) meaning *individual* (private) property and, correspondingly, the capitalist as individual owner of capital, is *pre-Marxian*. As a juridical category it is as old as the Roman law taken over later by bourgeois jurisprudence. This is the juridical form in which capital appears at its beginning period. But with the progress of accumulation this form increasingly loses its relevance. Marx shows clearly that at a certain stage of capitalist development, for the needs of increasing accumulation of capital – the "independent variable" in capitalist production – this form tends to be largely inadequate and there appears increasingly (as is seen in the rise of share capital) what Marx calls "directly social capital in opposition to private capital" together with the "associated capitalist." This signals the "abolition of private property within the limits of the capitalist mode of production itself" (Marx 1987: 572; 1992: 502). However, Marx does not speak only of individual private property in the means of production. In his work we also read about another kind of private property largely left aside by the Marx readers. In this second and more important sense, private property in the means of production exists as property of the few in the face of non-property of the great majority who are compelled to sell their labor power in order to live. In this sense the objective conditions of labor are the "*private property* of a part of society" (Marx 1956: 21; emphasis added). It is then "class property." This is the sense which appears in the assertion of the *Communist Manifesto* that communists could sum up their theory in a single expression: "abolition of

9. The discussion of socialism in Lenin's case was purely theoretical, the outcome of his specific (mis)reading of Marx, while for Stalin the theorization came as a rationalization of the actually existing regime he was heading.
10. In the expression the term "separate" (*otdelnyi*) does not appear in Moscow's English version.

private property," and the latter is explicitly used in the sense of "disappearance of class property" (Marx & Engels 1966: 71, 73).

The same idea reappears in Marx's address on the 1871 Commune: "The Commune intended to abolish that class property which makes the labor of the many the wealth of the few" (1971: 75). Hence even with the (juridical) abolition of individual private property, if the great majority continues to earn its living by exchange of labor power against wage/salary, this would signify that private property continues to exist as "class property." It is not with (working-class) state property but only with *society's* direct appropriation of the conditions of production – implying necessarily the disappearance of the wage system – that private property finally goes out of existence. Only then does capitalism end. The idea of socialism as the lower phase of and transition to communism based on public (mainly state) ownership of the means of production and wage labor and with the state form under a single party – introduced by Lenin and perfected by Stalin (with the additional introduction of commodity production) – remained the central idea of socialism, accepted uncritically by the rulers of the whole system of TCS across the globe and their international sympathizers. In this ironclad frame of socialism, state substituted for society and party substituted for (working) class totally. It should be clear that this socialism has nothing in common with Marx's socialism, which was not transitional but equivalent to communism: a society of free and associated individuals with social ownership of the means of production and without state, commodity production or wage labor.

The Soviet Union was not considered socialist by its rulers till the late 1930s. Until then it was considered a proletarian dictatorship. The victory of socialism was proclaimed on the basis of fulfillment of the second five-year plan (1933–37), showing 98.7 percent of the means of production coming under state and cooperative/collective ownership. The party declared that "in our country...the first phase of communism, socialism, has been basically realised" (*KPSS v resoliutsiakh* 1971: 335). The basic structure of this socialism remained more or less the same till the end of the regime. And only towards the end, with the introduction of relative freedom of opinion and expression, do we start to learn the real nature of this socialism from the *internal* witnesses of the regime. Thus an eminent Soviet economist of the period wrote: "Removed from direct administration and disposal of social ownership, having no influence on the system of remuneration, and participating in no way in the distribution of national income and produced product," the soviet workers "perceived" such "state ownership" as "alien" and "not their own" (Butenko 1988: 16, 18). Similarly, the doyen of labor economics underlined: "The state ownership was neither public nor socialist. Surplus labor and the corresponding surplus value belonged not to the people or to those who generated them. Profit was appropriated by the state ... the directors of enterprises hired labor power in the name of the state. Wages, in these conditions, were, as in any capitalist society, the transformed form of the value of labor power as a commodity (*prevrashchennoi formoi stoimosti tovara rabochaya sila*)" (Manevich 1991: 139). It is in this situation of "apathy enveloping millions" and "exhausting all motivational basis," as another economist observed, that the "standard 'socialist toiler' (*sotsialisticheskoi truzhenik*), a product of 70 years of Soviet rule," has worked (Loginov 1992).

China and Mao: concept and reality

Mao Zedong proclaimed that "the salvos of the October revolution brought Marxism-Leninism to China," and he characterized his party as the "bolshevized communist party" (Mao 1972: 175). Materially China was even more backward than pre-October Russia. China's revolution – abstracting from its anti-imperialist character – was essentially a peasant war led by the Communist Party of China (CPC), directed against the pre-capitalist social order. The CPC under Mao, unlike the Bolsheviks under Lenin, came to represent China's great majority, firmly rooted in the country's rural laboring masses. The supposed leadership by the proletariat was more theoretical and ideological than real, the party having only tenuous links with the industrial working class. In fact Mao wrote: "The more backward a country is, the easier is its passage to socialism" (Mao 1975: 81). He was even inclined, like the nineteenth-century Russian "populists," to think that the Chinese revolution could "avoid the capitalist path in order to reach socialism directly" (Mao 1972: 131).

According to the regime's spokespersons, the CPC's victory in 1949 meant the triumph of the "new democratic revolution" accomplishing the anti-feudal and anti-imperialist tasks. The subsequent period until the end of the first five-year plan (1953–57) was a transition period of "socialist construction." From 1956–57 on, China was called a socialist country. Remaining well within Leninist tradition, Mao considered socialism as the lower phase of and the transition to communism. About the nature of the Chinese society for the period beginning with the late 1950s, Mao is ambiguous. Thus in two texts separated by a few months, he speaks curiously of "socialist relations of production" in February and of "proletarian dictatorship" in October as existing in China (Mao 1977: 394, 507). Referring positively to Stalin, Mao affirms, reversing Marx's materialist position, like Stalin before him, that the "system of ownership is the basis of the relations of production" (Mao 1977: 139). Again, following Stalin, Mao proclaimed the establishment of socialism in China on the basis of the abolition of *individual* private ownership in the means of production. Correctly taking account of the existence of commodity production and wage system in China's "socialist" reality, Mao, unlike Stalin, did not resort to subterfuges to hide their incompatibility with socialism (in Marx's sense). He stated: "China is a socialist country... At present our country practices the commodity system, an eight-grade wage system, and the wage system is unequal, and in all this scarcely different from the old society; the difference is that the system of ownership has changed" (Mao cited in *Biography* 2004: 1475).[11] Mao also asserted, going beyond even Lenin, the "existence of classes and class struggle" – insisting on the latter's "protracted and sometimes violent character" – under "socialism" (Schram 1974: 168). This sharpening class struggle included the struggle within the CPC itself against the "capitalist roaders" through a series of "cultural revolutions."

The Great Proletarian Cultural Revolution (GPCR) began with a lot of fanfare on the initiative of the "Chairman in person." The 16-point decision proclaimed the need "for the masses to liberate themselves." Here undoubtedly Mao was in advance of the Bolsheviks, in whose writings such a clearly stated emancipatory message for the laboring people is difficult to come by. The nearest for them was the slogan "all power to the soviets" whose rapid liquidation in reality we have seen. The "Sixteen Articles" of August 1966 called for a system of general elections like that of the Paris Commune. However, that was not how things turned out. Within a very short period Mao himself rejected the attempt made in Shanghai to follow faithfully the example of the Paris Commune. Mao favored rather the military-dominated revolutionary committees. "Whatever may have been Mao's intention at the beginning of the Cultural Revolution, in the end he settled for the reestablishment of a presumably ideologically rectified Party and a presumably reformed state bureaucracy" (Meisner 1999: 370). Far from establishing a system of election and recall at all levels of administration, all functionaries continued to be nominated. Finally the old bureaucratic machinery emerged from the Cultural Revolution almost intact, as in Russia after October 1917.

Speaking in general, as regards the pretension of having proletarian dictatorship and then socialism, the reality showed that the laboring

11. Translated from Chinese and transmitted to us by the distinguished Chinese scholar Wang Hui, in a private communication.

people of China, as in Russia earlier, had no role in the fundamental decisions and the enforcement of those decisions affecting their own lives. This was the exclusive privilege of the Party leadership. The "task" of the "masses" (how condescending the term became in the communist movement!) was to *follow* the "instructions" from above. Going beyond the Russian experience, it was a single individual – Mao – who was the ultimate reference point. Whether it was the system of "people's communes" or the launching of the GPCR, the initiative came from "the Chairman in person." In a society supposed to be marching toward communism every move was centered on following the Chairman's "latest instructions." What a contrast between the emphasis on Mao being the "great teacher/leader/supreme commander, great helmsman" and Marx's self-emancipatory perspective of the "proletariat organized as the ruling class," let alone of socialism as the "association of free individuals"!

Conclusion: the relevance of Marx

It appears that the revolutions of the last century that claimed to be socialist were really all minority revolutions in the name of the majority. Though we discussed only two specimens of TCS above, it would not be difficult to show that the pattern that emerges from these two applies *mutatis mutandis* to all the members of TCS. To go back to a remarkable text by Engels, "Even when the majority participated in them [in these revolutions], this participation was only in the service of a minority. Because of this [participation] and because of the unopposed attitude of the majority, the minority acquired the impression that it was the representative of the whole people" (Engels 1966: 227). All these societies have been "state socialist" (to use an oxymoron from the point of view of Marx), the state "entoiling [enmeshing] the living civil society like a boa constrictor " instead of "society reabsorbing the state [power]," and in the process "perfecting the state machinery instead of throwing off this deadening incubus" (Marx 1971: 149, 150, 153).[12] The theoretical ground and justification (in advance) of this enslaving system one already finds in the anti-emancipatory reading of Marx's *Gothacritique* by Lenin in his *apparently* libertarian brochure *State and Revolution*, where the two fundamental instruments for

12. Che Guevara, with his otherwise refreshingly critical notes on the Soviet *Textbook on Political Economy* in his recently published manuscripts, does not cross the bounds of the "state socialist" framework, including its commodity production and wage system. See Guevara (2006).

enslaving the human individual – the state and wage labor – are explicitly made to appear in the lower phase of communism, (mis)interpreted as the "transition to communism." It is no wonder that this is about the only text of Marx on the future society with its division into a lower and a higher phase which is the constantly mentioned reference point for spokespersons of the party-states, for showing the concordance of their socialism with the socialism envisaged by Marx, inasmuch as this two-phase division could easily be manipulated – given Lenin's particular reading – to justify the existence of state, commodity production, and wage labor in the first phase seen as only the *transition* to "full communism." Indeed the practice of twentieth century "socialism" has been a vast exercise in the enslavement of the human individual whose emancipation was the ultimate goal of the socialist revolution as envisioned by Marx.

The situation of the individual in the future Association in Marx's different texts does not find much echo in the discussion on socialism by the partisans of TCS. Marx's relevant discussion appears in his texts beginning as early as 1843–44, dealing with the problem of the individual's alienation in commodity-capitalist society. In the *Communist Manifesto* appears the essence of his position: "freedom of each is the condition of the freedom of all." His basic criterion for judging a society was the extent to which the individual was free in the society bereft of alienation and the constraints of labor and division of labor imposed on the (laboring) individual from outside. Up to now, the individual has been subordinated to an alien external power which has prevented the "development of all the human powers as such" (Marx 1953: 387). Marx's 1859 characterization of prior human evolution as the "pre-history of human society" should be understood precisely in this sense. There is a remarkable passage in Marx's 1857–58 manuscripts summing up the evolution of the status of the laboring individual through three stages:

> The relations of personal dependence (first wholly natural) are the first social form in the midst of which human productivity develops [but] only in reduced proportions and in isolated places. Personal independence based on material dependence is the second great form only within which is constituted a general social metabolism made of universal relations, faculties and needs. Free individuality based on the universal development of individuals and their domination of their common social productivity as their [own] social power is the third stage. The second creates the conditions of the third. (Marx 1953: 75)

The remarkable fourth section of the first chapter of *Capital I* carries over from the 1844 manuscripts the central theme of the alienation of the individual under commodity production and opposes it to the dealienated "association of free individuals" (Marx 1987: 109–10). In the same book Marx refers to the transformation of capital's private property into "individual property" under the future association of free individuals (683).[13] Again, Marx's famous discussion of necessity and liberty in the manuscript for the third volume of *Capital* is precisely built around the "socialized individual" in free association (Marx 1992: 832). This whole emancipatory message has been conspicuously absent from the reality of "socialism" of the last century. The only human and humane alternative to the inhuman reign of capital is *socialism* – the "association of free individuals" - as Marx envisaged it.

References

Akademiya Nauk SSSR. 1954. *Politicheskaya Ekonomiya* Moscow: Gosudarstvennoe Izdatel'stva Politicheskoi Literatury.

Anweiler, Oskar. 1958. *Die Rätebewegung in Russland 1905–1921.* Leiden: E.J.Brill.

Biography of Mao Zedong (in Chinese). 2004. Beijing: Zhongyangwenxian Press.

Bunyan, James and Fisher H. H. 1934. *The Bolshevik Revolution 1917-1918, Documents and Materials.* London: Humphrey Milford.

Butenko, A.P. 1988. "O Kharaktere sobstvennosti v usloviyakh real'nogo sotsializma" (On the character of ownership in conditions of real socialism). *EKO* 2.

Carr, E.H. 1964. *The Bolshevik Revolution*, vol. 1. London: Macmillan.

Daniels, Robert V. 1967. *The Red October*. New York: Charles Scribner.

Deutscher, Isaac. 1960. *Russia in Transition*. New York: Grove Press.

Deutscher, Isaac. 1963. *The Prophet Armed: Trotsky, 1879–1921.* New York: Oxford University Press.

Engels, Friedrich. 1966 [1895]. "Einleitung zu Karl Marx, 'Klassenkämpfe in Frankreich 1848 bis 1850.'" In *Marx-Engels Studienausgabe*, vol. 3. Frankfurt/M: Fischer Taschenbukh Verlag.

Engels, Friedrich. 1972 [1847]. "Die Kommunisten und Karl Heinzen." In *Marx-Engels Werke* (hereafter MEW), vol. 4. Berlin: DietzVerlag.

Ferro, Marc. 1980. *Des soviets au communisme bureaucratique*. Paris: Gallimard.

Guevara, Ernesto Che. 2006. *Apuntes críticos a la economia política.* Havana: Editorial de ciencias sociales.

KPSS v Resoliutsiyakh i Resheniyakh vol. 5, 1971. Moscow: Izdatel'stvo politicheskoi literaturi.

13. This echoes what Marx had said in his 1871 Address on the Commune: that it had made "individual property a truth" by transforming the means of production "into instruments of free and associated labor" (Marx 1971: 75).

Lenin, V.I. 1982a. *Izbrannye Proizvedeniya* (hereafter IP) (Selected Works), vol. 1. Moscow: Izdatel'stvo politicheskoi literaturi.

Lenin, V.I. 1982b. IP, vol. 2. Moscow: Izdatel'stvo politicheskoi literaturi.

Lenin, V.I. 1982c. IP, vol. 3. Moscow: Izdatel'stvo politicheskoi literaturi.

Loginov, V. 1992. "Prichiny krizisa sovetskoi ekonomiki: vosproizvodstvennyi aspekt," (Causes of crisis of the Soviet economy: aspect of reproduction). Voprosy ekonomiki no. 4-6 (Causes of crisis of the Soviet economy: aspect of reproduction). Voprosy ekonomiki no. 4-6.

Manevich, E. 1991. "Zárabotnaya pláta v uslovyakh rynochnoi ekonomiki" (Wage in the conditions of market economy). Voprosy ekonomiki no. 7.

Mao Tsetoung. 1972. *Textes Choisis*. Pekin: Editions en Langues Etrangères.

Mao Tsetoung. 1975. *Mao Tsetoung et la construction du socialisme*. Textes inédits, traduits et présentés par Hu Chi-His. Paris: Éditions du Seuil.

Mao Tse-tung. 1977. *Selected Works*, vol. V. Peking: Foreign Languages Press.

Marx, Karl. 1932 [1844]. "Aus den Exzerptheften: Ökonomische Studien." Marx/Engels *Gesamtausgabe* (hereafter MEGA) I/3. Berlin: Marx-Engels Verlag.

Marx, Karl. 1953 [1857-58]. *Grundrisse der Kritik der Politischen Ökonomie*. Berlin: Dietz Verlag.

Marx, Karl. 1956 [1861-63]. *Theorien über den Mehrwert*, vol. 1. Berlin: Dietz.

Marx, Karl. 1962a [1861-63]. *Theorien über den Mehrwert*, vol. 3. Berlin: Dietz.

Marx, Karl. 1962b [1880]. *Randglossen zu Adolph Wagners "Lehrbuch..."* MEW 19. Berlin: Dietz.

Marx, Karl. 1964a [1894]. *Das Kapital*, vol. 3. Berlin: MEW 25.

Marx, Karl. 1964b [1871-72]. "*Statuts Généraux de L'Association Internationale des Travilleurs.*" *The General Council of the First International: Minutes*. Moscow: Progress Publishers.

Marx, Karl. 1964c [1875]. *Randglossen zum Programm der deutschen Arbeiterpartei*, (Critique of the Gotha Programme). In Marx-Engels *Ausgewäwalte Shriften*, vol. 2. Berlin: Dietz.

Marx, Karl. 1965 [1875]. *Le Capital*. In *Oeuvres: Économie*, vol. 1. Paris: Gallimard.

Marx, Karl. 1971 [1871]. *On the Paris Commune*. Moscow: Progress.

Marx, Karl. 1972 [1847]. *Die moralisierende Kritik und die kritisierende Moral*. MEW 4. Berlin: Dietz.

Marx, Karl. 1973b [1874-77]. *Konspekt von Bakunins Buch 'Staatlichkeit und Anarchie.'* MEW 18. Berlin: Dietz.

Marx, Karl. 1976a [1844]. *Kritische Randglossen zu dem Artikel 'Der König von Preussen...'* MEW 1. Berlin: Dietz.

Marx, Karl. 1976b [1861-63]. *Zur Kritik der Politischen Ökonomie (Manuskript 1861-63)*. MEGA II/3.1. Berlin: Dietz.

Marx, Karl. 1980 [1858-61]. *Ökonomische Manuskripte und Schriften*. MEGA II/2. Berlin: Dietz.

Marx, Karl. 1987 [1872]. *Das Kapital*, vol. 1. MEGA II/6. Berlin: Dietz.

Marx, Karl. 1988 [1863-67]. *Ökonomische Manuskripte*. MEGA II/4.1. Berlin: Dietz.

Marx, Karl. 1992 [1863–67]. *Ökonomische Manuskripte*. MEGA II/4.2. Berlin: Dietz.

Marx, Karl. 2008 [1868–81]. *Manuskripte Zum Zweiten Buch des "Kapitals."* MEGA. Berlin: Akademie Verlag.

Marx, Karl and Friedrich Engels. 1966 [1848]. *Manifest der kommunistischen Partei*. In *Marx-Engels Studienausgabe*, vol. 3. Frankfurt/M: Fischer Taschenbuch.

Marx, Karl and Friedrich Engels. 1973a [1845–46]. *Die deutsche Ideologie*. MEW 3. Berlin: Dietz.

Meisner, Maurice. 1999. *Mao's China and After*. New York: The Free Press.

Most, Johann. 1989 [1876]. *Kapital und Arbeit*. MEGA II/8. Berlin: Dietz.

Rabinowitch, Alexander. 2004. *The Bolsheviks Come to Power*. Chicago: Haymarket.

Schram, Stuart. 1974. *Mao Tse-Tung Unrehearsed*. Harmondsworth: Penguin.

Serge, Victor. 2001. *Mémoires d'un révolutionnaire*. Paris: Robert Laffont.

Stalin, J. 1970. *Selected Writings*. Westport: Greenwood.

Stalin, J. 1980. *Oeuvres choisies*. Tirana: Nëntori.

Sweezy, Paul. 1993. "Socialism, Legacy and Renewal." *Monthly Review*, January.

Change the System, Not Its Barriers

Michael A. Lebowitz

"System-change, not climate-change!" More and more, this demand has emerged in response to the overwhelming signs of environmental destruction around us. It reflects a growing understanding of the incompatibility of capitalism and life. However, many do *not* understand this. Many people concerned about what is happening to the planet think that what is necessary are regulations which can check the destructiveness of current patterns. Measures which try to limit carbon emissions by offering big carrots and small sticks, which propose taxes to encourage rational economic actors to choose less harmful options, which offer subsidies for forms of power generation deemed less harmful to the environment – all these efforts to patch up the problems which have emerged remain the first choice of those who look upon themselves as realists in the real world.

That idea that we can regulate abuses within capitalism is not unique to environmental issues. We see the same pattern when it comes to the current financial crisis of capitalism. New regulations, new limits, new forms of oversight are seen as a solution to abuse and excess. They are proposed as ways to encourage good behaviour on the part of the actors who have created the situation. Bad capitalists rather than capitalism itself are identified as the evil. And the problem of the newly homeless, the unemployed? Everywhere the same approach: protect those who are being evicted, protect the victims of the system, repair the excesses and all will go (more or less) well.

The common element is the failure to understand the system, the failure to grasp the very nature of capital and capitalism. It is the failure to recognise that the logic of capital is the logic of cancer – the tendency to expand without limits.

Capital's tendency to go beyond all barriers

Like every other social process of production, capitalism is a system of reproduction (Marx 1977: 711). It develops as an organic

Socialism and Democracy, Vol.24, No.3, November 2010, pp.46–59
ISSN 0885-4300 print/ISSN 1745-2635 online
DOI: 10.1080/08854300.2010.513617

system by taking the historic premises it inherits and by "subordinating all elements of society to itself, or in creating out of it the organs which it still lacks. This is historically how it becomes a totality." And, once capital stands upon its own foundations, "every economic relation presupposes every other in its bourgeois economic form, and everything posited is thus also a presupposition; this is the case with every organic system" (Marx 1973: 278).

Thus, the result of capitalist production is the reproduction of its premises: capitalists, capitalist ownership of the means of production, and workers separated from the means of production and compelled to sell their labour-power in order to reproduce themselves. As long as that process is not interrupted, capital can replace the means of production consumed and can continue to exploit workers, thereby producing the surplus value which underlies the reproduction of the capitalist. However, capitalism is much more than a system of reproduction of its initial conditions. Rather than a steady-state system, capitalism by its nature requires *expanded* reproduction.

Inherent in the logic of capital, Marx argued, is its "ceaseless striving" to go beyond its quantitative barrier: "The goal-determining activity of capital can only be that of growing wealthier, i.e. of magnification, of increasing itself" (Marx 1973: 270). Accordingly, in its drive for profits, capital presses to increase the exploitation of producers – by increasing both the degree of exploitation and the numbers exploited. Capital constantly attempts to expand by extending the length and intensity of the workday, driving down the wages it pays, and increasing productivity relative to real wages. And. it can succeed in increasing the surplus value generated in production because it has the power to decide how and where to expand and is constantly engaged in finding ways to divide and separate workers in order to weaken them.

The surplus value generated through the exploitation of workers in production and latent in commodities, however, is only made real by the exchange of those impregnated commodities for money. Therefore, if capital is to grow, so also must the consumption capacity: "a precondition of production based on capital is therefore the production of a *constantly widening sphere of circulation*" (Marx 1973: 407). Accordingly, in its "ceaseless striving" to expand the "consuming circle within circulation," capital turns to the "production of *new* needs and discovery and creation of new use values," to the "discovery, creation and satisfaction of new needs arising from society itself" – that expansion of the needs of workers upon which "the contemporary power of capital rests" (Marx 1973: 408–9, 287; Lebowitz 2003: 32–39).

Further, capital confronts quantitative limits in the existing sphere of circulation by driving to widen that sphere. "The tendency to create the *world market* is directly given in the concept of capital itself. Every limit appears as a barrier to be overcome" (Marx 1973: 408). And, as capital strives "to tear down every spatial barrier" to exchange, and to "conquer the whole earth for its market," it also strives "to annihilate this space with time, i.e. to reduce to a minimum the time spent in motion from one place to another" (Marx 1973: 539). In short, "capital," Marx accordingly declared, "is the endless and limitless drive to go beyond its limiting barrier. Every boundary is and has to be a barrier for it" (Marx 1973: 334).

This language is not incidental to Marx's argument. In Hegelian terms, if capital has a Limit, this means that it is *finite,* that "its perishing is not merely contingent, so that it could be without perishing." In contrast, if a system has *no* limit, then it is infinite. The use of the concept of Barrier accordingly reveals that there *is* no limit: "by the very fact that something has been determined as barrier, it has already been surpassed" (Lebowitz 2009: Ch. 7). Thus, when Marx spoke of capital's drive to take all limits (or boundaries) and to transform them into mere barriers, he was describing its endless drive to expand, its ceaseless striving to be infinite.

So, is it possible, then, to *regulate* capital? Certainly on specific questions, it is possible to create barriers, regulations which target specific outcomes. Capital always comes up against barriers, and its history is one of driving beyond barriers and transforming and developing itself in the process. Indeed, Growth-Barrier-Growth is the law of motion of capital. But what *cannot* be regulated is capital's tendency to grow without limits. After all, it is the very essence of capitalism to expand. *So, does capital have no limit?* Will this system, which looks upon human beings and nature as mere means to its growth and tends to destroy both these "original sources of all wealth," continue infinitely until it has destroyed everything (Marx 1977: 638)? In short, is the only limit to capital the total destruction of human beings and nature?

Certainly, the classical political economists worried that there was a limit to the growth of capital – "a day of judgement" signalled by the tendency of the rate of profit to fall. Ironically, this has become a matter of faith since for many opponents of capitalism. However, in "Marx's Falling Rate of Profit: A Dialectical View" (reprinted in Lebowitz 2009), I stressed that there was no built-in limit to capital in the mathematics of the so-called "falling rate of profit." In fact, as further developed in "The General and Specific in Marx's Theory of Crisis" (and expanded in Lebowitz 2009), it is clear that Marx repeatedly stressed that the classic FROP argument presented in Volume III of *Capital* depends upon the assumption of lagging productivity growth in Department I – i.e., where "the productive power of labour does not rise *equally* and *simultaneously* in all the branches of production which contribute to produce the commodity" (Lebowitz 2009: 133–43; Marx 1994: 33–4). If the rate of profit falls, though, because of uneven productivity growth, it is merely a barrier that capital can drive beyond.

So, if FROP does not point to the finiteness of capital, does it mean that there is no limit this side of the mutual destruction of the contending parties? In "Marx's Falling Rate of Profit," I argued that for Marx it was "conscious human beings who recognize that capital is its own barrier, who are the Limit to capital." The Limit that Marx identified was "the proletariat, created, united, and expanded by capital in the course of its development. What capital produces, "above all, is its own grave-diggers. Its fall and the victory of the proletariat are equally inevitable" (quoted, Lebowitz 2009: 127–8).

The products of capital

Yet, that assertion of inevitability seems a bit problematic. Who are those real subjects that will put an end to capital? After all, it is not the Abstract Proletariat who acts in the real world. Rather, it is always people who have produced themselves through their own activities – through that simultaneous "changing of circumstances and of human activity or self-change" which is the essence of Marx's view of "the self-creation of man as a process" (Lebowitz 2003: 178–81). Every act of production, every labour process, indeed every human activity has as its result a "joint product" – both the change in the object of labour and the change in the labourer herself.

So, what about human activity under capitalist relations of production? What is the joint product that develops alongside the commodities containing surplus value that emerge from this particular labour process? What is the nature of the people produced within capitalism?

In *Capital*, Marx described the mutilation, the impoverishment, the "crippling of body and mind" of the worker "bound hand and foot for life to a single specialized operation" that occurs in the division of labour characteristic of the capitalist process of manufacturing. Did the development of machinery rescue workers under capitalism? Certainly, the potential to permit workers to develop their capabilities was there; however, you can detect the horror with which Marx explained how machinery provided a technical basis for the capitalist "inversion" – how it *completed* the "separation of the intellectual faculties of the production process from manual labour" (Marx 1977: 482–4, 548, 607–8, 614).

In this situation, head and hand become separate and hostile, "every atom of freedom, both in bodily and in intellectual activity" is lost. "All means for the development of production undergo a dialectical inversion," Marx indicated; "they distort the worker into a fragment of a man," they degrade him and "alienate from him the intellectual potentialities of the labour process" (Marx 1977: 548, 643, 799). In short, in addition to producing commodities and capital itself, capitalism produces a fragmented, crippled human being, whose enjoyment consists in possessing and consuming things.

Indeed, consumerism is another way that capitalism deforms people. Within capitalist relations of production, people are subjected to "the powerful will of a being outside them, who subjects their activity to his purpose." The creative power of the worker's labour here "establishes itself as the power of capital, as an *alien power* confronting him" (Marx 1977: 450; 1973: 453, 307). Thus, fixed capital, machinery, technology, all "the general productive forces of the social brain," appear as attributes of capital and as independent of workers (Marx 1973: 694; 1977: 1053–4, 1058). Workers produce products which are the property of capital, which are turned against them and dominate them as capital. The world of wealth, Marx commented, faces the worker "as an alien world dominating him" (Marx 1977: 1062).

And, that alien world dominates the worker more and more *precisely* because (as noted above) capital constantly creates new needs to consume as the result of its requirement to realise the surplus value contained in commodities (Lebowitz 2003: 37–9). For workers, producing within this relationship is a process of a "complete emptying-out," "total alienation," the "sacrifice of the human end-in-itself to an entirely external end" (Marx 1973: 488). How else but with money, the true need that capitalism creates, can we fill the vacuum? We fill the vacuum of our lives with *things* – we are driven to consume.

What we observe here is *the vicious circle of capitalism*. Beginning with (a) people who are separated from the means of production and with needs that they must fulfill, we see that these people (b) must go into the labour market to sell their labour power – competing with other people in the same situation. They (c) enter into capitalist production, that process which yields as its result impoverished workers with both the need and the means to consume. Having (d) consumed the products they are able to purchase, however, those workers are once again without the means to maintain themselves and must present themselves again to capital; they must once again produce for capital's goals. Within the wage-labour relation, workers remain dependent upon capital.

But there is another reason for the reproduction of capitalism. Precisely because the nature of capital as the product of exploitation is hidden, there is the tendency not to recognise that the productive power of capital is in essence the productive power of combined past and present social labour (Lebowitz 2010b: 35–40). As a result, we attribute all progress to capital. And, the more the system develops, the more that production relies upon fixed capital, the "organs of the human brain, created by the human hand," that social heritage that takes the form of instruments of labour – the more that capital (and the capitalist) appear to be necessary to workers. Capital continues to rule over production and society because workers think capital is *necessary*. Indeed, capital tends to produce the working class it *needs*, workers who treat capitalism as common sense:

> The advance of capitalist production develops a working class which by education, tradition and habit looks upon the requirement of that mode of production as self-evident natural laws. The organization of the capitalist process of production, once it is fully developed, breaks down all resistance (Marx 1977: 899).

Thus, "in the completed bourgeois system, every economic relation presupposes every other in its bourgeois economic form" (Marx 1973: 278).

Of course, workers *do* struggle against capital for specific goals – they struggle for better wages, workdays of lower length and intensity, and benefits that will allow them to satisfy more of their needs within this wage-labour relation. However, as long as workers do not understand that capital is the result of exploitation, they will always be dependent upon it – no matter how much they may struggle on particular questions, such as questions of "fairness" (e.g., "fair" wages, "fair" day's work). And, that is why Marx wrote *Capital*. Precisely because of capital's inherent tendency to develop a working class that looks upon capital's requirements as "self-evident natural laws," Marx's purpose was to explain the nature of capital to workers and to help them to understand the necessity to go beyond capitalism (Lebowitz 2003: 177).

Understanding that capitalism is a perverse society that deforms people, and that capital itself is the result of exploitation, however, is not enough. If people think that there is no alternative, then they will struggle to do their best within capitalism but will not waste their time and energy trying to achieve the impossible. If workers accept the logic of capital as essential, then even a working class in motion will not be the Limit to capital. Rather, the successes of their struggles will be mere barriers that workers have erected, because capital will find ways to get around them.

Ideas become a material force when they grip the minds of masses. And the idea that capitalism may be unjust but that there is no alternative – an idea that was strengthened by the experience of attempts to build socialism in the last century – supports the reproduction of capital; it ensures that when capitalism is in crisis, the dominant tendency among workers will be to *give in* rather than to *move in* (Lebowitz 2006: 39; Lebowitz 2010b: 136). For this very reason, to change the system requires the development of a new common sense – a vision of an alternative.

A vision of socialism for the 21st century

Marx had such a vision – the society of associated producers, "a society of free individuality, based on the universal development of individuals and on their subordination of their communal, social productivity as their social wealth" (Marx 1973: 158). Socialism for him was a society which removes all obstacles to the full development of human beings; it was one in which "the worker's own need for development" guides society (Marx 1977: 772). The possibility of that alternative society, indeed, was the perspective from which he criticized capitalism; it is the *premise* of his book, *Capital* (Lebowitz 2003: 203, 209).

Rather than this focus upon the full development of human potential, however, the dominant conception of 20th-century socialism stressed the development of productive forces, a development that someday (and somehow) would produce a society which negated the unsatisfied needs characteristic of capitalism – a society characterized by the abundance that would allow everyone to consume and consume in accordance with their needs. An important part of the socialist vision was lost – human beings at the centre.

Unfortunately, too, a significant part of the image conveyed by "socialism" and "communism" was that of a state standing over and above society, one that directs and oppresses working people – a bitter irony, given Marx's contempt for the "all-directing bureaucracy" and the "state parasites, richly paid sycophants and sinecurists" of the state of mid-19th-century France, a state that squeezed "the living civil society like a boa constrictor" (quoted, Lebowitz 2003: 193–5).

That is why Venezuelan President Hugo Chávez's very public distinction between the experience of the 20th century and what we must build now was so important. "We have to re-invent socialism," Chávez announced to assembled activists at the January 2005 World Social Forum in Porto Alegre, Brazil. "It can't be the kind of socialism that we saw in the Soviet Union," he stressed, "but it will emerge as we develop new systems that are built on cooperation, not competition." If we are ever going to end the poverty of the majority of the world, capitalism must be transcended, Chávez argued. "But we cannot resort to state capitalism, which would be the same perversion as the Soviet Union. We must reclaim socialism as a thesis, a project and a path, but a new type of socialism, a humanist one, which puts humans and not machines or the state ahead of everything" (Lebowitz 2006: 109; Sojo 2005).

The spectre of socialism for the 21st century thus made its public debut, and characteristic of the vision that it embodied was that neither expansion of the means of production nor direction by the state should define the new socialist society; rather, human beings must be at its centre. It is a conception of socialism that returns to Marx and to his focus upon the development of "rich human beings," the development of "the rich individuality," that real wealth which is the development of human capacity (Lebowitz 2003: 131–3; Lebowitz 2010b: 42–4).

But Venezuela? As I indicated in *Build It Now*, this "most unpredictable site" for "reinventing socialism" was an example of the surprises that history offers. Here, after all, was a country with a very small organised working class (especially in the private sector), a minuscule peasantry, a substantial informal sector, massive poverty, and a warped oil economy characterised by a parasitic capitalist class and a rentist culture of clientelism and corruption (Lebowitz 2006: 86–8). Definitely not the textbook case memorised by metropolitan radicals. True, there were rebellions against the ravages of neoliberal policy measures which created the environment leading to the election of Chávez in 1998. But, it took the coup and the bosses' lockout in 1992–3 (both sponsored by US imperialism and both defeated by mobilisation from below) to turn Chávez away from his earlier belief in the possibility of a "Third Way."

2003 was the year in which the Bolivarian Revolution really started – when the new social missions which bypassed the inefficient and sabotaged state began and when Chávez denounced capitalism ("the logic of capital is a perverse logic") and contrasted it to the "social economy," which "bases its logic on the human being" and "generates mainly use-value" (Lebowitz 2006: 95–101). And, as this process advanced, so also did Chávez's reading about socialism.

Particularly influential now was the work of István Mészáros – especially his *Beyond Capital* (1994). From Mészáros's reading of the *Grundrisse*, Chávez in 2005 drew a critique of exchange relations and commodity exchange in contrast to a society oriented toward communal needs and communal purposes (Lebowitz 2006: 106–9). While this focus upon community vs. self-interest reinforced the influence of liberation theology upon Chávez, the part played by Mészáros was entirely contingent.[1]

From Mészáros, Chávez also subsequently drew the concept of socialism as an organic system – a specific combination in which all the elements coexist simultaneously and support one another. Considering the failure of "real socialism," Mészáros had stressed the need for "the radical reconstitution of the dialectic of production-distribution-consumption, setting out from the genuine social control of the means of production." Here, then, was the starting point for what in January 2007 Chávez called "the elementary triangle of socialism" – the combination of social property, social production and satisfaction of social needs (Lebowitz 2010b: 24–5).[2]

Consider the logic of this socialist combination, this developed conception of socialism for the 21st century that has surfaced in Venezuela. Unifying those three sides of the socialist triangle is the theme of human development:

A. Social ownership of the means of production is critical within this structure because it is the only way to ensure that our communal, social productivity is directed to the free development of all rather than used to satisfy the private goals of capitalists, groups of producers, or state bureaucrats. But, this concerns more than our current activity. Social ownership of our social heritage, the results of past social labour, is an assertion that all living human beings have the right to the full development of their potential – to real wealth, the

1. Chávez had been introduced to Mészáros and his work by Jorge Giordani (his thesis advisor when in prison and subsequently the long-standing economics minister). Giordani, who promoted the translation of *Beyond Capital* into Spanish, had been a student at Sussex where he had developed a close friendship with Mészáros. Through this unlikely set of coincidences, *Beyond Capital* became the bible which Chávez studied and regularly exhorted all to read.
2. See the discussion of these elements in Lebowitz (2007a).

development of human capacity. It is the recognition that "the free development of each is the condition for the free development of all."

B. Social production organized by workers builds new relations among producers – relations of cooperation and solidarity. It allows workers to end "the crippling of body and mind" and the loss of "every atom of freedom, both in bodily and in intellectual activity" that comes from the separation of head and hand. As long as workers are prevented from developing their capacities by combining thinking and doing in the workplace, they remain alienated and fragmented human beings whose enjoyment consists in possessing and consuming things. Organization of production in all spheres by workers, thus, is a condition for the full development of the producers, for the development of their capabilities – a condition for the production of rich human beings.

C. Satisfaction of communal needs and purposes as the goal of productive activity means that, instead of interacting as separate and indifferent individuals, we function as members of a community. Rather than looking upon our own capacity as our property and as a means of securing as much as possible in an exchange, we start from the recognition of our common humanity and, thus, of the importance of conditions in which everyone is able to develop his/her full potential. When our productive activity is oriented to the needs of others, it both builds solidarity among people and produces socialist human beings.

These three sides of the "socialist triangle" form members of a whole. Parts of a structure in which "all the elements coexist simultaneously and support one another," they mutually interact. "This is the case with every organic whole." There is here the "universal, all-sided, *vital*, connection of everything with everything" that Lenin found in Hegel, that whole composed of various elements which "stand to one another in a necessary connection arising out of the nature of the organism" (Lebowitz 2003: 52–4; Lebowitz 2010b: 85–6).

Consider that mutual dependence. Social ownership of the means of production is a necessary condition for worker management and production for the needs of the community. In the absence of social ownership, the character of production and production decisions will not stress the joint product of socialist production – the development of rich human beings. Further, in its focus upon the entitlement to the fruits of our social heritage, social ownership supports the development of solidarity based upon recognition of our common humanity and, thus, the development of communal institutions (such as communal councils and worker councils) in order to make communality real.

In its turn, worker and community management ensures that decisions are not conceived and executed through a "systematic and hierarchic division of labour" but, rather, are democratic, participatory, and protagonistic. For the means of production to remain social property, it is essential to prevent the emergence of a "trained caste" above workers, "absorbing the intelligence of the masses" and developing the capacity to rule production in place of workers. Through worker management, the producers transform themselves and develop qualitatively different needs; they express themselves through their collective productive activity rather than by possessing things and thus create the conditions for development of a solidarian society.

Finally, productive activity oriented toward communal needs and purposes has as its condition the development of communality. Without this focus upon the community, production tends to be self-oriented in its character and exists as a *means* rather than as an expression of one's capabilities and self. Communality guards against worker-managers viewing their labour-power as property and as the basis of an *exchange* with society as well as against a tendency to treat social property as belonging to a particular group. By stressing the principle that the free development of each is the condition for the free development of all, the solidarian society insists upon the existence of democratic, participatory and protagonistic institutions which ensure for all members of society "their complete development, both individual and collective" (Lebowitz 2006: 89).

The socialist triangle is a system of reproduction. Its premises are results of the system; and its products are social ownership of the means of production, social production organized by workers, and a solidarian orientation to communal needs and purposes. "Every economic relation presupposes every other in its [socialist] economic form, and everything posited is thus also a presupposition; this is the case with every organic system" (Marx 1973: 278).

Struggling to make the vision real

The conception of such an alternative is essential if we are ever to offer more than mere barriers to the logic of capital. To end capitalism – i.e., to make capital finite – we must (like even the worst architect) build the goal in our minds before we can construct it in reality. "At the end of every labour process, a result emerges which had already been conceived by the worker at the beginning, hence already existed ideally" (Marx 1977: 284). To struggle against a situation in which workers "by education, tradition and habit" look upon capital's needs "as self-evident natural laws" (i.e., as common sense), we must struggle for an *alternative* common sense.

The Battle of Ideas, in short, is an essential part of the revolutionary labour process. In the ideological struggle against capital, we need to counterpose to capital's "ought," that drive of capital for self-expansion, the *workers' "ought"* – "the inverse situation in which objective wealth is there to satisfy the worker's own need for development" (Marx 1977: 772). In *The Socialist Alternative: Real Human Development*, starting from the concept of the socialist triangle, I have tried to sketch out some dimensions for such an ideological struggle by introducing the concept of a Charter for Human Development:

> A. Everyone has the right to share in the social heritage of human beings, has an equal right to the use and benefits of the products of the social brain and the social hand, in order to be able to develop her full potential.
> B. Everyone has the right to be able to develop her full potential and capacities through democracy, participation and protagonism in the workplace and society – a process in which these subjects of activity have the requisite health and education which permit them to make full use of this opportunity.
> C. Everyone has the right to live in a society in which human beings and nature can be nurtured – a society in which we can develop our full potential in communities based upon cooperation and solidarity. (Lebowitz 2010b: 131)

The vision of a new society oriented to human development, however, is only a vision. There are many obstacles to its realisation. Certainly, this is true in the case of Venezuela, where, despite its successes, building socialism still faces US imperialism and, among other things, pervasive clientelism, corruption and bureaucracy within the Bolivarian Revolution itself. Whether these prove to be barriers or limits will only be determined by struggle.[3]

How do we turn this preconceived goal into a real result? Success in the revolutionary labour process, as in every labour process, depends upon the determination to achieve that purpose consciously:

> And this is a purpose he is conscious of, it determines the mode of his activity with the rigidity of a law, and he must subordinate his will to it. This subordination is no mere momentary act. Apart from the exertion of the working organs, a purposeful will is required for the entire duration of the work (Marx 1977: 284).

More, in short, than the Battle of Ideas is essential for this revolutionary process. Real struggles, based upon "the worker's own need for

3. See this repeated theme in (Lebowitz 2006: 112–6; Lebowitz 2007b; Lebowitz 2010a).

development," are the way workers transform themselves – the way they rid themselves of "the muck of ages." Through revolutionary practice, that simultaneous changing of circumstances and human activity or self-change, they produce themselves as other than the products of capital. By going beyond the barriers presented by capital, the "ought" of workers allows them to develop the capacities to "found society anew." It is through that process of struggle that the conditions are created for going beyond capital: "the present "spontaneous action of the natural laws of capital and landed property" can only be superseded by "the spontaneous action of the laws of the social economy of free and associated labour" in a long process of development of new conditions" (Lebowitz 2003: 180–3 204–5).

As explored in *The Socialist Alternative: Real Human Development,* that struggle for human development goes far beyond a narrow focus upon struggles within the workplace. Rather, it involves a struggle against every barrier to the full development of human potential, to that free development of each which is the condition for the free development of all. Capital, we must understand, is the obstacle to human development. We can go beyond specific barriers it presents, but capital will always present new barriers, and only struggle itself will determine whether capital itself proves to be the Limit or only the Barrier. In place of that system which destroys the "original sources of all wealth," we must build "the inverse situation, in which objective wealth is there to satisfy the worker's own need for development."

Be realistic – change the system, not its barriers!

References

Lebowitz, Michael A. 2003. *Beyond CAPITAL: Marx's Political Economy of the Working Class*. 2nd ed. New York: Palgrave Macmillan.

Lebowitz, Michael A. 2006. *Build It Now: Socialism for the Twenty-First Century*. New York: Monthly Review Press.

Lebowitz, Michael A. 2007a. "New Wings for Socialism," *Monthly Review* (April).

Lebowitz, Michael A. 2007b. "Venezuela: A Good Example of the Bad Left of Latin America," *Monthly Review* (July-August).

Lebowitz, Michael A. 2009. *Following Marx: Method, Critique and Crisis*. Chicago: Haymarket Books.

Lebowitz, Michael A. 2010a. "Exploring the Dialectic of the Bolivarian Revolution," *Monthly Review* (February).

Lebowitz, Michael A. 2010b. *The Socialist Alternative: Real Human Development*. New York: Monthly Review Press.

Marx, Karl. 1973. *Grundrisse*. New York: Vintage Books.

Marx, Karl. 1977. *Capital*, Vol. I. New York: Vintage Books.

Marx, Karl. 1994. *Economic Manuscript of 1861–63. Conclusion.* In Marx and Engels, *Collected Works*, Vol. 34. New York: International Publishers.

Mészáros, István. 1994. *Beyond Capital: Toward a Theory of Transition*. New York: Monthly Review Press.

Sojo, Cleto A. 2005. "Venezuela's Chávez Closes WSF with Call to Transcend Capitalism," *Venezuelanalysis.com*, (January 31).

Emancipation in Marx's Early Work

George Comninel

One does not often hear serious discussion of human emancipation these days, and yet the idea is at the core of critical thinking about the human condition, and remains the ultimate goal of truly transformative politics. Although a range of issues concerning political liberty emerged earlier in the modern age, and some can be traced back still earlier through the history of popular struggles and the history of political thought, it really was in the era of the French Revolution and its aftermath that the question of human emancipation as such came to the fore. While other thinkers contributed to understanding the issues, it remains particularly the theoretical achievements of the young Karl Marx that help illuminate what human emancipation entails, and how it is to be achieved.

The modern problem of emancipation

Marx grew up in Trier, an ancient and formerly free Rhineland city that embraced the French Revolution, but which, due to the defeat of Bonaparte shortly before his birth, was subjected to the reactionary rule of the Prussia. Marx's father had been compelled to set aside his Enlightenment principles, and formally abandon his Jewish identity to become a Lutheran, in order to continue his career in law. Karl himself, a brilliant and philosophical youth, was from an early age deeply committed to a radical realization of freedom. Frustrating his father by turning towards philosophy and away from a career in law, then abandoning even the pretence of legal studies after his father died,[1] Marx devoted himself as student, journalist, and activist to clarifying the meaning of human emancipation and how it was to be achieved. As was also the case for virtually every other thinker and activist of the time, the immediate and inescapable starting point

1. On this period of Marx's life, see especially Francis Wheen, *Karl Marx* (London: Fourth Estate, 1999), pp. 21–30.

Socialism and Democracy, Vol.24, No.3, November 2010, pp.60–78
ISSN 0885-4300 print/ISSN 1745-2635 online
DOI: 10.1080/08854300.2010.513612

for Marx's ideas required coming to terms with the politics, objectives, and limitations of the French Revolution.

In its opposition first to aristocratic privilege, and then to monarchy, the politics of the Revolution revolved about issues of liberty, equality, and sociality.[2] The radical Jacobins conceived the Revolution in terms of a fundamentally *political* emancipation, and the lawyers, office holders, and professionals who constituted their majority came to understand this almost entirely in terms of building a democratically representative republican "Nation." They saw their mission as - and increasingly they became - functionaries of the state as a revolutionary instrument devoted to instilling democratic republican citizenship. This project of realizing a republic in accord with Rousseau's conception, embodying the "General Will" of the people, went far beyond the relatively mild forms of previous liberal politics, from the most tentative of original revolutionaries through the moderate Girondins.[3]

Yet from the perspective of the still more radical popular movement in the Revolution, which embraced not only direct democracy, but increasingly also ideas of *social* equality - political tendencies that culminated in Gracchus Babeuf's "Conspiracy of Equals" - even the most radical Jacobins fell far short of advocating true emancipation. Babeuf's ideas in turn constituted a key contribution of the French Revolution to the development of "socialism" in the first half of the 19th century. Indeed, it was in reference to raising "the social question" that a distinctive radical politics emerged within the broad "left" - comprising democratic, republican, and even merely liberal-constitutionalist ideologies - defined by a shared opposition to absolute monarchy following the Revolution.

It was in this context that, by early 1844, it had become clear to Marx that *both* the social question *and* the political notion of power[4]

2. *Fraternité* might be translated as "fraternity" or "brotherhood," but its implications went beyond the sense generally conveyed by those terms in the context of Anglo-American liberal ideology. Inherent in early modern French political thought was a robust idea of the centrality of society in human experience, both informing and informed by the ideas of Jean-Jacques Rousseau. See Ellen Wood, "The State and Popular Sovereignty in French Political Thought: A Genealogy of Rousseau's 'General Will'," *History of Political Thought*, vol. 4, no. 2 (1983).
3. See George C. Comninel, *Rethinking the French Revolution: Marxism and the Revisionist Challenge* (London: Verso, 1987).
4. This is the term Jean Bruhat used (in "La Révolution française et la formation de la pensée de Marx," *Annales historique de la Révolution française*, XXXVIII (2) 1966, p. 141) to describe the focus of Marx's interest during the first half of 1844, a period of "preoccupation" with the radically Jacobin Convention of 1792–94. At

urgently had to be addressed, and he simultaneously undertook the critique of political economy and a close study of the radical politics of the French Revolution. It was also in this period, after completing his articles for the *Deutsch-Französische Jahrbücher* he had edited with Arnold Ruge, that Marx definitively abandoned the idea that human emancipation was either a project of philosophy or a collaboration between philosophy and the proletariat. From the spring of 1844 onwards, Marx was clear that the emancipation of humanity belonged to a historical process grounded in the development of social relations (the material history of social humanity), and that the processes of class struggle that drove and informed the realization of real emancipation emerged from the interests of the working class in their immediate character as "common humanity," and not from philosophy.

Indeed, in examining Marx's manuscripts and texts from 1843 through mid-1844, we can discern – in language that is sometimes daunting in its dense philosophical analysis, if also at times poignant, scathing, or breathtaking in its vision – the process through which his immanent critique of both Hegel and the philosophy of the Young Hegelians culminated in his transcending the idea that philosophy was action. This new stance was most famously articulated in Marx's eleventh "Thesis on Feuerbach" the following year: "The philosophers have only *interpreted* the world, in various ways; the point, however, is to change it."[5] What, then, we are led to ask, is the form of change that is necessary – what is the nature of the emancipation that must be achieved?

That even the most conservative forms of liberalism still embodied genuine elements of emancipation was due to the legacy of feudalism. At the core of the "feudal revolution" that swept the territories of Charlemagne's empire (*circa* 1000 CE) and spread from there, was a reduction of virtually all previously free persons to a status of

---

the time, Marx wrote to Arnold Ruge of his plan to write a history of the Convention, and he urged the publication in *Vorwärts* of excerpts from the memoirs of the Jacobin René Levasseur, which he had studied. While it is important to take note of this interest in the radical politics of revolution, his most significant work in this period was undoubtedly the *Economic and Philosophic Manuscripts of 1844*, in which he first developed the critique of political economy. The brief notes on Levasseur, however, were his only writings on the French Revolution proper, aside from passages in such other political works as the *Communist Manifesto* and *The Eighteenth Brumaire of Louis Bonaparte*. In moving ever more decisively beyond the politics of the French Revolution, he also moved beyond studying it as such.

5. Robert C. Tucker, ed., *The Marx-Engels Reader*, 2nd ed. (New York: Norton, 1978), p. 145. This is my preferred translation from the German, but there are many alternatives.

unfreedom. This followed from the sudden appropriation of all sovereign powers of state authority by great landlords, who constituted themselves in a directly political sense as *lords* not only over tenants of their own properties, but also over all who lived nearby.[6] This transformation wiped out the surviving traces of a public sphere, first established in the ancient world, in which free men (if only men) enjoyed political rights, and were protected in their freedom. In the early modern period, after the demise of feudalism in the mid 15th century, re-establishment of a meaningful public sphere - accompanied by much debate over constitutional forms, legal rights, and the proper limits of sovereign power - emerged as the most fundamental and enduring issue of politics within the dominant classes. The circumscribed limits of this project of minimal political emancipation were, however, blown open by the experience of the Revolution.

In light of this historical contextualization, emancipation in its broadest sense can be seen to be a particular political project of the modern age. The politics of the ancient world had been characterized in fundamental ways by the possession of liberty (though of course many were excluded from it). With the introduction of feudalism proper, however, citizenship and liberty were extinguished for the great majority of even the formerly free male population relative to lordly bearers of sovereign power.

The republics and republicanism of late medieval Italy were neither ancient survivals nor prematurely modern political forms, but historically specific developments of the Middle Ages integrally connected to the feudal societies to the north.[7] It is telling that in the wake of the Renaissance, Italian cities generally lost their ascendancy even within the peninsula, and slipped into a long political somnolence. Early in the modern era, few other than the Swiss had won back the essentially republican form of liberty characteristic of the ancient world,[8] liberty that was thereafter jealously preserved in

6. See Jean-Pierre Poly and Eric Bournazel, *The Feudal Transformation: 900-1200* (New York: Holmes & Meier, 1991); George C. Comninel, "English Feudalism and the Origins of Capitalism," *Journal of Peasant Studies*, 27 (4): 1-53. As I note in the latter, England had a unique form of "feudalism" in which sovereignty was not truly parceled among lords, and in which as many as one-quarter of the peasantry remained legally free, and protected (as freeholders) in the public courts.

7. See Justin Rosenberg, "Secret Origins of the State," in *The Empire of Civil Society* (London: Verso, 1994).

8. Even in the period of the Empire, both in theory and generally in practice, Roman citizens enjoyed protection of their liberty under law, and the state in principle remained "the public thing" - the literal meaning of *res publica*.

their cantons. It is because of the general imposition of unfreedom during the Middle Ages, and the limited extent to which emancipation had since been realized, that the Genevan Rousseau was prompted to confront the conundrum that men were born free, yet everywhere were in chains.

Simultaneously, at the level of culture, there emerged in "the Enlightenment" a growing rejection of superstition and revealed faith as the basis for public discourse and the regulation of public activity. The feudalism of the Middle Ages devolved upon the Church virtually complete control over culture – regulation of morality, legitimate ideas, the forms of social intercourse, artistic expression, acceptable knowledge – while the lords enjoyed almost untrammeled political power as bearers of the sword. As issues of public rights and freedom re-emerged, so also did challenges to the power of the Church. Contrary to much recent opinion, this cannot be reduced to a single dimension of modern discourse, such as liberalism – neither Voltaire nor de Sade can in any way be said to have been liberals, nor is it easy even to reconcile Rousseau with specifically liberal ideas. The emancipation of thought and cultural production during the modern era took many and varied forms, framed within a broad rejection of received knowledge, leading to the profound displacement of religion as guardian of ideas, values, and legitimacy.

Nor can the modern era be associated with a single form of social and economic development. As Robert Brenner and Ellen Meiksins Wood have demonstrated, capitalism did not develop across Europe, but uniquely in England; and not in the context of town life, but in agriculture.[9] In France, by contrast, the social property relations of modern era increasingly took the form of politically constituted property within the monarchy, centered upon increasingly formal property rights in personally owned, heritable, and saleable "public" offices, supplanting the immediately political property form of territorial sovereignty characteristic of the feudal era. This led to a society characterized by intense bureaucratism and statism – unlike both feudal society and

9. Robert Brenner, "Agrarian Class Structure and Economic Development in Pre-Industrial Europe," and "The Agrarian Roots of European Capitalism," in T.H. Aston and C.H.E. Philpin, eds., *The Brenner Debate: Agrarian Class Structure and Economic Development in Pre-Industrial Europe* (Cambridge: Cambridge University Press, 1985); Ellen Meiksins Wood, "The Separation of the Economic and the Political in Capitalism," in *Democracy Against Capitalism: Renewing Historical Materialism* (Cambridge: Cambridge University Press, 1995); and Comninel, *Rethinking the French Revolution* and "English Feudalism and the Origins of Capitalism."

modern England – with intense and frequent struggles over interests that were simultaneously "political" and "economic."

States and property after the French Revolution

It is in this light that we must interpret the "nation building" that the Jacobins undertook as professional administrators of the Republic. With every major political development between the calling of the Estates General in 1788 and the consolidation of Bonaparte's Empire, the number of state officials grew. Much like the absolutist monarchy of the old régime, this burgeoning apparatus of power both played a vital role in the social and economic life of France, and provided income and career to the already rich and powerful, the talented and ambitious, and the merely comfortable *bourgeois*.[10] This is evident in Marx's commentary on the state at the founding of the Second Empire by Louis Bonaparte:

> the executive power commands an army of officials numbering more than half a million individuals and therefore constantly maintains an immense mass of interests and livelihoods in the most absolute dependence; where the state enmeshes, controls, regulates, superintends, and tutors civil society from its most comprehensive manifestations of life down to its most insignificant stirrings, from its most general modes of being to the private existence of individuals; where through the most extraordinary centralization this parasitic body acquires a ubiquity, an omniscience, a capacity for accelerated mobility, and an elasticity which finds a counterpart only in the helpless dependence, the loose shapelessness of the actual body politic... But it is precisely with the maintenance of that extensive state machine in its numerous ramifications that the material interests of the French bourgeoisie are interwoven in the closest fashion. Here it finds posts for its surplus population and makes up in the form of state salaries for what it cannot pocket in the form of profit, interest, rents, and honorariums.[11]

It is striking to what extent, not only in this passage but throughout the work, Marx identifies the material interests of the French dominant classes in terms of finance, state incomes, and rents, and the slight extent to which any industrial bourgeoisie is even noted, let alone credited with a significant role. Moreover, Marx clearly identified the peasantry as bearing the burden of supporting the dominant classes through their astounding level of mortgage indebtedness, together with the heavy taxes that were the "life source" of the apparatuses of

10. See Comninel, *Rethinking the French Revolution*.
11. Karl Marx, *The Eighteenth Brumaire of Louis Napoleon* (online), Ch. 4.

state.[12] The French state, through its successive absolutist, Republican, and Bonapartist forms, erected an ever more stupendous edifice of administration, rule, and war – nominally for the good of the people, or the glory and General Will of the Nation, but always on the backs of impoverished peasant masses, and to the great benefit of its architects and overseers.

There were, then, different paths of social and political development in the modern era, emerging from the Middle Ages in accord with the historical specificities of each country. In Italy, robust industry and commercial dominance, together with strong republican institutions, subsided into undistinguished centuries of aristocratic dominance over sharecropping peasant tenants, aside from a few surviving enclaves of commerce. France and England increasingly diverged as a result of fundamentally different feudal forms.[13] In France, the central state developed as a means for politically constituted property to appropriate peasant surplus. England, however, became the unique locus for the development of agrarian capitalism, from which its generalized industrial form subsequently developed, with considerable direct assistance from the state.[14] Not only, then, were the forms of state different in different European societies, but the differences directly reflected structures of social property relations through which class exploitation was realized.

In 1843, Engels first distinguished England as having priority in the sphere of the economic; France, with priority in the political; and Germany, in the philosophical. He drew out this idea specifically in relation to how the *doctrine* of communism emerged in each country.[15] This focus on ideas is telling: socialists in England were driven to communist ideas "*practically*, by the rapid increase of misery, demoralisation, and pauperism in their own country," with little awareness of the ideas and movements on the Continent. French socialists instead came to the same conclusion "*politically*, by first asking for political liberty and equality; and, finding this insufficient, joining social liberty, and social equality to their political claims." Since, however, "the Germans became Communists philosophically, by reasoning upon first principles," it is not hard to appreciate

12. *Ibid.*, Ch. 7.
13. Comninel, "English Feudalism."
14. See Michael Zmolek, *Rethinking the Industrial Revolution: An Inquiry into the Transition from Agrarian to Industrial Capitalism in Britain*, Ph.D. Diss., York University, Toronto, 2008.
15. Frederick Engels, "Progress of Social Reform on the Continent," *Marx-Engels Collected Works* (MECW), vol. 3, (New York: International Publishers, 1975), p. 392.

that this development was not grounded in the economic or political experiences of working people. This German priority in philosophy was associated by both Engels and Marx with its priority in the development of modern theology.[16] Not only did Germany produce the Reformation, but almost immediately the ideas of religious reform were appropriated by German peasants, with the radical preacher Thomas Münzer as leader, to justify demands for social equality, elimination of private property, and an end to the right of political power over others.[17] Luther exploded in vituperation against this presumption that a return to original Christian values might thus be applied to social life outside the ecclesiastical structure, and exhorted those in power to "Kill them like dogs!"

The role of religion alongside property and political power as a specific form of oppression was particularly clear in Germany. The Holy Alliance of 1815 brought together the Christian states of Orthodox Russia, Catholic Austria, and Lutheran Prussia - with tacit support from Anglican-dominated Britain - to suppress the liberal, democratic, and socialist ideas that emerged during the French Revolution. Then, in pursuit of a more complete Christian union, Frederick William III forced a merger of Lutheran and Calvinist faiths in Prussia, generating not only resistance from "Old Lutherans" who rejected the apparent incorporation of Calvinist doctrine, but a profound awareness of the politicization of religious belief. Whereas the French state, both during the Revolution, and after the overthrow of the restored Legitimist Bourbon monarchy in July 1830, stood opposed to the claims of the Church, while in Britain the established Church was becoming ever less significant to the state, the absolutism of the Prussian state was manifestly grounded in a re-confirmation of faith.

It is this confluence of religious oppression, political oppression, and the suppression of all "socialist" ideas challenging inequality and immiseration that provided the context for the development of Marx's ideas with respect to the meaning of human emancipation. Since his youth, he had become increasingly critical of oppression in each of these forms. Forced by state censorship in 1843 from his position as editor of the *Rheinische Zeitung*, he returned to a critical reading of Hegel's *Philosophy of Right* to clarify his thought.[18]

16. *Ibid.*, p. 400; Karl Marx, *Economic and Philosophic Manuscripts of 1844*, MECW, vol. 3, pp. 182, 290.
17. Engels, "Progress of Social Reform," p. 400.
18. Karl Marx, "Preface" to *A Contribution to the Critique of Political Economy*, in *Early Writings* (London: Penguin, 1975), p. 425.

Marx's critique of Hegelian philosophy in 1843

Marx had initially rejected the philosophy of Hegel – the comfortable academic who provided an apologia for the Prussian monarchy – but subsequently found himself drawn to the "Young Hegelians," who pursued an atheist and materialist re-grounding of Hegel's original historical conception of social totality. Recognizing humanity in its collectivity as the real embodiment of consciousness in the universe, Hegel brought together philosophy, religion, and history to conceive the development of humanity as the realization of the divine in the world over historical time. Without reprising the complex developmental unity of his thought, its key contribution was the way he incorporated into philosophy the already pervasive liberal conception of history as progress. Where the philosophy of Aristotle conceived the world in fundamentally fixed terms, and the *telos* of a thing was simply the end towards which it developed within this given frame, Hegel conceived the social whole – indeed, the whole of humanity – in terms of its development as a totality through history, through discernible stages of growing realization and increasing complexity, towards a final form of fully realized human potential.

Where political economy in England conceived progress largely in terms of economic development, and political ideology in France saw it in terms of historical class struggles, progress found its expression in Germany primarily in philosophical terms, culminating in reconciliation with the Prussian theocratic monarchy. In opposition to Hegel's accommodation with the monarchy,[19] the Young Hegelians sought to turn his ideas against the reactionary state. It was this combination of theoretical sophistication with a left political agenda that attracted Marx, despite his initial distaste for Hegel.

Hegel's work elaborated upon the longstanding philosophical (and theological) concept of *alienation*, particularly pursuing the integration of its sense of the sale of property with a more profound sense that involved personal identity, informed by the idea of being a "stranger" to God.[20] The Young Hegelians turned this conception back against Hegel's concessions to Prussian official religion, articulating the view that religious belief constituted alienation from our own humanity. In this critical conception of alienation, putting faith in an imaginary divinity was a denial of our own responsibility for the forms of life

19. This is not to say that there were not, implicit in Hegel's work, significant points that looked beyond the existing absolutist state. What he did not do, however, was elaborate such points in explicit criticism of the existing state.
20. István Mészáros, *Marx's Theory of Alienation* (London: Merlin Press, 1970).

and achievements that we realize in and through the social whole. In the course of worship, "religion alienates our own nature from us,"[21] we project the potency of our own collective existence as something apart, a divine "other" to which we are subject - a subjection made palpable in subordination to religious authorities, and particularly to the "holy" form of the monarchy. Rejecting the conservative view that human freedom and rationality, as conceived by Hegel, had already been realized in the Prussian state (however explicit his texts seemed on that point), the Young Hegelians sought to make reason and emancipation real.

For the most part, as is especially evident in Bruno Bauer's book *The Jewish Question* (1873), they conceived the emancipation of humanity in terms of its release from religious alienation. The authority of the Prussian state was said to be grounded in religion, and it directed much of its attention towards religious issues. The philosophical freedom of humanity from the alienation of religion, embodied in the freedom of the state from religion, would result in realization of freedom in the republic, or *Freistaat*. It was this reduction of human emancipation to nothing more than achieving the merely political objective of the French Revolution - the "free state" rather than free humanity - that elicited Marx's caustic criticism of Bauer in the first part of "On *The Jewish Question*."[22] He concluded this critique by demanding a great deal more:

> All emancipation is a *reduction* of the human world and relationships to man *himself.*
>
> Political emancipation is the reduction of man, on the one hand, to a member of civil society, to an *egoistic, independent* individual, and, on the other hand, to a *citizen*, a juridical person.
>
> Only when the real, individual man re-absorbs in himself the abstract citizen, and as an individual human being has become a *species-being* in his everyday life, in his particular work, and in his particular situation, only when man has recognized and organized his *"forces propres"* as *social* powers, and, consequently, no longer separates social power from himself in the shape of *political* power, only then will human emancipation have been accomplished.[23]

In his first published work of theory, then, Marx declared the need to go beyond the "merely political" politics of the French Revolution: human emancipation required the transformation of our "own powers" into a truly social form.

---

21. Ludwig Feuerbach, *Essence of Christianity*, trans. George Eliot (New York: Dover Publications, 2008), Ch. 25.
22. Karl Marx, "On *The Jewish Question*", MECW, vol. 3, pp. 146–168.
23. *Ibid.*, p. 168.

Among the Young Hegelians, however, Moses Hess had begun to take the idea of alienation an important step further, in ideas best known from *The Essence of Money* (1845). Hess had first advanced this approach in a Swiss publication of 1843 that contained pieces by several Young Hegelians, as well as Frederick Engels, and Marx's critique of Bauer was directed towards a piece in this collection as well as toward *The Jewish Question*.[24] As Hess articulated his ideas in 1845, he conceived "the human essence" to be "the collaboration of individuals of the human species" in the social whole of life activity, and he saw in money the alienation (estrangement) of humans from that essence, in terms drawn from the critique of religion:

> in the old mutual estrangement of men, an external symbol had to be invented to represent the spiritual and material exchange of products. Through this abstraction from real, spiritual and living intercourse the capacity, the creative force of men was increased during their estrangement; in other words, they found in this abstract means of intercourse a mediating essence for their own estrangement; they had to seek the unifying essence outside of themselves, i.e., an inhuman, super-human essence, since they were not men, i.e., were not united. Without this inhuman means of intercourse they would never have entered into intercourse. But as soon as men unite, as soon as a direct intercourse between them can take place the inhuman, external, dead means of intercourse must necessarily be abolished.[25]

In the second part of "On *The Jewish Question*," referring specifically to Bauer's piece in the Swiss collection, Marx developed a critique of money as alienation in conjunction with his critique of merely political emancipation. In passages that are too often misread because their subject is not the question of Jews as such, but rather the preoccupation with money that *Christianity* created and imposed as the day-to-day meaning of being "Jewish," Marx's point is that this preoccupation with money has finally reached its highest development in *bourgeois society* "under the dominance of Christianity."[26] In this sense, he argues, Christians have themselves become "Jews" (as, he notes ironically, it was Jews who first became Christians). The real object of emancipation, therefore, is not the merely political freedom of the secular state – which is insufficient even to end the religious form of alienation – but achievement of social life without the alienation from ourselves embodied in the pursuit of money.

---

24. Moses Hess, *Einundzwanzig Bogen aus der Schweiz*, Pt. 1, Zurich (1843), p. 329. I am greatly indebted to Marcello Musto for bringing this point to my attention.
25. Moses Hess, *The Essence of Money*, Ch. 14, Marxists Internet Archive, www.marxists.org/archive/hess/1845/essence-money.htm.
26. Marx, "On *The Jewish Question*," p. 173.

In this first of his published "early works," therefore, Marx advanced a philosophical position that went beyond the Jacobinism of the French Revolution and explicitly incorporated "the social question." He had, however, already developed an even more far-reaching contribution to the idea of emancipation than that contained in "On *The Jewish Question*," marking, indeed, a remarkably original and profound contribution to political theory. Through his return to Hegel's *Philosophy of Right* earlier in 1843, Marx had come to appreciate that the state as such was inherently a form of human alienation.

This point emerges through his critique of Hegel's ideas in relation to their fawning embrace of the Prussian monarchy. At one level, Hegel's claims do go beyond merely legitimizing or apologizing for that monarchy, but in their toadying they are immediately open to the most cutting criticism, which Marx did his best to provide. In taking these ideas seriously, however, Marx moves from Hegel's assertion that "the general interest" is the purpose of the state, to its implications for the nature of the constitution. Here, where Hegel abases himself to assert that without a monarchy the state "is no longer a state," Marx focuses upon the meaning of the constitution in relation to the people, and observes that the constitution is *always* grounded in the people:

> Democracy is the genus Constitution. Monarchy is one species, and a poor one at that.... Democracy is the solved *riddle* of all constitutions. Here, not merely *implicitly* and in essence but *existing* in reality, the constitution is constantly brought back to its actual basis, the *actual human being*, the *actual people*, and established as the people's *own* work.[27]

From this point on, as he increasingly loses patience with Hegel's dodges, Marx has in mind that the real social collectivity of the people – which is not comprised even within the democratic form of the *political* state[28] – stands in opposition to the state as such. The political form of the state, in other words, is itself inherently a form of alienation. It is for this reason that Marx's conception of emancipation – in all of the work that follows in 1843, and still more in the life-work that he truly takes up from 1844 – always requires transcending the state as such. "It is not the *radical* revolution, not the *general human*

---

27. Karl Marx, *Contribution to the Critique of Hegel's Philosophy of Law*, MECW, vol. 3, p. 29.
28. In his critique of Hegel's conception of the development of the state from the family and civil society, Marx distinguished between the state as political apparatus and the substantive social reality of the people in their totality, even going so far as to oppose the "the political state" to "the non-political state."

emancipation which is a utopian dream for Germany, but rather the partial, the *merely* political revolution," he asserted in his published critique of Hegel, identifying the agents for this emancipation as the proletariat, whose lack of *particular* interest compelled them to realize the interests of humanity as a whole.[29] He still, however, conceived this in relation to philosophy as such, "which finds its *material* weapons in the proletariat."

In these writings of 1843, Marx advanced the concept of emancipation beyond that of any other political theorist.[30] Alienation was the projection of forms of material human sociality – the social relations through which we realize our collective existence, the necessary condition for human existence – into artificial institutions and ideas treated as real; not merely *alien* to us as individual human beings, but having power over us. Emancipation was overcoming *alienation*, in all of its forms, to return the human world to real human beings themselves. Alienation existed in the form of religion, as the Young Hegelians first claimed. It also existed in the form of money (and hence property), by which the social intercourse of humanity became a means to exercise power over others, reducing them to mere things. Then, in identifying the very form of the state as a form of alienation, Marx found the solution to the "riddle of all constitutions," as well as to Rousseau's conundrum. So long as the state existed in its political form, as alienated social power that acted back upon us as individual humans, we could never be free. For humanity to live without chains, the General Will had to be realized freely, without alienation.

The alienation of labour and true human emancipation

Yet, Marx's achievement in his Paris manuscripts of 1844 dwarfs even these profound contributions of 1843. Having been alerted to the real import of the ideas of the political economists by Engels' "Outlines of a Critique of Political Economy," Marx read each of the authors cited in it, and undertook a detailed critique of his own.[31] He began by dividing his pages into columns under the headings of the three basic classes and corresponding forms of income identified by the political economists: Wages of Labour, Profit of Capital, and Rent of Land.

29. *Ibid.*, p. 186.
30. Both Thomas Münzer and the English "Digger" Gerrard Winstanley argued that human freedom required abolition of both the state and private property, but their works are not accepted as part of the "canon" of political thought.
31. Comninel, "Marx's Context," *History of Political Thought*, Vol. XXI, No. 3, Autumn 2000, pp. 467–83.

Writing down the columns of "Wages of Labour," he drew out what the political economist asserts, and what it actually means for workers:

> He tells us that originally and in theory the whole product of labour belongs to the worker. But at the same time he tells us that in actual fact what the worker gets is the smallest and utterly indispensable part of the product - as much, only, as is necessary for his existence, not as a human being, but as a worker, and for the propagation, not of humanity, but of the slave class of workers.[32]

From this, Marx rises above the point of view of political economy, and in subsequent passages (known on the basis of their content as "Estranged Labour") he conceives of *the alienation of labour*. The alienation of labour is not a product of property or monetary wealth - rather, property is itself the form of the alienation of labour.[33]

This realization had the most profound impact upon Marx's thought, posing the problem of human emancipation in entirely new terms, as is evident in the two questions he posed at the end of his original analysis under "Wages of Labour":

> (1) What in the evolution of mankind is the meaning of this reduction of the greater part of mankind to abstract labour?
> (2) What are the mistakes committed by the piecemeal reformers, who either want to raise wages ... or regard equality of wages ... as the goal of social revolution?[34]

The first question takes Hegel's conception of human society developing through the course of history, and reconceives it in relation to the development of the alienation of labour. It is this reconception that leads Marx to assert in the *Communist Manifesto* that "The history of all hitherto existing society is the history of class struggles." This follows from the fact that the differences of wealth between classes arise from the alienation of labour. As he noted in the opening words of "Wages of Labour," this basic social relationship between worker and capitalist involves antagonistic struggle.

Where other forms of alienation may have predominantly negative effects upon those who labour, they are not constituted antagonistically in the way that the alienation of labour is. The worker can use the form of money to meet his or her own needs, and even the capitalist may fall victim to money. The alienation of labour is profoundly different in making the life-activity of some humans alien to themselves in the

32. Marx, *Economic and Philosophic Manuscripts of 1844*, p. 239.
33. *Ibid.*, pp. 271–3.
34. *Ibid.*, p. 241.

immediate form of benefit to others. It is for this reason that in conceiving a general relationship of antagonism between classes at the start of the *Manifesto*, Marx summarized it as "in a word, oppressor and oppressed."

This historical conception of human society developing through particular forms of the alienation of labour is not developed to any great extent in the 1844 manuscripts, but it is already present. Marx asserts here that labour and capital in their opposition "constitute *private property* as its developed state of contradiction," and he refers to earlier social forms ("ancient Rome, Turkey, etc.") as having an "antithesis between *lack of property* and *property*" that is as yet undeveloped.[35] He conceives "the entire movement of history" in relation to "*Communism* as the *positive* transcendence of *private property* as *human self-estrangement*, and therefore as the real *appropriation* of the *human essence* by and for man... the complete return of man to himself as a *social* (i.e., human) being."[36]

And communism, in this conception, is a movement of real, historical struggle against the alienation of labour. It is not the weapon of philosophy, but the movement of humanity recovering itself, by itself. This movement is a material historical process grounded in the development of social production:

> The entire movement of history, just as its [communism's] *actual* act of genesis – the birth act of its empirical existence – is, therefore, also for its thinking consciousness the *comprehended* and *known* process of its *becoming*.[37]

That is, rather than following the dictates of philosophy, or seeking historical verification in "disconnected historical phenomena opposed to private property," communism as a mature movement "finds both its empirical and its theoretical basis in the movement of *private property* – more precisely in that of the economy."

> This *material*, immediately *perceptible* private property is the material perceptible expression of *estranged human* life. Its movement – production and consumption – is the *perceptible* revelation of the movement of all production until now, *i.e.*, the realisation or the reality of man.[38]

It is for these reasons that the revolution of proletarian workers is the basis for the general emancipation of humanity. To transcend the "reduction of the greater part of mankind to abstract labour" is to

35. *Ibid.*, pp. 293–4.
36. *Ibid.*, p. 296.
37. *Ibid.*, p. 297.
38. *Ibid.*

redeem humanity as a whole by and for humans. The long, historical, one-sided development of human social capacities through forms of the alienation of labour culminates in those who have nothing to lose but their chains transforming social existence for all humanity into a form that will have no chains on anyone. This, then, is a complete resolution of Rousseau's conundrum.

It is for this reason that the paltry aspirations of "piecemeal reformers" always remain inadequate. What is at issue is not "better wages for the slave," but full emancipation of all humankind. This requires above all an end to the alienation of labour, but the general emancipation of humanity requires an end to alienation in all of its forms. Alienation in the form of the state exists primarily to ensure that alienation in the form of private property – the alienation of labour – is maintained.[39] Thus the political form of the state must itself be transcended.

There is, however, necessarily a dialectical character to this. Unless the state's defence of property is overcome, there can be no overcoming the alienation of labour. At the same time, without overcoming the alienation of labour there can be no transcendence of the political form of the state. Anarchists understand that both the state and private property must be superseded, but offer no solution beyond ending both at the same time. There are substantial reasons for recognizing that human emancipation cannot, however, be so simply realized. One significant issue, of course, is that the forces defeated in any revolutionary transformation will not simply disappear, even if there is simultaneous revolution across the globe. This is, however, far less profound a problem than the fact that social production in all its forms, the institutions and patterns of daily social life, and the built-form of the infrastructure of our social existence, have taken form over long generations of social inequality and political power. Who will live where, how people will travel to work, what jobs will continue to exist, how needs will continue to be met where current production relations are inherently abusive, how environmentally destructive production upon which entire communities depend should be dealt with: these are not questions that can be resolved through simple consensus on the morrow of the revolution. Alienation in all of its forms will bequeath to any social process of human emancipation an enormous range of challenges, problems that are not without solution, but which will vex persons of reason and good will for a considerable period of time.

39. This point is apparent in much of anthropology and sociology, and figures centrally in the history of political thought.

Emancipation and revolution

In his later political writing, especially his "Critique of the Gotha Programme," Marx briefly sketched an approach to these problems. Asserting both the need for revolution to make possible an end to capitalist social relations of production, and the need not only to change the immediate form of the state, but to eliminate the state as such as a condition of full emancipation, Marx nonetheless accepted the need for a political form of the state to continue for some time (and one might well expect not a short time). Here – using the phrase "dictatorship of the proletariat" in one of a very few places in the whole of his writing – he explicitly (if briefly) explored the implications of it not being possible to transform social life completely all at once. He recognized that a transformation in social life was required to make possible a move from the principles of what he described as "bourgeois right." In capitalist society, "bourgeois right" does not apply to workers, in that their returns from production are not proportional to the labour that they contributed.[40] The first stage of revolutionary transformation must necessarily end the alienation of labour by which workers inherently produce wealth for their capitalist employers, but it cannot immediately go very far beyond that. Only

> after the enslaving subordination of the individual to the division of labor, and therewith also the antithesis between mental and physical labor, has vanished; after labor has become not only a means of life but life's prime want; after the productive forces have also increased with the all-around development of the individual, and all the springs of co-operative wealth flow more abundantly

is it possible to move to a form of society in which it is not necessary to maintain the principles of "bourgeois right" in distributing the proceeds of collective social labour. And only then, therefore, would no state be required.

Thus, the state must be defeated in revolution to end the most immediate manifestations of alienation, as well as the most oppressive and undemocratic characteristics of the state itself. Yet only after a far more profound transcendence of alienation and a reconfiguration of the real social landscape – to allow free human interaction on the basis of "from each according to his ability, to each according to his need" – can the state truly wither away.

On the one hand, human emancipation requires that the state itself must truly be transcended, in time. On the other hand, the political form of the state cannot simply be dispensed with on the morrow of

40. Marx, "Critique of the Gotha Programme" (many editions), Section I.

the revolution. It is, therefore, essential to recognize the ways in which the alienation inherent in the state has been partially constrained through the construction of human rights during the modern era. States long ago generally ceased to be embodiments of relatively simple communities of like-minded persons, among whom a General Will might be said to exist at the political level.

Notwithstanding the revolutionary conception of liberty, equality, and sociality that informed the Jacobin project of building a Rousseauan republic, such a state cannot achieve true human emancipation. Relative to the alienation inherent in state power, however, the establishment of individual and collective rights has been a profound political achievement. The state's alien potency has not been replaced by benign, freely determined self-governance, but it is potentially held in check in its power over individuals. There is no certainty that rights will be respected, of course, and they can never simply be taken for granted, but must be preserved and extended through struggle. It is, indeed, precisely because rights are limited and uncertain that the state as such must, in the end, be transcended. It is, therefore, important to acknowledge the potential for what Bakunin – in diatribes that otherwise offered little that could survive Marx's scathing criticism – had called the "dictatorship *over* the proletariat," a form of alienation that is not to be trivially dismissed. The post-revolutionary state should not, *must not,* be allowed yet again to render the people the impotent subjects of their own collective power. Rights and democratic practice must be zealously guarded, not taken for granted.

Conclusion

The struggles for human emancipation must have, at their core, class struggle to end the alienation of labour. This is not, however, the only form of alienation through which humanity has been, and continues to be, oppressed. Ultimately, the realization of full human freedom requires the elimination of our collective subordination to any form of sovereign power – we must not be subjected to some "other" that is constituted as more than "us." Since this transcendence cannot be realized all at once, however, we must recognize and preserve that partial recovery of liberty relative to the state that has been one of the signal achievements of the modern age. As part of an ongoing struggle for the realization of emancipation – necessarily dialectical in pursuing real ends through real contradictions – we must hold on to the rights that we have constructed, without holding them to be either above criticism, or the essence of freedom.

In this regard, it is equally important to recognize that even if the structures of power – not only the state, but other forms of oppression – have roots in the systemic reproduction of fundamental inequality through the alienation of labour, it is not only class from which humanity must be emancipated. Religion is potentially a relatively benign form of alienation. Other forms of alienation – the objectification of some humans for the benefit of others – are far less benign; these include the reduction of women to subjects of men's will, as well as the reduction of persons of colour to subordinate means of satisfying needs (or worse still, to threats to security) – in short, all forms of objectifying the autonomy of persons that reduce one human to mere means to an end (or mere obstacle) for another.

As Marx first put it in "On *The Jewish Question*," the emancipation of humanity requires the "*reduction* of the human world and relationships to [humanity] *itself*." This "reduction" is not a form of alienation, but of *realization* – humans in their relations with each other must recognize themselves in others, and so realize their *species-being*. Through his lifework, Marx focused upon the fundamental challenge of the alienation of labour, through which the historical development of society consistently has been bent towards the interests of the wealthy and powerful. Yet, from his earliest exploration of the forms of alienation, to his mature observations on the need and the capacity to achieve a society founded on the principle of "from each according to ability to each according to need," nothing less than the complete emancipation of humanity ever would suffice for Marx.

Revisiting Marx's Concept of Alienation

Marcello Musto

I. Introduction

Alienation was one of the most important and widely debated themes of the twentieth century, and Karl Marx's theorization played a key role in the discussions. Yet contrary to what one might imagine, the concept itself did not develop in a linear manner, and the publication of previously unknown texts containing Marx's reflections on alienation defined significant moments in the transformation and dissemination of the theory.

The meaning of the term changed several times over the centuries. In theological discourse it referred to the distance between man and God; in social contract theories, to loss of the individual's original liberty; and in English political economy, to the transfer of property ownership. The first systematic philosophical account of alienation was in the work of G.W.F. Hegel, who in *The Phenomenology of Spirit* (1807) adopted the terms *Entäusserung* (literally self-externalization or renunciation) and *Entfremdung* (estrangement) to denote Spirit's becoming other than itself in the realm of objectivity. The whole question still featured prominently in the writings of the Hegelian Left, and Ludwig Feuerbach's theory of religious alienation in *The Essence of Christianity* (1841) – that is, of man's projection of his own essence onto an imaginary deity – contributed significantly to the development of the concept. Alienation subsequently disappeared from philosophical reflection, and none of the major thinkers of the second half of the nineteenth century paid it any great attention. Even Marx rarely used the term in the works published during his lifetime, and it was entirely absent from the Marxism of the Second International (1889–1914).

During this period, however, several thinkers developed concepts that were later associated with alienation. In his *Division of Labour* (1893) and *Suicide* (1897), Émile Durkheim introduced the term "anomie" to indicate a set of phenomena whereby the norms guaranteeing social cohesion enter into crisis following a major extension of the division of labour. Social trends concomitant with huge changes

Socialism and Democracy, Vol.24, No.3, November 2010, pp.79–101
ISSN 0885-4300 print/ISSN 1745-2635 online
DOI: 10.1080/08854300.2010.544075

in the production process also lay at the basis of the thinking of German sociologists: Georg Simmel, in *The Philosophy of Money* (1900), paid great attention to the dominance of social institutions over individuals and to the growing impersonality of human relations; while Max Weber, in *Economy and Society* (1922), dwelled on the phenomena of "bureaucratization" in society and "rational calculation" in human relations, considering them to be the essence of capitalism. But these authors thought they were describing unstoppable tendencies, and their reflections were often guided by a wish to improve the existing social and political order - certainly not to replace it with a different one.

II. The rediscovery of alienation

The rediscovery of the theory of alienation occurred thanks to György Lukács, who in *History and Class Consciousness* (1923) referred to certain passages in Marx's *Capital* (1867) - especially the section on "commodity fetishism" (*Der Fetischcharakter der Ware*) - and introduced the term "reification" (*Verdinglichung, Versachlichung*) to describe the phenomenon whereby labour activity confronts human beings as something objective and independent, dominating them through external autonomous laws. In essence, however, Lukács' theory was still similar to Hegel's, since he conceived of reification as a structural given. Much later, after the appearance of a French translation[1] had given this work a wide resonance among students and left-wing activists, Lukács decided to republish it together with a long self-critical preface (1967), in which he explained that "*History and Class Consciousness* follows Hegel in that it too equates alienation with objectification."[2]

Another author who focused on this theme in the 1920s was Isaak Rubin, whose *Essays on Marx's Theory of Value* (1928) argued that the theory of commodity fetishism was "the basis of Marx's entire economic system, and in particular of his theory of value."[3] In the view of this Russian author, the reification of social relations was "a real fact of the commodity-capitalist economy."[4] It involved "'materialization' of production relations and not only 'mystification' or illusion.

1. *Histoire et conscience de classe*, trans. Kostas Axelos and Jacqueline Bois, Paris: Minuit, 1960.
2. Georg Lukács, *History and Class Consciousness*, Cambridge: MIT Press, 1971, xxiv.
3. Isaak Illich Rubin, *Essays on Marx's Theory of Value*, Detroit: Black & Red, 1972, 5.
4. Ibid., 28 (trans. mod.).

This is one of the characteristics of the economic structure of contemporary society.... Fetishism is not only a phenomenon of social consciousness, but of social being."[5]

Despite these insights - prescient if we consider the period in which they were written - Rubin's work did not promote a greater familiarity with the theory of alienation; its reception in the West began only with its translation into English in 1972 (and from English into other languages).

The decisive event that finally revolutionized the diffusion of the concept of alienation was the appearance in 1932 of the *Economic-Philosophical Manuscripts of 1844*, a previously unpublished text from Marx's youth. It rapidly became one of the most widely translated, circulated and discussed philosophical writings of the twentieth century, revealing the central role that Marx had given to the theory of alienation during an important period for the formation of his economic thought: the discovery of political economy.[6] For, with his category of alienated labour (*entfremdete Arbeit*),[7] Marx not only widened the problem of alienation from the philosophical, religious and political sphere to the economic sphere of material production; he also showed that the economic sphere was essential to understanding and overcoming alienation in the other spheres. In the *Economic-Philosophical Manuscripts of 1844*, alienation is presented as the phenomenon through which the labour product confronts labour "as something alien, as a power independent of the producer." For Marx:

> ...the externalization [*Entäusserung*] of the worker in his product means not only that his labour becomes an object, an *external* existence, but that it exists *outside him*, independently of him and alien to him, and begins to confront

5. Ibid., 59.
6. In fact, Marx had already used the concept of alienation before he wrote the *Economic-Philosophical Manuscripts of 1844*. In one text he published in the *Deutsch-Französische Jahrbücher* (February 1844) he wrote: "It is [...] the task of history, once the other-world of truth has vanished, to establish the truth of this world. It is the immediate task of philosophy, which is in the service of history, to unmask self-estrangement in its unholy forms once the holy form of human self-estrangement has been unmasked. Thus the criticism of heaven turns into the criticism of earth, the criticism of religion into the criticism of law and the criticism of theology into the criticism of politics." Karl Marx, "A Contribution to the Critique of Hegel's Philosophy of Right. Introduction," in Karl Marx, *Early Writings*, London: Penguin, 1992, 244–5.
7. In Marx's writings one finds the term *Entfremdung* as well as *Entäusserung*. These had different meanings in Hegel, but Marx uses them synonymously. See Marcella D'Abbiero, *Alienazione in Hegel. Usi e significati di Entäusserung, Entfremdung Veräusserung*, Rome: Edizioni dell'Ateneo, 1970, 25-7.

> him as an autonomous power; that the life which he has bestowed on the object confronts him as hostile and alien.'[8]

Alongside this general definition, Marx listed four ways in which the worker is alienated in bourgeois society: (1) from the product of his labour, which becomes "an alien object that has power over him"; (2) in his working activity, which he perceives as "directed against himself," as if it "does not belong to him";[9] (3) from "man's species-being," which is transformed into "a being alien to him"; and (4) from other human beings, and in relation to their labour and the object of their labour.[10]

For Marx, in contrast to Hegel, alienation was not coterminous with objectification as such, but rather with a particular phenomenon within a precise form of economy: that is, wage labour and the transformation of labour products into objects standing opposed to producers. The political difference between these two positions is enormous. Whereas Hegel presented alienation as an ontological manifestation of labour, Marx conceived it as characteristic of a particular, capitalist, epoch of production, and thought it would be possible to overcome it through "the emancipation of society from private property."[11] He would make similar points in the notebooks containing extracts from James Mill's *Elements of Political Economy*:

> Labour would be the free expression and hence the enjoyment of life. In the framework of private property it is the alienation of life since I work in order to live, in order to procure for myself the means of life. My labour is not life. Moreover, in my labour the specific character of my individuality would be affirmed because it would be my individual life. Labour would be authentic, active, property. In the framework of private property my individuality has been alienated to the point where I loathe this activity, it is torture for me. It is in fact no more than the appearance of activity and for that reason it is only a forced labour imposed on me not through an inner necessity but through an external arbitrary need.[12]

So, even in these fragmentary and sometimes hesitant early writings, Marx always discussed alienation from a historical, not a natural, point of view.

---

8. Karl Marx, "Economic and Philosophical Manuscripts (1844)," in *Early Writings*, 324.
9. Ibid., 327.
10. Ibid., 330. For an account of Marx's four-part typology of alienation, see Bertell Ollman, *Alienation*, New York: Cambridge University Press, 1971, 136–52.
11. Karl Marx, "Economic and Philosophical Manuscripts (1844)," 333.
12. Karl Marx, "Excerpts from James Mill's *Elements of Political Economy*," in *Early Writings*, 278.

III. Non-Marxist conceptions of alienation

Much time would elapse, however, before a historical, non-ontological, conception of alienation could take hold. In the early twentieth century, most authors who addressed the phenomenon considered it a universal aspect of human existence. In *Being and Time* (1927), for instance, Martin Heidegger approached it in purely philosophical terms. The category he used for his phenomenology of alienation was "fallenness" (*Verfallen*): that is, the tendency of Being-There (*Dasein* – ontologically constituted human existence) to lose itself in the inauthenticity and conformism of the surrounding world. For Heidegger, "fallenness into the world means an absorption in Being-with-one-another, in so far as the latter is guided by idle talk, curiosity, and ambiguity" – something truly quite different from the condition of the factory worker, which was at the centre of Marx's theoretical preoccupations. Moreover, Heidegger did not regard this "fallenness" as a "bad and deplorable ontical property of which, perhaps, more advanced stages of human culture might be able to rid themselves," but rather as an ontological characteristic, "an *existential mode* of Being-in-the-world."[13]

Herbert Marcuse, who, unlike Heidegger, knew Marx's work well, identified alienation with objectification as such, not with its manifestation in capitalist relations of production. In an essay he published in 1933, he argued that "the burdensome character of labor"[14] could not be attributed merely to "specific conditions in the performance of labor, to the social-technical structuring of labor"[15], but should be considered as one of its fundamental traits:

> In laboring, the laborer is always "with the thing": whether one stands by a machine, draws technical plans, is concerned with organizational measures, researches scientific problems, instructs people, etc. In his activity he allows himself to be directed by the thing, subjects himself and obeys its laws, even when he dominates his object.... In each case he is not "with himself" ... he

---

13. Martin Heidegger, *Being and Time*, San Francisco: Harper, 1962, 220–1. In the 1967 preface to his republished *History and Class Consciousness*, Lukács observed that in Heidegger alienation became a politically innocuous concept that "sublimated a critique of society into a purely philosophical problem" (Lukács, xxiv). Heidegger also tried to distort the meaning of Marx's concept of alienation: in his *Letter on "Humanism"* (1946), he noted approvingly that, "by experiencing alienation, [Marx] attains an essential dimension of history" (Martin Heidegger, "Letter on Humanism," in *Basic Writings*, London: Routledge, 1993, 243) – a misleading formulation which has no basis in Marx's writings.
14. Herbert Marcuse, "On the Philosophical Foundation of the Concept of Labor in Economics," *Telos* 16 (Summer, 1973), 25.
15. Ibid., 16–17.

> is with an "Other than himself" – even when this doing fulfils his own freely assumed life. This externalization and alienation of human existence . . . is ineliminable in principle.'[16]

For Marcuse, there was a "primordial negativity of laboring activity" that belonged to the "very essence of human existence."[17] The critique of alienation therefore became a critique of technology and labour in general, and its supersession was considered possible only in the moment of play, when people could attain a freedom denied them in productive activity: "In a single toss of a ball, the player achieves an infinitely greater triumph of human freedom over objectification than in the most powerful accomplishment of technical labor."[18]

In *Eros and Civilization* (1955), Marcuse took an equally clear distance from Marx's conception, arguing that human emancipation could be achieved only through the abolition of labour and the affirmation of the libido and play in social relations. He discarded any possibility that a society based on common ownership of the means of production might overcome alienation, on the grounds that labour in general, not only wage labour, was:

> ...work for an apparatus which they [the vast majority of the population] do not control, which operates as an independent power to which individuals must submit if they want to live. And it becomes the more alien the more specialized the division of labor becomes.... They work ... in *alienation* [... in the] absence of gratification [and in] negation of the pleasure principle.'[19]

The cardinal norm against which people should rebel was the 'performance principle' imposed by society. For, in Marcuse's eyes,

> 'the conflict between sexuality and civilization unfolds with this development of domination. Under the rule of the performance principle, body and mind are made into instruments of alienated labor; they can function as such instruments only if they renounce the freedom of the libidinal subject-object which the human organism primarily is and desires.... Man exists ... as an instrument of alienated performance.'[20]

Hence, even if material production is organized equitably and rationally, "it can never be a realm of freedom and gratification.... It is the

16. Ibid., 25.
17. Ibid.
18. Ibid., 14–15.
19. Herbert Marcuse, *Eros and Civilization*, Boston: Beacon Press, 1966, 45.
20. Ibid., 46–7. Georges Friedmann was of the same view, arguing in *The Anatomy of Work* (New York: Glencoe Press, 1964) that the overcoming of alienation was possible only after liberation from work.

sphere outside labor which defines freedom and fulfilment."[21] Marcuse's alternative was to abandon the Promethean myth so dear to Marx and to draw closer to a Dionysian perspective: the "liberation of eros."[22] In contrast to Freud, who had maintained in *Civilization and Its Discontents* (1929) that a non-repressive organization of society would entail a dangerous regression from the level of civilization attained in human relations, Marcuse was convinced that, if the liberation of the instincts took place in a technologically advanced "free society"[23] in the service of humanity, it would not only favour the march of progress but create "new and durable work relations."[24] But his indications about how the new society might come about were rather vague and utopian. He ended up opposing technological domination in general, so that his critique of alienation was no longer directed against capitalist relations of production, and his reflections on social change were so pessimistic as to include the working class among the subjects that operated in defence of the system.

The two leading figures in the Frankfurt School, Max Horkheimer and Theodor Adorno, also developed a theory of generalized estrangement resulting from invasive social control and the manipulation of needs by the mass media. In *Dialectic of Enlightenment* (1944) they argued that "a technological rationale is the rationale of domination itself. It is the coercive nature of society alienated from itself."[25] This meant that, in contemporary capitalism, even the sphere of leisure time - free and outside of work - was absorbed into the mechanisms reproducing consensus.

After World War II, the concept of alienation also found its way into psychoanalysis. Those who took it up started from Freud's theory that man is forced to choose between nature and culture, and that to enjoy the securities of civilization he must necessarily renounce his impulses.[26] Some psychologists linked alienation with the psychoses that appeared in certain individuals as a result of this conflict-

21. Marcuse, *Eros and Civilization,* 156.
22. Ibid., 155.
23. Ibid., 198.
24. Ibid., 155. Cf. the evocation of a 'libidinal rationality which is not only compatible with but even promotes progress toward higher forms of civilized freedom' (199). On the relationship between technology and progress, see Kostas Axelos, *Alienation, Praxis, and Techné in the Thought of Karl Marx,* Austin/London: University of Texas Press, 1976.
25. Max Horkheimer, Theodor W. Adorno, *Dialectic of Enlightenment,* New York: Seabury Press, 1972, 121.
26. See Sigmund Freud, *Civilization and its Discontents,* New York: Norton, 1962, 62.

ridden choice, thereby reducing the whole vast problematic of alienation to a merely subjective phenomenon.

The author who dealt most with alienation from within psychoanalysis was Erich Fromm. Unlike most of his colleagues, he never separated its manifestations from the capitalist historical context; indeed, his books *The Sane Society* (1955) and *Marx's Concept of Man* (1961) used the concept to try to build a bridge between psychoanalysis and Marxism. Yet Fromm likewise always put the main emphasis on subjectivity, and his concept of alienation, which he summarized as "a mode of experience in which the individual experiences himself as alien,"[27] remained too narrowly focused on the individual. Moreover, his account of Marx's concept based itself only on the *Economic-Philosophical Manuscripts of 1844* and showed a deep lack of understanding of the specificity and centrality of alienated labour in Marx's thought. This lacuna prevented Fromm from giving due weight to objective alienation (that of the worker in the labour process and in relation to the labour product) and led him to advance positions that appear disingenuous in their neglect of the underlying structural relations.

> Marx believed that the working class was the most alienated class.... [He] did not foresee the extent to which alienation was to become the fate of the vast majority of people.... If anything, the clerk, the salesman, the executive, are even more alienated today than the skilled manual worker. The latter's functioning still depends on the expression of certain personal qualities like skill, reliability, etc., and he is not forced to sell his "personality", his smile, his opinions in the bargain.[28]

One of the principal non-Marxist theories of alienation is that associated with Jean-Paul Sartre and the French existentialists. Indeed, in the 1940s, marked by the horrors of war and the ensuing *crise de conscience*, the phenomenon of alienation – partly under the influence of Alexandre Kojève's neo-Hegelianism[29] – became a recurrent reference both in philosophy and in narrative literature. Once again, however, the concept is much more generic than in Marx's thought, becoming

27. Erich Fromm, *The Sane Society*, New York: Fawcett, 1965, 111.
28. Erich Fromm, *Marx's Concept of Man*, New York: Frederick Ungar, 1961, 56–7. This failure to understand the specific character of alienated labour recurs in his writings on alienation in the 1960s. In an essay published in 1965 he wrote: "One has to examine the phenomenon of alienation in its relation to narcissism, depression, fanaticism, and idolatry to understand it fully." "The Application of Humanist Psychoanalysis to Marx's Theory," in Erich Fromm, ed., *Socialist Humanism*, New York: Doubleday, 1965, 221.
29. See Alexandre Kojève, *Introduction to the Reading of Hegel: Lectures on the Phenomenology of Spirit*, Ithaca: Cornell University Press, 1980.

identified with a diffuse discontent of man in society, a split between human individuality and the world of experience, and an insurmountable *condition humaine*. The existentialist philosophers did not propose a social origin for alienation, but saw it as inevitably bound up with all "facticity" (no doubt the failure of the Soviet experience favoured such a view) and human otherness. In 1955, Jean Hippolyte set out this position in one of the most significant works in this tendency:

> [alienation] does not seem to be reducible solely to the concept of the alienation of man under capitalism, as Marx understands it. The latter is only a particular case of a more universal problem of human self-consciousness which, being unable to conceive itself as an isolated *cogito*, can only recognize itself in a word which it constructs, in the other selves which it recognizes and by whom it is occasionally disowned. But this manner of self-discovery through the Other, this objectification, is always more or less an alienation, *a loss of self and a simultaneous self-discovery*. Thus objectification and alienation are inseparable, and their union is simply the expression of a dialectical tension observed in the very movement of history.[30]

Marx helped to develop a critique of human subjugation, basing himself on opposition to capitalist relations of production. The existentialists followed an opposite trajectory, trying to absorb those parts of Marx's work that they thought useful for their own approach, in a merely philosophical discussion devoid of a specific historical critique.[31]

IV. The debate on Marx's early writings about alienation

The alienation debate that developed in France frequently drew upon Marx's theories. Often, however, it referred only to the *Economic-Philosophical Manuscripts of 1844*; not even the sections of *Capital* that Lukács had used to construct his theory of reification were taken into consideration. Moreover, some sentences from the 1844 Manuscripts were taken out of context and transformed into sensational quotes supposedly proving the existence of a radically different "new Marx," saturated with philosophy and free of the economic determinism that critics attributed to *Capital* (often without having read it). Again on the basis of the 1844 texts, the French existentialists laid by far the greatest emphasis on the concept of self-alienation (*Selbstentfremdung*), that is, the alienation of the worker from the human species and from others like himself – a phenomenon that

30. Jean Hyppolite, *Studies on Marx and Hegel*, New York/London: Basic Books, 1969, 88.
31. Cf. István Mészáros, *Marx's Theory of Alienation*, London: Merlin Press, 1970, 241 ff.

Marx did discuss in his early writings, but always in connection with objective alienation.

The same glaring error appears in a leading figure of post-war political theory, Hannah Arendt. In *The Human Condition* (1958), she built her account of Marx's concept of alienation around the *Economic-Philosophical Manuscripts of 1844*, even then isolating only one of the types mentioned there by Marx: subjective alienation. This allowed her to claim:

> ...expropriation and world alienation coincide, and the modern age, very much against the intentions of all the actors in the play, began by alienating certain strata of the population from the world. [...] World alienation, and not self-alienation as Marx thought, has been the hallmark of the modern age.[32]

Evidence of her scant familiarity with Marx's mature work is the fact that, in conceding that Marx "was not altogether unaware of the implications of world alienation in capitalist economy," she referred only to a few lines in his very early journalistic piece, "The Debates on the Wood Theft Laws" (1842), not to the dozens of much more important pages in *Capital* and the preparatory manuscripts leading up to it. Her surprising conclusion was: "such occasional considerations play[ed] a minor role in his work, which remained firmly rooted in the modern age's extreme subjectivism."[33] Where and how Marx prioritized "self-alienation" in his analysis of capitalist society remains a mystery that Arendt never elucidated in her writings.

In the 1960s, the theory of alienation in the *Economic-Philosophical Manuscripts of 1844* became the major bone of contention in the wider interpretation of Marx's work. It was argued that a sharp distinction should be drawn between an "early Marx" and a "mature Marx" – an arbitrary and artificial opposition favoured both by those who preferred the early philosophical work and those for whom the only real Marx was the Marx of *Capital* (among them Louis Althusser and the Russian scholars). Whereas the former considered the theory of alienation in the *Economic-Philosophical Manuscripts of 1844* to be the most significant part of Marx's social critique, the latter often exhibited a veritable "phobia of alienation" and tried at first to downplay its relevance;[34] or, when this strategy was no longer possible, the whole theme of alienation was written off as "a youthful indiscretion, a

32. Hannah Arendt, *The Human Condition*, Chicago: University of Chicago Press, 1958, 253–4.
33. Ibid., 254.
34. The directors of the Institute of Marxism–Leninism in Berlin even managed to exclude the *Economic-Philosophical Manuscripts of 1844* from the numbered

residue of Hegelianism"[35] that Marx later abandoned. Scholars in the first camp retorted that the 1844 manuscripts were written by a man of 26 just embarking on his major studies; but those in the second camp still refused to accept the importance of Marx's theory of alienation, even when the publication of new texts made it clear that he never lost interest in it and that it occupied an important position in the main stages of his life's work.

To argue, as so many did, that the theory of alienation in the 1844 Manuscripts was the central theme of Marx's thought was so obviously wrong that it demonstrated no more than ignorance of his work.[36] On the other hand, when Marx again became the most frequently discussed and quoted author in world philosophical literature because of his newly published pages on alienation, the silence from the Soviet Union on this whole topic, and on the controversies associated with it, provided a striking example of the instrumental use made of his writings in that country. For the existence of alienation in the Soviet Union and its satellites was dismissed out of hand, and any texts relating to the question were treated with suspicion. As Henri Lefebvre put it, "in Soviet society, *alienation could and must no longer be an issue*. By order from above, for reasons of State, the concept had to disappear."[37] Therefore, until the 1970s, very few authors in the "socialist camp" paid any attention to the works in question.

A number of well-known Western authors also played down the complexity of the phenomenon. Lucien Goldmann, for instance, thought it possible to overcome alienation in the social-economic conditions of the time, and in his *Recherches dialectiques* (1959) argued that it would disappear, or recede, under the mere impact of planning. "Reification," he wrote, "is in fact a phenomenon closely bound up with the absence of planning and with production for the market"; Soviet socialism in the East and Keynesian policies in the West were resulting "in the first case in the elimination of reification, and in the second case in its progressive weakening."[38] History has demonstrated the faultiness of his predictions.

---

volumes of the canonical *Marx-Engels Werke*, relegating them to a supplementary volume with a smaller print run.

35. Adam Schaff, *Alienation as a Social Phenomenon*, Oxford: Pergamon Press, 1980, 21.
36. Cf. Daniel Bell, "The Rediscovery of Alienation: Some notes along the quest for the historical Marx," *Journal of Philosophy*, vol. LVI, 24 (November, 1959), 933–52, which concludes: "while one may be sympathetic to the idea of alienation, it is only further myth-making to read this concept back as the central theme of Marx," 935.
37. Henri Lefebvre, *Critique of Everyday Life*, London: Verso, 1991, 53.
38. Lucien Goldmann, *Recherches dialectiques*, Paris: Gallimard, 1959, 101.

V. The irresistible fascination of the theory of alienation

In the 1960s a real vogue began for theories of alienation, and hundreds of books and articles were published on it around the world. It was the age of alienation *tout court*. Authors from various political backgrounds and academic disciplines identified its causes as commodification, overspecialization, anomie, bureaucratization, conformism, consumerism, loss of a sense of self amid new technologies, even personal isolation, apathy, social or ethnic marginalization, and environmental pollution.

The concept of alienation seemed to express the spirit of the age to perfection, and indeed, in its critique of capitalist society, it became a meeting ground for anti-Soviet philosophical Marxism and the most democratic and progressive currents in the Catholic world. However, the popularity of the concept, and its indiscriminate application, created a profound terminological ambiguity.[39] Within the space of a few years, alienation thus became an empty formula ranging right across the spectrum of human unhappiness – so all-encompassing that it generated the belief that it could never be modified.[40]

With Guy Debord's book *The Society of the Spectacle*, which, after its first publication in 1967, soon became a veritable manifesto for the generation of students in revolt against the system, alienation theory linked up with the critique of immaterial production. Building on the theses of Horkheimer and Adorno, according to which the manufacturing of consent to the social order had spread to the leisure industry, Debord argued that the sphere of non-labour could no longer be considered separate from productive activity:

> Whereas during the primitive stage of capitalist accumulation "political economy considers the proletarian only as a *worker*", who only needs to be allotted the indispensable minimum for maintaining his labour power, and never considers him "in his leisure and humanity", this ruling-class perspective is revised as soon as commodity abundance reaches a level that requires an additional collaboration from him. Once his workday is over, the worker

39. Thus Richard Schacht (*Alienation*, Garden City: Doubleday, 1970) noted that "there is almost no aspect of contemporary life which has not been discussed in terms of 'alienation'" (lix); while Peter C. Ludz ("Alienation as a Concept in the Social Sciences," reprinted in Felix Geyer and David Schweitzer, eds., *Theories of Alienation*, Leiden: Martinus Nijhoff, 1976) remarked that "the popularity of the concept serves to increase existing terminological ambiguity" (3).
40. Cf. David Schweitzer, "Alienation, De-alienation, and Change: A critical overview of current perspectives in philosophy and the social sciences," in Giora Shoham, ed., *Alienation and Anomie Revisited*, Tel Aviv: Ramot, 1982, for whom "the very meaning of alienation is often diluted to the point of virtual meaninglessness" (57).

> is suddenly redeemed from the total contempt toward him that is so clearly implied by every aspect of the organization and surveillance of production, and finds himself seemingly treated like a grownup, with a great show of politeness, in his new role as a consumer. At this point the *humanism of the commodity* takes charge of the worker's "leisure and humanity" simply because political economy now can and must dominate those spheres.[41]

For Debord, then, whereas the domination of the economy over social life initially took the form of a "degradation of *being* into *having*," in the "present stage" there had been a "general shift from *having* to *appearing*."[42] This idea led him to place the world of spectacle at the centre of his analysis: "The spectacle's social function is the concrete manufacture of alienation,"[43] the phenomenon through which "the fetishism of the commodity ... attains its ultimate fulfilment."[44] In these circumstances, alienation asserted itself to such a degree that it actually became an exciting experience for individuals, a new opium of the people that led them to consume and "identify with the dominant images,"[45] taking them ever further from their own desires and real existence:

> the spectacle is the stage at which the commodity has succeeded in *totally* colonizing social life.... Modern economic production extends its dictatorship both extensively and intensively. [...] With the "second industrial revolution", alienated consumption has become just as much a duty for the masses as alienated production.[46]

In the wake of Debord, Jean Baudrillard has also used the concept of alienation to interpret critically the social changes that have appeared with mature capitalism. In *The Consumer Society* (1970), distancing himself from the Marxist focus on the centrality of production, he identified consumption as the primary factor in modern society. The "age of consumption," in which advertising and opinion polls create spurious needs and mass consensus, was also "the age of radical alienation."

> Commodity logic has become generalized and today governs not only labour processes and material products, but the whole of culture, sexuality, and human relations, including even fantasies and individual drives.... Everything

41. Guy Debord, *The Society of the Spectacle*, Canberra: Hobgoblin 2002, 13.
42. Ibid., 9.
43. Ibid., 11.
44. Ibid., 12.
45. Ibid., 11.
46. Ibid., 13.

> is spectacularized or, in other words, evoked, provoked and orchestrated into images, signs, consumable models.[47]

Baudrillard's political conclusions, however, were rather confused and pessimistic. Faced with social ferment on a mass scale, he thought "the rebels of May 1968" had fallen into the trap of "reifying objects and consumption excessively by according them diabolic value"; and he criticized "all the disquisitions on 'alienation,' and all the derisive force of pop and anti-art" as a mere "indictment [that] is part of the game: it is the critical mirage, the anti-fable which rounds off the fable."[48] Now a long way from Marxism, for which the working class is the social reference point for changing the world, he ended his book with a messianic appeal, as generic as it was ephemeral: "We shall await the violent irruptions and sudden disintegrations which will come, just as unforeseeably and as certainly as May 1968, to wreck this white Mass."[49]

VI. Alienation theory in North American sociology

In the 1950s, the concept of alienation also entered the vocabulary of North American sociology, but the approach to the subject there was quite different from the one prevailing in Europe at the time. Mainstream sociology treated alienation as a problem of the individual human being, not of social relations,[50] and the search for solutions centred on the capacity of individuals to adjust to the existing order, not on collective practices to change society.[51]

Here, too, there was a long period of uncertainty before a clear and shared definition took shape. Some authors considered alienation to be a positive phenomenon, a means of expressing creativity, which was inherent in the human condition in general.[52] Another common view was that it sprang from the fissure between individual and society;[53] Seymour Melman, for instance, traced alienation to the split between

47. Jean Baudrillard, *The Consumer Society*, London: Sage, 1998, 191.
48. Ibid., 195–6.
49. Ibid., 196.
50. See for example John Clark, "Measuring alienation within a social system," *American Sociological Review*, vol. 24, n. 6 (December 1959), 849–52.
51. See Schweitzer, "Alienation, De-alienation, and Change" (note 40), 36–7.
52. A good example of this position is Walter Kaufman's "The Inevitability of Alienation," his introduction to Schacht's previously quoted volume, *Alienation*. For Kaufman, "life without estrangement is scarcely worth living; what matters is to increase men's capacity to cope with alienation" (lvi).
53. Schacht, *Alienation*, 155.

the formulation and execution of decisions, and considered that it affected workers and managers alike.[54] In "A Measure of Alienation" (1957), which inaugurated a debate on the concept in the *American Sociological Review*, Gwynn Nettler used an opinion survey as a way of trying to establish a definition. But, in sharp contrast to the rigorous labour-movement tradition of investigations into working conditions, his questionnaire seemed to draw its inspiration more from the McCarthyite canons of the time than from those of scientific research.[55] For in effect he identified alienation with a rejection of the conservative principles of American society: "consistent maintenance of unpopular and averse attitudes toward familism, the mass media and mass taste, current events, popular education, conventional religion and the telic view of life, nationalism, and the voting process."[56]

The conceptual narrowness of the American sociological panorama changed after the publication of Melvin Seeman's short article "On the Meaning of Alienation" (1959), which soon became an obligatory reference for all scholars in the field. His list of the five main types of alientation – powerlessness, meaninglessness (that is, the inability to understand the events in which one is inserted), normlessness, isolation and self-estrangement[57] – showed that he too approached the phenomenon in a primarily subjective perspective. Robert Blauner, in his book *Alienation and Freedom* (1964), similarly defined alienation as

---

54. Seymour Melman, *Decision-making and Productivity*, Oxford: Basil Blackwell, 1958, 18, 165–6.
55. Among the questions that Nettler put to a sample considered susceptible to "alien orientation" were: "Do you enjoy TV? What do you think of the new model of American automobiles? Do you read *Reader's Digest*? ... Do you like to participate in church activities? Do national spectator-sports (football, baseball) interest you?" ("A measure of alienation," *American Sociological Review*, vol. 22, no. 6 [December 1957], 675). He concluded that negative answers were evidence of alienation; and elsewhere he added: "there seems little doubt that this scale measures a dimension of estrangement from our society."
56. Ibid., 674. To prove his point, Nettler noted that "to the question, 'Would you just as soon live under another form of government as under our present one?' all responded with some indication of possibility and none with rejection" (674). He even went so far as to claim "that alienation is related to creativity. It is hypothesized that creative scientists and artists ... are alienated individuals ... that alienation is related to altruism [and] that their estrangement leads to criminal behavior" (676–7).
57. Melvin Seeman, "On the Meaning of Alienation," *American Sociological Review*, vol. 24, no. 6 (December 1959), 783–91. In 1972 he added a sixth type to the list: "cultural estrangement." (See Melvin Seeman, "Alienation and Engagement," in Angus Campbell and Philip E. Converse, eds., *The Human Meaning of Social Change*, New York: Russell Sage, 1972, 467–527.)

"a quality of personal experience which results from specific kinds of social arrangements,"[58] even if his copious research led him to trace its causes to "employment in the large-scale organizations and impersonal bureaucracies that pervade all industrial societies."[59]

American sociology, then, generally saw alienation as a problem linked to the system of industrial production, whether capitalist or socialist, and mainly affecting human consciousness.[60] This major shift of approach ultimately downgraded, or even excluded, analysis of the historical-social factors that determine alienation, producing a kind of hyper-psychologization that treated it not as a social problem but as a pathological symptom of individuals, curable at the individual level.[61] Whereas in the Marxist tradition the concept of alienation had contributed to some of the sharpest criticisms of the capitalist mode of production, its institutionalization in the realm of sociology reduced it to a phenomenon of individual maladjustment to social norms. In the same way, the critical dimension that the concept had had in philosophy (even for authors who thought it a horizon that could never be transcended) now gave way to an illusory neutrality.[62]

Another effect of this metamorphosis was the theoretical impoverishment of the concept. From a complex phenomenon related to man's work activity and social and intellectual existence, alienation became a partial category divided up in accordance with academic research specializations.[63] American sociologists argued that this methodological choice enabled them to free the study of alienation from any political connotations and to confer on it scientific objectivity. But, in reality, this a-political 'turn' had evident ideological implications, since support for the dominant values and social order lay hidden behind the banner of de-ideologization and value-neutrality.

So, the difference between Marxist and American sociological conceptions of alienation was not that the former were political and the

58. Robert Blauner, *Alienation and Freedom*, Chicago: University of Chicago Press, 1964, 15.
59. Ibid., 3.
60. Cf. Walter R. Heinz, eds., "Changes in the Methodology of Alienation Research," in Felix Geyer and Walter R. Heinz, eds., *Alienation, Society and the Individual*, New Brunswick/London: Transaction, 1992, 217.
61. See Felix Geyer and David Schweitzer, "Introduction," in idem, eds., *Theories of Alienation* (note 39), xxi–xxii, and Felix Geyer, "A General Systems Approach to Psychiatric and Sociological De-alienation," in Giora Shoham, ed. (note 40), 141.
62. See Geyer and Schweitzer, 'Introduction', xx–xxi.
63. David Schweitzer, "Fetishization of Alienation: Unpacking a Problem of Science, Knowledge, and Reified Practices in the Workplace," in Felix Geyer, ed., *Alienation, Ethnicity, and Postmodernism*, Westport/London: Greenwood Press, 1996, 23.

latter scientific. Rather, Marxist theorists were bearers of values opposed to the hegemonic ones in American society, whereas the US sociologists upheld the values of the existing social order, skilfully dressed up as eternal values of the human species.[64] In the American academic context, the concept of alienation underwent a veritable distortion and ended up being used by defenders of the very social classes against which it had for so long been directed.[65]

VII. Alienation in *Capital* and the preparatory manuscripts

Marx's own writings played an important role for those seeking to counter this situation. The initial focus on the *Economic-Philosophical Manuscripts of 1844* tended to shift after the publication of new texts, making it possible to reconstruct the development of his thought more accurately.

In the second half of the 1840s, Marx no longer made frequent use of the term "alienation"; the main exceptions were his first book, *The Holy Family* (1845), jointly authored with Engels, where it appears in some polemics against Bruno and Edgar Bauer, and one passage in *The German Ideology* (1845–6), also written with Engels. Once he had abandoned the idea of publishing *The German Ideology*, he returned to the theory of alienation in *Wage Labour and Capital*, a collection of articles based on lectures he gave to the German Workers' League in Brussels in 1847, but the term itself does not appear in them, because it would have had too abstract a ring for his intended audience. In these texts, he wrote that wage labour does not enter into the worker's "own life activity" but represents a "sacrifice of his life." Labour-power is a

64. Cf. John Horton, "The Dehumanization of Anomie and Alienation: a problem in the ideology of sociology," *The British Journal of Sociology*, vol. XV, no. 4 (1964), 283–300, and David Schweitzer, "Fetishization of Alienation," 23.

65. See Horton, "Dehumanization." This thesis is proudly championed by Irving Louis Horowitz in "The Strange Career of Alienation: how a concept is transformed without permission of its founders," in Felix Geyer, ed. (note 63), 17–19. According to Horowitz, "alienation is now part of the tradition in the social sciences rather than social protest. This change came about with a broadening realization that terms like *being alienated* are no more and no less value-laden than *being integrated*." The concept of alienation thus "became enveloped with notions of the human condition – … a positive rather than a negative force. Rather than view alienation as framed by 'estrangement' from a human being's essential nature as a result of a cruel set of industrial-capitalist demands, alienation becomes an inalienable right, a source of creative energy for some and an expression of personal eccentricity for others" (18).

commodity that the worker is forced to sell "in order to live," and "the product of his activity [is] not the object of his activity:"[66]

> the worker, who for twelve hours weaves, spins, drills, turns, builds, shovels, breaks stones, carries loads, etc. – does he consider this twelve hours' weaving, spinning, drilling, turning, building, shovelling, stone-breaking as a manifestation of his life, as life? On the contrary, life begins for him where these activities cease, at table, in the public house, in bed. The twelve hours' labour, on the other hand, have no meaning for him as weaving, spinning, drilling, etc. but as *earnings*, which bring him to the table, to the public house, into bed. If the silk-worm were to spin in order to continue its existence as a caterpillar, it would be a complete wage-worker.[67]

Until the late 1850s there were no more references to the theory of alienation in Marx's work. Following the defeat of the 1848 revolutions, he was forced to go into exile in London; once there, he concentrated all his energies on the study of political economy and, apart from a few short works with a historical theme,[68] did not publish another book. When he began to write about economics again, however, in the *Foundations of the Critique of Political Economy* (better known as the *Grundrisse*), he more than once used the term "alienation." This text recalled in many respects the analyses of the *Economic-Philosophical Manuscripts of 1844*, although nearly a decade of studies in the British Library had allowed him to make them considerably more profound:

> The social character of activity, as well as the social form of the product, and the share of individuals in production here appear as something alien and objective, confronting the individuals, not as their relation to one another, but as their subordination to relations which subsist independently of them and which arise out of collisions between mutually indifferent individuals. The general exchange of activities and products, which has become a vital condition for each individual – their mutual interconnection – here appears as something alien to them, autonomous, as a thing. In exchange value, the social connection between persons is transformed into a social relation between things; personal capacity into objective wealth.[69]

---

66. Karl Marx, "Wage Labour and Capital," in *Marx-Engels Collected Works*, vol. 9, New York: International Publishers, 1977, 202.
67. Ibid., 203.
68. *The Eighteenth Brumaire of Louis Bonaparte, Revelations concerning the Communist Trial in Cologne* and *Revelations of the Diplomatic History of the Eighteenth Century*.
69. Karl Marx, *Grundrisse*, London: Penguin, 1993, 157. In another passage on alienation (158), we read: "Rob the thing of this social power and you must give it to persons to exercise over persons."

The account of alienation in the *Grundrisse*, then, is enriched by a greater understanding of economic categories and by more rigorous social analysis. The link it establishes between alienation and exchange-value is an important aspect of this. And, in one of the most dazzling passages on this phenomenon of modern society, Marx links alienation to the opposition between capital and "living labour-power:"

> The objective conditions of living labour appear as *separated, independent* values opposite living labour capacity as subjective being.... The objective conditions of living labour capacity are presupposed as having an existence independent of it, as the objectivity of a subject distinct from living labour capacity and standing independently over against it; the reproduction and *realization*, i.e. the expansion of these *objective conditions*, is therefore at the same time their own reproduction and new production as the wealth of an alien subject indifferently and independently standing over against labour capacity. What is reproduced and produced anew is not only the *presence* of these objective conditions of living labour, but also their presence as independent values, i.e. values belonging to an alien subject, confronting this living labour capacity. The objective conditions of labour attain a subjective existence *vis-à-vis* living labour capacity – capital turns into capitalist.[70]

The *Grundrisse* was not the only text of Marx's maturity to feature an account of alienation. Five years after it was composed, the "Results of the Immediate Process of Production" – also known as "*Capital, Volume One*: Book 1, Chapter VI, unpublished" (1863–4) – brought the economic and political analyses of alienation more closely together. "The rule of the capitalist over the worker," Marx wrote, "is the rule of things over man, of dead labour over the living, of the product over the producer."[71] In capitalist society, by virtue of "the transposition of the social productivity of labour into the material attributes of capital,"[72] there is a veritable "personification of things and reification of persons," creating the appearance that "the *material conditions of labour* are not subject to the worker, but he to them."[73] In reality, he argued:

> Capital is not a thing, any more than money is a thing. In capital, as in money, certain specific social relations of production between people appear as relations of things to people, or else certain social relations appear as the natural properties of things in society. Without a class dependent on wages,

70. Ibid., 461–2.
71. Karl Marx, 'Results of the Immediate Process of Production', in idem, *Capital, Volume 1*, London: Penguin, 1976, 990.
72. Ibid., 1058.
73. Ibid., 1054.

> the moment individuals confront each other as free persons, there can be no production of surplus-value; without the production of surplus-value there can be no capitalist production, and hence no capital and no capitalist! Capital and wage-labour (it is thus we designate the labour of the worker who sells his own labour-power) only express two aspects of the self-same relationship. Money cannot become capital unless it is exchanged for labour-power, a commodity sold by the worker himself. Conversely, work can only be wage-labour when its *own* material conditions confront it as autonomous powers, alien property, value existing for itself and maintaining itself, in short as capital. If capital in its material aspects, i.e. in the use-values in which it has its being, must depend for its existence on the material conditions of labour, these material conditions must equally, on the formal side, confront labour *as alien, autonomous powers*, as value – objectified labour – which treats living labour as a mere means whereby to maintain and increase itself.[74]

In the capitalist mode of production, human labour becomes an instrument of the valorization process of capital, which, "by incorporating living labour-power into the material constituents of capital,... becomes an animated monster and ... starts to act 'as if consumed by love'."[75] This mechanism keeps expanding in scale, until co-operation in the production process, scientific discoveries and the deployment of machinery – all of them social processes belonging to the collective – become forces of capital that appear as its natural properties, confronting the workers in the shape of the capitalist order:

> The productive forces ... developed [by] social labour ... appear as the *productive forces of capitalism*. [...] Collective unity in co-operation, combination in the division of labour, the use of the forces of nature and the sciences, of the products of labour, as machinery – all these confront the individual workers as something *alien, objective, ready-made*, existing without their intervention, and frequently even hostile to them. They all appear quite simply as the prevailing forms of the instruments of labour. As objects they are independent of the workers whom they dominate. Though the workshop is to a degree the product of the workers' combination, its entire intelligence and will seem to be incorporated in the capitalist or his understrappers, and the workers find themselves confronted by the *functions* of the capital that lives in the capitalist.[76]

Through this process capital becomes something 'highly mysterious.' "The conditions of labour pile up in front of the worker as social forces, and they assume a capitalized form."[77]

74. Ibid., 1005–6 (emphasis in the original).
75. Ibid., 1007.
76. Ibid., 1054 (emphasis in the original)
77. Ibid., 1056.

Beginning in the 1960s, the diffusion of "*Capital, Volume One*: Book 1, Chapter VI, unpublished" and, above all, of the *Grundrisse*[78] paved the way for a conception of alienation different from the one then hegemonic in sociology and psychology. It was a conception geared to the overcoming of alienation in practice – to the political action of social movements, parties and trade unions to change the working and living conditions of the working class. The publication of what (after the *Economic-Philosophical Manuscripts of 1844* in the 1930s) may be thought of as the "second generation" of Marx's writings on alienation therefore provided not only a coherent theoretical basis for new studies of alienation, but above all an anti-capitalist ideological platform for the extraordinary political and social movement that exploded in the world during those years. Alienation left the books of philosophers and the lecture halls of universities, took to the streets and the space of workers' struggles, and became a critique of bourgeois society in general.

VIII. Commodity fetishism and de-alienation

One of Marx's best accounts of alienation is contained in the famous section of *Capital* on "The Fetishism of the Commodity and Its Secret," where he shows that, in capitalist society, people are dominated by the products they have created. Here, the relations among them appear not "as direct social relations between persons…, but rather as material relations between persons and social relations between things";[79]

> The mysterious character of the commodity-form consists … in the fact that the commodity reflects the social characteristics of men's own labour as objective characteristics of the products of labour themselves, as the socio-natural properties of these things. Hence it also reflects the social relation of the producers to the sum total of labour as a social relation between objects, a relation which exists apart from and outside the producers. Through this substitution, the products of labour become commodities, sensuous things which are at the same time supra-sensible or social. […] It is nothing but the definite social relation between men themselves which assumes here, for them, the fantastic form of a relation between things. In order, therefore, to find an analogy we must take flight into the misty realm of religion. There the products of the human brain appear as autonomous figures endowed with a life of their own, which enter into relations both with each other and with the human race. So it is in the world of commodities with the products of men's hands. I call this the

78. See Marcello Musto, ed., *Karl Marx's Grundrisse: Foundations of the Critique of Political Economy 150 years Later,* London/New York: Routledge, 2008, 177–280.
79. Karl Marx, *Capital, Volume 1,* 166.

> fetishism which attaches itself to the products of labour as soon as they are produced as commodities, and is therefore inseparable from the production of commodities.[80]

Two elements in this definition mark a clear dividing line between Marx's conception of alienation and the one held by most of the other authors we have been discussing. First, Marx conceives of fetishism not as an individual problem but as a social phenomenon, not as an affair of the mind but as a real power, a particular form of domination, which establishes itself in market economy as a result of the transformation of objects into subjects. For this reason, his analysis of alienation does not confine itself to the disquiet of individual women and men, but extends to the social processes and productive activities underlying it. Second, Marx fetishism manifests itself in a precise historical reality of production, the reality of wage labour; it is not part of the relation between people and things as such, but rather of the relation between man and a particular kind of objectivity: the commodity form.

In bourgeois society, human qualities and relations turn into qualities and relations among things. This theory of what Lukács would call reification illustrated alienation from the point of view of human relations, while the concept of fetishism treated it in relation to commodities. *Pace* those who deny that a theory of alienation is present in Marx's mature work, we should stress that commodity fetishism did not replace alienation but was only one aspect of it.[81]

The theoretical advance from the *Economic-Philosophical Manuscripts of 1844* to *Capital* and its related materials does not, however, consist only in the greater precision of his account of alienation. There is also a reformulation of the measures that Marx considers necessary for it to be overcome. Whereas in 1844 he had argued that human beings would eliminate alienation by abolishing private production and the division of labour, the path to a society free of alienation was much more complicated in *Capital* and its preparatory manuscripts. Marx held that capitalism was a system in which the workers were subject to capital and the conditions it imposed. Nevertheless, it had created the foundations for a more advanced society, and by generalizing its benefits humanity would be able to progress along the faster road of social development that it had opened up. According to Marx, a system that produced an enormous accumulation of wealth for the few and deprivation and exploitation for the general mass of workers must be replaced with "an association of free men, working

80. Ibid., 164–5.
81. Cf. Schaff, *Alienation as a Social Phenomenon*, 81.

with the means of production held in common, and expending their many different forms of labour-power in full self-awareness as one single social labour force."[82] This type of production would differ from wage labour because it would place its determining factors under collective governance, take on an immediately general character and convert labour into a truly social activity. This was a conception of society at the opposite pole from Hobbes's "war of all against all"; and its creation did not require a merely political process, but would involve transformation of the sphere of production. But such a change in the labour process had its limits:

> Freedom, in this sphere, can consist only in this, that socialized man, the associated producers, govern the human metabolism with nature in a rational way, bringing it under their collective control instead of being dominated by it as a blind power; accomplishing it with the least expenditure of energy and in conditions most worthy and appropriate for their human nature.[83]

This post-capitalist system of production, together with scientific-technological progress and a consequent reduction of the working day, creates the possibility for a new social formation in which the coercive, alienated labour imposed by capital and subject to its laws is gradually replaced with conscious, creative activity beyond the yoke of necessity, and in which complete social relations take the place of random, undifferentiated exchange dictated by the laws of commodities and money.[84] It is no longer the realm of freedom for capital but the realm of genuine human freedom.

---

82. *Capital, Volume 1*, 171.
83. Karl Marx, *Capital, Volume 3*, London: Penguin, 1981, 959.
84. For reasons of space, a consideration of the unfinished and partly contradictory nature of Marx's sketch of a non-alienated society will have to be left to a future study.

Marx and the Politics of Sarcasm

Terrell Carver

"Theory is capable of gripping the masses as soon as it demonstrates *ad hominem* ...." (*Karl Marx*)[1]

What we see is what we get

Marx is well known as a theorist. He is constructed as such in biographies, works of reference and scholarly works of critique. He is excerpted in readers for college students[2] and is a touchstone for famous philosophers.[3] He is about as exciting politically as any other long-dead intellectual whose career is over, and he is rapidly invading the territory where – like Socrates or Nietzsche – he is loved and admired, mocked and pitied, for his eccentricities and foibles[4] as much as for his ideas. Indeed anyone approaching the ideas has been strongly advised – since the late 1870s – to do so with some trepidation, and a great need for guidance.

Originally it was Friedrich Engels who was our Virgil on this descent, succeeded in the twentieth century by guides who were less *parti pris* and more familiarly "liberal": Isaiah Berlin, David McLellan and others who were in general safely academic. Engels's contextualization of Marx and his précis of Marx's work as "theory" were already necessary even before Marx himself was dead; Marx's rhetorical idiom was already dead and thus difficult to grasp. By the late 1850s, how to read Hegel was no longer a political issue in German politics (and had

1. Karl Marx and Frederick Engels, *Collected Works* (London: Lawrence & Wishart, 1975–2004); hereafter *CW*; Karl Marx, "Contribution to the Critique of Hegel's Philosophy of Law: Introduction", *CW* 3, p. 182.
2. Such as Robert Tucker's much reprinted and revised *The Marx-Engels Reader*, 2nd ed. (New York: W.W. Norton, 1978).
3. Such as Jacques Derrida's *Specters of Marx: State of the Debt, the Work of Mourning and the New International*, trans. Peggy Kamuf (New York: Routledge, 1994).
4. See Francis Wheen's "humanizing" biography *Karl Marx* (London: Fourth Estate, 1999, new ed. 2010).

Socialism and Democracy, Vol.24, No.3, November 2010, pp.102–118
ISSN 0885-4300 print/ISSN 1745-2635 online
DOI: 10.1080/08854300.2010.513608

never been elsewhere), and indeed Marx's published writings on that score were of the day - largely in the 1840s - and difficult to re-read later. In the 1860s and 1870s then, as Marx labored on his critique of political economy, how to read the political economists he was involved with engaged neither "the German professors"[5] nor the workers in the way that Marx seems to have envisaged; not even Engels risked a snappy and popular summary of Marx's lengthy and apparently "technical" critique on its own. Rather the cut and thrust of Marx's *anti*-Hegelian and *anti*-economistic politics got absorbed into "theory," in particular a theory of history and a theory of capitalism. The former is a critique of prior historiography and a deductive account - from present trends - of the shape of the future. The latter is a critical parody of economic theory, but also a substantive theorization of capitalism as a self-destructive system. In both cases the intellectual and political contexts had moved on, but Marx apparently had not. Reading Marx was therefore not *au courant* and straightforward. He had become "an author."

But what was Marx doing in the first place? Marx was actually a trouble-making journalist during the 1840s. He wrote notable articles on local economic conditions in the Rhineland, linking impoverished workers to state structures and thus to collective public responsibility; these were his first published works of 1842, printed in a regional newspaper.[6] His subsequent works were polemics - *The Holy Family* (1845), the unfinished projects known as "the German Ideology" manuscripts (1845-46)[7] and *The Poverty of Philosophy* (1847). The last named work marked his move from the small-time world of German émigré radicalism to the larger world of European socialism, via an attack on Proudhon, the already well-known reformer-guru. The little-circulated *Manifesto of the Communist Party* (1848), an anonymous publication by Marx and his fellow journalist Engels, attacks all previous historiography and thus rewrites the future.

After the 1840s Marx was still a trouble-making journalist, albeit semi-retired and devoting himself to a *magnum opus*. Two of his works, oddly framed now as "historical," made a splash in his day: *The Eighteenth Brumaire of Louis Bonaparte* (1852, 2nd ed. 1869), and *The Civil War in France* (1871). This was "instant history," perhaps,

5. See Marx's Afterword to the second German edition of *Capital*, vol. 1; *CW* 35, p. 13.
6. See *CW* 1, pp. 132-81, 224-63.
7. For a radical revisioning of these manuscripts and their historical context, see Terrell Carver, "*The German Ideology* Never Took Place," *History of Political Thought*, vol. 31, no. 1 (2010), pp. 107-27.

but rather more like docu-drama. Predictably these works are regularly criticized by academic historians for bias and error, though this begs obvious questions about audience and authorial intent in the first place, and is really a commentary on the framing, rather than the works. *Capital,*[8] by contrast, was Marx's attempt to be serious and not to be an overt polemicist, at least not in terms of framing and argumentative content. If ever there was a place to look for "theory," this was it. However, sadly, the parodic qualities of the presentation – and subtle ironies of the covertly critical wit – misled many if not most readers into reproducing as truth the very "truths" that Marx was painstakingly – and with considerable patience – deconstructing as collective delusions. The raw materials of political economy which Marx took up were doubly recondite even to his colleagues, and this was so even by 1859: political economy was not their *métier* (and indeed that was Marx's complaint about them, hence also his originality in their circles), but also the "economics" that he worked on went out of date (with the "marginalist" revolution) not long after his first volume began to circulate with any degree of notice.

Ironically then, Marx's framing as a "theorist" – for most commentators ever since – is not centered on his most self-consciously precise and refined work in this vein (his critique of political economy), but rather on the "outlook" [*Ansicht*] – subsequently known as "theory of history" – through which his deconstruction of capitalism was supposed to make sense. The "outlook" tells us that capitalism is a human historical construction, not a timeless condition of humanity. Marx's parodic re-presentation of political economy as a "critical theory" of his own tells us how capitalism works: its everyday categories prevent us from seeing the exploitation of one class by another, hence the need for his critique to wake us up politically. Marx's "theory" is a *demystification* of the categories value, money, commodity and capital, which is what makes his thought critical. Unfortunately many readers of this "economics" take it to be "positive" and thus descriptive – and most of these readers inevitably conclude that as "theory" it is false, at least in some of its propositions.

Thus because Marx became a "theorist" his early polemics became "theory," his midlife philippics became "history," and his mature critical thought has been marginalized and misread. My argument here is that there is not much point to re-reading Marx today in these ways, familiar as they are. Nice as it is to return to what we know,

8. And its precursor, *A Contribution to the Critique of Political Economy* (1859); *CW* 29, pp. 257–417.

I propose that we take a leap towards something else. In the discussion which follows, my aim is to align the textual surface – rhetoric and communicative strategy – with what we know of Marx's politics: his views, tactics, goals.[9] This requires not simply a "turn" to reading his journalism alongside or within his framing as a "theorist," but rather a re-reading of his *oeuvre* and thought as essentially that of a journalist. I mean this in the literal sense that he always wrote for money, and thus was audience-aware in his writing (and in his negotiations with colleagues and publishers). And I mean it in the metaphorical sense that he aimed to stir up trouble and cause controversy at the moment – "grab the headlines" if you will – *rather than* to write "theory" for philosophers and historians to contemplate.

There is thus a double re-orientation involved here: we adjust our view as to exactly what Marx was doing while he was writing, and we adjust our view as to the importance of the textual surface, and specifically as to which words and expressions are the important ones for us to notice. The goal here is to construct "the engaged Marx" in a way that revivifies him today, and perhaps makes us think better of some of the journalistic political commentators (and perforce political actors) that we are lucky enough to have on our radar lately. It may be that "the engaged Marx" is a model writer for today, or maybe not – that is a matter for individuals to call. There are also different ways that his political projects, particular motivations and presumed goals can be aligned with different aspects of his textual surfaces. I propose here to take his least read, most despised and comprehensively neglected work, *Herr Vogt*[10] (1860), as a case in point, and to consider in this respect a similarly deprecated and maligned rhetorical device – sarcasm.

What we don't want to see is what we'll never get

Marx has been roundly drubbed throughout the literature for being "difficult," bad tempered, rude, paranoid and obsessively *ad hominem*, over and above his love-affair with polemic as a way of tearing down others' ideas and erecting his own upon the ruins.

9. For further reading on this general approach, see Quentin Skinner, *Visions of Politics*, vol. 1: *Regarding Method* (Cambridge: Cambridge University Press, 2002); and Alan Finlayson, "From Beliefs to Arguments: Interpretive Methodology and Rhetorical Political Analysis," *British Journal of Politics and International Relations*, vol. 9, no. 4 (2007), pp. 545–63.
10. Rare amongst Marx's works of any length, *Herr Vogt* was never re-published in a separate edition, appearing in a complete English translation only in 1981; *CW* 17, p. 535 n. 12.

Virtually no commentator or biographer admires this aspect of his character. At its worst, of course, this kind of characterization is a no-win/catch-22: if Marx sticks to his guns and takes no prisoners, he is obnoxiously bigoted and pig-headed; if he changes his mind or makes allowances, then he is power-driven and deceptive. The less extreme view is simply that he had his "buttons" and sensitivities like the rest of us and was human, all too human. The idea that he based his views on reason and principle, that from such a point he could criticize others with validity, and – above all – that he was right to think that their views and his criticisms *mattered*, is really foreign to "liberal" commentary, where good manners are universal precisely because nothing very crucial ever seems to be at stake. I leave aside, to be sure, the hagiographical commentary where Marx is simply right about everything and everyone, but even there, his rhetorical flights of scorn and invective fall stone dead.

The "liberal" view of Marx is founded on a number of presuppositions: that anger is bad and must be controlled; that compromise rather than intransigence is good; and that everyone will live to fight another day without too much problem. However, these criteria are not applied at all consistently in the "liberal" problematique. Washington, Lincoln, Churchill, Franklin D. Roosevelt and any number of other historical figures (on "our" side) are praised for standing firm, not negotiating, and risking their all. And any number of compromisers and milquetoasts get blamed for their failures: Macdonald, Chamberlain, George H.W. Bush. The consistency here is in the success, and Marx – despite the periodic upsurges of highly qualified respect he gets from time to time – is not in the victors' ring for liberals. As a historical failure, he must be a philosophical failure, and his character cannot be good either. Sarcasm in this reading is simply the rhetorical marker for everything that is wrong with Marx as a non-"liberal," at least in terms of sensibility.

Ad hominem attacks can't be good, either, given that liberals want politics to be about ideas, principles and reason, not "personalities." The fact that democratic politics, whatever the system, is *performed* through personalization, is something that has generally eluded liberal theorists, at least on paper. Locke, author of the most influential political tract of all time, *Two Treatises of Government* (and in particular the "second" one on "Civil Government")[11] has nothing to say about personalities in politics, preferring an impersonal discourse of

11. John Locke, *Two Treatises of Government*, ed. Peter Laslett, student ed. (Cambridge: Cambridge University Press, 1988).

impartial magistracy. Oddly his work was thought to reflect on, and provide justification for, the Glorious Revolution of 1688–9, through which a constitutional *monarchy* was established in England and Ireland by specific act of Parliament (not least declaring the throne vacant in the first place, when it obviously wasn't). Locke was even of the (new) royal party when they sailed in from The Netherlands, and was hardly unacquainted with the idea of personality in politics. Yet "theory" on this point was omitted from the classic text of liberalism, and indeed several hundred years of meditation on the relationship between character and rulership completely vanished. The aspect of Locke's text that receives the least attention is his overall rhetorical and political strategy: a withering attack on Sir Robert Filmer, frequently blistered with sarcasm, lightened up with schoolboy sniggers. Filmer, of course, was personally quiet in his grave at the time, and more importantly, in liberal terms, Locke was flogging a dead horse – absolutism by divine right – anyway.

My point is that Marx's "liberal" commentators, educated as they are in societies where Lockean ideals rule in theory, are ill-prepared to take on Marx's world where this is simply not the case (and arguably they are not particularly well prepared to take on their own world where tabloid values run riot through popular journalism and are themselves the subject of soberer reportage in the "quality" press). Similarly, given the Lockean emphasis (from *An Essay on Human Understanding,* also of 1689) on plain speech and literal expression over and above "fancy" or metaphor or other figure of speech,[12] liberals are disadvantaged in dealing with the ironies involved in sarcasm. Sarcasm may be direct speech that is derogatory or hurtful, intended to damage feelings or reputation, to mock or taunt. But more often than not it is wrapped in an irony, that is, making a remark with due sincerity but meaning the opposite, e.g. praising someone in an arch or knowing way that actually conveys disdain or criticism. This can of course be communicated through tone of voice or manner of address, and on the printed page through a number of devices, such as the inserted exclamation mark, drawing the reader's attention to the inverse relationship between literal sense and intended meaning. Marx's use of such exclamation marks within square brackets (to show that they are ironic insertions) has been noted, as it happens (and nowhere else that I know of), by Wikipedia.[13]

12. See the discussion on this point in Michael J. Shapiro, "Metaphor in the Philosophy of the Social Sciences," *Culture and Critique,* vol. 2 (1985–86), pp. 192–3.
13. http://en.wikipedia.org/wiki/Sarcasm (accessed May 11, 2010).

Liberals and liberalism are inclined to see Marx as a failure for a number of reasons, most recently his alleged involvement (in some associative way) with the "Eastern Bloc" regimes of the Cold War years, and more historically with his espousal of revolution, by violent means if necessary. However, virtually all liberal democratic states were established with violence, most usually that of revolution and civil war, but for the purpose, as Locke states, to *exclude* force from politics (through the operation of the impartial magistracy by rule of law, and "all for the public good").[14] Other than rather tepid memorializations, however, liberal theory and liberal regimes produce erasure on this score, celebrating stability, often at the expense of the liberal principles that revolutionary and other civil settlements were meant to institute in perpetuity. In his time Marx was a revolutionary when even to be liberal was to be revolutionary, and to be socialist or communist was barely intelligible. Had he played a statesmanlike role in electoral politics (in England or Prussia, conceivably, if had he managed to acquire or regain citizenship in either), then he might be perceived differently. His hypothetical revolutionary triumphs would have been erased through the magic of the liberal "social contract," where – somehow, and contrary to almost all fact – government emerges *peaceably* from amongst "the people."

Even more seriously, and much more plausibly, liberals want to make Marx a failure – with attendant character and rhetorical flaws – because he put his finger on an area of ambiguity and nervousness for them, namely the intimate association between representative democracy and capitalist power.[15] This is not only the famous line that "the modern state" is merely "the executive committee of the bourgeoisie"[16] but also the very tricky issue that Marx tackles in "On *The Jewish Question*" (1844) – another work of sarcastic polemic (against philosopher-pamphleteer Bruno Bauer, not against Jews). Marx discerned that the modern state, even when based on popular sovereignty (which of course was *not* the case in Prussia), has created for itself in "theory" (which of course Marx is demystifying) a world of citizens where freedom and equality characterize their properly "political" relationship. His problem with this is that this "political" realm has little to do with the life-experiences of those who cannot but enter

14. Locke, *Two Treatises*, II.§§131, 226.
15. Marx also charged Christianity (in *Capital*, vol. 1) with being particularly suited to both liberalism and capitalism, but I shall leave that particular issue aside here; *CW* 35, p. 90
16. Karl Marx and Frederick Engels, *Manifesto of the Communist Party*, *CW* 6, p. 486.

the world of modern commercial relations. In that real world, where property-owners confront the property-less, freedom and equality as "theory" are a mockery of what they should be in practice. Or to put it even more simply, the life of citizens has an abstract character that - so Marx argues - makes the harsh world of individualized property relations possible in the first place.[17]

Both worlds are implicated in the entrenched tensions and suffering brought on by extremes of wealth and poverty, precisely because the "heaven" of citizen-life is used to mystify the "earthly" life where hard labor (for most) gets no property, and easy property (for some) obviates any need to work. Liberal democracy - and liberal social democracy - have a bad conscience on this point,[18] and cannot allow the contradiction. Indeed, class compromise is better than class war, one has to admit. But liberal theory has never faced up to the issue, so unsurprisingly Marx's harping on it is little to their liking. The nastier and crazier he becomes at the edges, the better for their view of him as an unpleasant character (and therefore poor thinker). What could be nastier and crazier (in Marx's career at least) than some kind of pathetic obsession with now forgotten personalities even more crabbed than his, worked up in an abhorrent authorial tone and with evident intent to hurt? Or in other words - sarcasm.

The Marx we wish we hadn't seen

Herr Vogt is a work that defies summary, and even an explanation as to what it is about would take an enormous amount of space. Suffice to say that Karl Vogt (1817–95) was a rebellious '48er and member of the revolutionary Frankfurt Assembly of 1848–49, and as such one of many figures in the swirling maelstrom of German politics known, one way or another, to Marx. In this context he emerges as an author and pamphleteer, publishing his thoughts on European foreign policy in 1859; he was then subject to anonymous allegations in print that he was an agent of Emperor Napoleon III of France. He denied this, though these allegations were later proved correct.[19] Vogt brought an action against a German newspaper for publishing this supposed libel, and, having lost, he published a pamphlet full of

17. Karl Marx, *On the Jewish Question*, *CW* 3, pp. 146–74.
18. See the controversies since 2007 surrounding the payments of management bonuses and shareholder dividends post-"credit crunch."
19. David McLellan, *Karl Marx: His Life and Thought* (London: Macmillan, 1973), p. 315; cf. Franz Mehring, *Karl Marx: The Story of His Life* (1918), www.marxists.org/archive/mehring/1918/marx/ch10b.htm, ch. 10, sec. 5.

stories and allegations about numerous figures in German politics, many of them '48er émigrés including Marx and Engels.

In *Herr Vogt* Marx responded to these tales and innuendos at very considerable length and in minute detail, thus providing in effect his own memoir of the political struggles he had been involved in, and taken account of, from the mid-1840s onwards. If we read him as a "theorist," the text is sometimes interesting in that it records his own summaries of, and comments on, such works as *The Poverty of Philosophy* (1847) and the *Manifesto of the Communist Party* (1848). These are of course major works in anyone's reading of "theory," though obviously at the time of publication they were first and foremost political interventions, deploying an "outlook" directed towards what we might describe as short- and medium-term ends. *Herr Vogt*, however, is admittedly very short-term, with an immediate goal of destroying the credibility of someone who had interjected himself, his political views and his discrediting accounts of the life and times of the left-wingers of his age, into the day-to-day flow of political journalism of 1859. Much of this was concerned with great-power politics, in particular European foreign policies including "England" (in the German terminology, rather than Great Britain, which was meant), Prussia, Austria, France, Russia and fought-over areas such as the Italian states and possessions and various realms in Eastern Europe.

For modern readers this makes the text largely "historical," as with the "historical" detail recounted in Marx's *The Eighteenth Brumaire of Louis Bonaparte*, published in 1852, and in effect a work of contemporary journalism, or "instant history" (up to December 1851), as we might say today. However, this move brackets the work off from "theory" and thus from mainstream Marx, marking it as "difficult" and protecting the reader, ironically, from seeing exactly how Marx's "outlook" operates in the nitty-gritty of political conflict.[20] *Herr Vogt* is not quite in this league, since Vogt was not an emperor or even an important politician, and Marx's critique is not so much oppositional and process-oriented as negative and *ad hominem*, since Vogt was not a

20. See my discussion of the way that an early draft of the outlook summarized in Marx's (now) famous Preface (1859) to *A Contribution to the Critique of Political Economy* emerges from, and gives way to, the supposedly "historical" (rather than "theoretical") discussion in *The Eighteenth Brumaire* without any change of gear; Terrell Carver, "Marx's *Eighteenth Brumaire of Louis Bonaparte*: Democracy, Dictatorship and the Politics of Class Struggle," in Peter Baehr and Melvin Richter (eds), *Dictatorship in History and Theory: Bonapartism, Caesarism, and Totalitarianism* (Cambridge: German Historical Institute, Washington, D.C. and Cambridge University Press, 2004), pp. 113–15.

movement. Nonetheless the two works have a considerable amount in common rhetorically as well as in content, and Marx himself draws attention to this at several points in his later text. He specifically recalls his satirical portrait of the Emperor, remarking that Vogt was even more risible and pathetic, and of course he also linked Vogt's ruminations on foreign policy to the regnant Emperor himself, whose political ambitions Marx considered to be semi-crazed and gangsterish.

Broadly speaking, of course, few historians of the period disagree all that much with the critical tenor of Marx's reasoning (even if few will admit to agreeing with Marx on points of detail), because hardly anyone – even in France – views the Second Empire as a particularly glorious or even very respectable era in French history, given the authoritarianism, corruption, scandal, adventurism and disasters involved, most specifically the emperor's humiliating capture by the Prussians in 1870. However, *Herr Vogt* is also bracketed off as "difficult" for another reason, namely the coruscations of recondite quotations, allusions, puns, tropes, metaphors, ironies and jokes which – on conventional views – merely burden Marx's argument. It would take numerous pages to list all the authors and works which Marx deploys in order to heap scorn on Vogt from a great height – and it doubtless took many hours and a large team to construct the learned footnotes required to pin all this down to sources and to explain precisely what Marx means – but we could start with Shakespeare, Goethe, Schiller, Cicero, Calderon, Dante, the Bible, German-language adaptations of Rabelais, middle-high-German poetry and numerous other sources. McLellan's view represents mainstream opinion, then and now, seeing *Herr Vogt* as "a striking example both of Marx's ability to expend tremendous labour on essentially trivial matters and also of his talent for vituperation."[21]

McLellan's account, and his views, are based closely on Franz Mehring's, as published in the first full-length biography of Marx in 1918:

> In reading the book one involuntarily experiences a sense of discomfort to hear Marx defending himself against slanderous attacks which did not touch him even remotely. On the other hand, the book [*Herr Vogt* – TC] offers an unusual treat to the literary gourmet. On the very first page Marx propounds a thesis which he pursues through the subsequent pages with the humour of a Shakespeare: "The original of Karl Vogt is the immortal Sir John Falstaff and in his zoological resurrection [Vogt was a zoologist; see note 28 below – TC] he

21. McLellan, *Karl Marx*, p. 311.

> has lost nothing of his character." Protracted as the theme is, it never becomes monotonous in Marx's hands and his vast acquaintance with classic and modern literature offers him arrow after arrow which he despatches with deadly accuracy against the insolent slanderer.[22]

In this article I am challenging the standard view on both counts: not so much that the matter wasn't trivial (of course it was to many at the time) but that the matter was not at all trivial *to Marx*, and for that reason we should give it serious consideration (if we are seriously interested in Marx). In other words, the standard view is one that trivializes as a welcome strategy (thus bracketing items off, or "humanizing" heroes with "feet of clay"). This then closes down our reading of certain texts in favor of others, because the favored reading strategy for the mainstream is to find the "theory" (and leave the rest to historians – if they want it, which in the case of Marx, they mostly don't). Moreover the standard view dismisses rhetoric generally as dispensable when finding the "theory," and in particular dismisses a rhetoric of scornful satire as mere "vituperation," which – given "liberal" sentiments of emotionless respect and good-natured compromise – can't be tolerated.

While I am not at all proposing the wholesale slaughter of liberal values and sentiments, it nonetheless seems to me well worth considering Marx's rhetoric as part of the package, since after all he wrote it that way, and even if one is only reading him for the "theory," the rhetorical dimension may still be pertinent. Moreover as a broader political strategy, most particularly in the present, perhaps it is also worth considering Marx as a model, or at least reviving some of his works (or some aspects of some of his works) as not out of line with scorn and satire as valid strategies in politics. Perhaps even in such forbidding (by reputation) works of "theory" as the volumes of *Capital* – so "forbidding," it seems, that of Marx's works of "theory" these are undoubtedly and shamefully the least read – it might be the case that the ironic and sometimes sarcastic "asides" are really the point, then as well as now.

My argument here is that rhetorically speaking (and not necessarily at all in terms of content), Michael Moore's movies, Jon Stewart's "Daily Show" and even *Private Eye* (the long-running British bi-weekly magazine of scandal and satire) are in the same frame as Marx, and for the same reasons. Note Mehring's view here below, downgrading Marx's contemporary political success as against the longer term

22. Mehring, *Karl Marx*, ch. 10, sec. 5.

interest he presumes in his readers as to what Marx was really supposed to be doing (for us):

> The deplorable business [to do with *Herr Vogt* – TC] won him a number of new friends and, in particular, it caused him to resume friendly relations with the Workers Educational League, which immediately supported him vigorously. On the other hand it tended to hamper the great work of his life rather than further it, despite, or rather just because of, the valuable sacrifice in strength and time which it demanded without offering any commensurate gain, and at the same time it caused him serious domestic difficulties.[23]

While I am not one to disparage "theory," it is arguably not the best way to intervene in politics as it happens, and may indeed be a displacement. Moreover Marx's skill as a sarcastic satirist may also be a productive way to read his "theory" – maybe not. But once rhetoric is bracketed off in general, and the cut-and-thrust politics of sarcasm is dismissed in no uncertain terms, then the exercise of deciding about this is not even possible in the first place.

To that end I intend to quote here below a number of characteristic examples of sarcasm from *Herr Vogt*. The reader is advised that my purpose in this exercise is to develop an appreciation of Marx's rhetorical strategies (and an admiration for the splendor of his performative executions), rather than to get at all involved with the content of the passages quoted, other than to give very basic hints just sufficient to make the rhetoric intelligible. Those interested in the content are referred to the notes in the English-language edition[24] (and to the MEGA^2 volume I/18, for the definitive text and *apparatus criticus*). After a few choice exemplars I shall return to considering how this way of reading, and in particular the reading of this text, can take us back productively to rather more familiar territory in the Marx canon.

The art of rhetoric

In the Preface to *Herr Vogt* Marx put his cards on the table:

> I know in advance that the same astute men who shook their heads sagely at the importance of Vogt's "revelations", when his concoction first appeared, will now be unable to comprehend why I am wasting my time refuting his childish allegations; while the "liberal" pen-pushers who gloatingly took up Vogt's commonplaces and worthless lies and hastened to hawk them around the German, Swiss, French and American press will now find my mode of

---

23. Ibid.
24. *CW* 17, pp. 21–329.

> dealing with themselves and their hero outrageously offensive. But never mind![25]

Being offensive was not an idle promise:

> Here then, in his research into my "activities", Vogt has at his disposal, as it were, the assistance of the Prussian state and he even had authentic material contained in my *Revelations Concerning the Communist Trial in Cologne*,[26] Basle, 1853, a copy of which he discovered in the Geneva Workers' Association and which he borrowed and "studied". This time, then, young Karl really will settle my hash. But no! For once Vogt is "at a loss", he just sets off a few of his home-made smoke-bombs and stink-bombs before beating a hasty retreat ... [Marx appends a learned footnote on the composition and use of "stink bombs" - TC].[27]

Marx continues the trope in more detail, alluding to Vogt's scientific writings on animals:[28]

> In America there is a small animal called a *skunk* which has only *one* method of defending itself at moments of extreme danger: its offensive smell. When attacked it releases a substance from certain parts of its body which, if it touches your clothes, will ensure that they have to be burnt and, if it touches your skin, will banish you for a period from all human society. The smell is so horribly offensive that when hunters see that their dogs have accidentally started a skunk they will hurriedly take to their heels in greater panic than if they had found that a wolf or a tiger was pursuing them. For powder and lead is an adequate defence against wolves and tigers, but no antidote has been found to the *a posteriori* of a skunk ... The shameless impertinence with which this "skunk" accuses me and my friends of *"living from the sweat of the workers' brow"*, when we have always sacrificed our private interests in order to defend those of the working class, and have done this *gratis*, is not even original. The *mouchards* [police spies - TC] of the December Gang [Marx's term for Louis Bonaparte's political cadres - TC] hurled similar slanders at Louis Blanc, Blanqui, Raspail [heroes of the French political left - TC], etc.[29]

Less scabrously, and with rather more wit, Marx has considerable fun at Vogt's expense:

> ... [Vogt writes that - TC] as the result of its secret "understanding" with Louis Bonaparte Prussia must and will "reach the coasts of the North Sea and the Baltic at the expense of its German brothers" (loc. cit., p. 14). On the other side,

25. *CW* 17, p. 26.
26. *CW* 11, pp. 395–457.
27. *CW* 17, pp. 64–5.
28. Vogt was in fact a professor of zoology, first at the University of Giessen, and then after his necessary emigration post-'48, at the University of Geneva.
29. *CW* 17, pp. 68–9; emphasis in original.

> "Prussia will have obtained a *natural frontier* only when the *watershed* of the Erzgebirge and the Fichtelgebirge is extended *through* the white Main and *along* the Main up to Mainz" (loc. cit., p. 93).
> Natural frontiers in the depth of Germany! Formed, moreover, by a *watershed* which passes *through a river*! It is this sort of discovery in the realm of physical geography ... that puts "the well-rounded character" [Marx's satirical pun on Vogt's physical appearance – TC] on a par with Alexander von Humboldt [the great German explorer and geographer – TC]. At the same ... Vogt, not satisfied with the "ancient rivalry between Prussia and Austria on German, etc., territory", invented another rivalry between these two states which "has so frequently broken out on *non-European* soil" (loc. cit., p. 20). This *non-European soil* is probably on the moon.[30]

And Marx comments more pertinently to the politics at hand:

> I have even seen a letter written by a "New Swiss" ... to a "Mr. P.B.B. of 78 Fenchurch Street, London" early in 1860 in which he *mentions a very considerable sum of money* which his ex-friend [Vogt – TC] had received from the [Imperial – TC] treasury in Paris, not as a *bribe*, but as *payment in advance*. Such items of news and worse have made their way to London, but for my part I would not give a brass farthing for them. I rather believe *Vogt* implictly when he says that
>
> > "it is no one's business where I" (*Vogt*) "get my money from. *I shall continue to try to obtain whatever resources are needed to achieve my political ends*, and conscious *that I am working for a good cause I shall continue to obtain them* **from wherever I can**" ...
>
> hence also from the Paris treasury.[31]

Marx connects his own satires directly to those of the popular press:

> I do not know if my readers have ever themselves seen a copy of *Punch*, the London equivalent of the [Berlin] *Kladderadatsch*. The title-page shows a picture of Punch sitting down and behind him stands his dog Toby with a grumpy expression on his face and a pen behind his ear, both of which point to his being a born penny-a-liner. If it is fair to compare small things with large [an allusion to Virgil – TC] then one could perhaps compare Vogt with Punch, especially since the latter has lost his wit....[32]

My final quotation in this brief selection of rhetorical wonders of invective, well in line with the classical models for public speech and political persuasion, is so good that even McLellan quotes it:

30. *CW* 17, p. 167; emphasis in Marx's original text.
31. *CW* 17, pp. 212–13.
32. *CW* 17, p. 238–9.

> By means of an ingenious system of concealed plumbing, all the lavatories of London empty their physical refuse into the Thames. In the same way every day the capital of the world spews out all its social refuse through a system of goose quills, and it pours out into a great central paper *cloaca* – the *Daily Telegraph*. [The chemist Justus von – TC] Liebig rightly criticises the senseless wastefulness which robs the Thames of its purity and the English soil of its manure.[33]

While the content connections between *Herr Vogt* and Marx's earlier analytical *and* satirical intervention – *The Eighteenth Brumaire of Louis Bonaparte* (1852) – are obvious (given that Marx is accusing Vogt of being a Bonapartist agent), it is however a rhetorical passage of *The Eighteenth Brumaire* that Marx quotes in *Herr Vogt*, and indeed incorporates into the later and less famous text, so the connection is seamless:

> To punish me for my many outrages, committed over a period of years, against the head and members of the "Gang of December 10" [Marx's term for Louis Bonaparte and his associates references the date in 1851 of his military *coup d'etat* suspending the Second Republic, of which he was president – TC], Vogt appointed me the leader of the Brimstone Gang [Vogt's term for a clique of post-48 émigrés in London – TC] . . . I may cite here some of the passages referring to the "December Gang" from my book [*The Eighteenth Brumaire* – TC] . . .
>
> "This gang dates from the year 1849. On the pretext of founding a benevolent society, the lumpenproletariat of Paris had been organised into secret sections, each section being led by Bonapartist agents, with a Bonapartist general at the head of the whole. Alongside decayed aristocratic *roués* with dubious means of subsistence and of dubious origin, alongside ruined and adventurous offshoots of the bourgeoisie, were vagabonds, discharged soldiers, discharged jailbirds, escaped galley slaves, rogues, mountebanks, *lazzaroni* [the Neapolitan mob – TC], pickpockets, tricksters, gamblers, *maquereaux* [pimps – TC], brothel-keepers, porters, casual labourers, organ-grinders, rag-pickers, knife-grinders, tinkers, beggars – in short, the whole indefinite, disintegrated mass, thrown hither and thither, which the French term *la bohème*; from this kindred element Bonaparte formed the core of the Gang of December 10. A 'benevolent society' – in so far as, like Bonaparte, all its members felt the need of benefiting themselves at the expense of the labouring nation . . . ."[34]

The above passage has long posed sociological and political puzzles for Marxists, viz. how does it fit into the ever-simplifying two-class model of bourgeois/capitalist society, as outlined, for example, in the *Manifesto of the Communist Party*?[35] How does it square with his political identification of the proletariat (in print as

33. *CW* 17, p. 243; McLellan, *Karl Marx*, p. 315.
34. *CW* 17, pp. 33–4.
35. *CW* 6, p. 485.

early as 1844)[36] as the emerging historical subject through which communism can and must be realized? However, read rhetorically, it makes partisan sense as a way of denigrating – with due dollops of sarcasm – the past and present of the current Emperor of France.

The other familiar work that Marx references in *Herr Vogt* is the *Manifesto*, but he draws the reader in to a relatively unfamiliar section; indeed Marx descriptively subsumes the canonical sections one and two of the *Manifesto* ("Bourgeois and Proletarians"; "Proletarians and Communists") into the little read and far less appreciated section three ("Socialist and Communist Literature"). The linkage, of course, is rhetorical and political: Marx is laying into rival thinkers, rival groups, rival ideas.

> Techow [a '48er and émigré author of a letter of 1850 used by Vogt to construct allegations against Marx – TC] thus "imagines" that I have written a "Proletarian Catechism". He means the *Manifesto* which criticises and, if he likes, "ridicules" socialist and critical utopianism of every kind. Only, this "ridiculing" was not such a simple matter as Techow "imagines", but required a fair amount of work ... Techow further "imagines" that I have "tailored" a "*system*", whereas, on the contrary, even in the *Manifesto* which was intended directly for workers, I rejected systems of *every* kind and in their place I insisted on "a critical insight into the conditions, the line of march and the ultimate general results of the real movement of society". Such an "insight" cannot be blindly repeated, nor can it be "tailored" like a cartridge pouch.[37]

Read this way, as Marx does, sections one and two of the *Manifesto* are the build-up to the crucial section three, and section four ("Position of the Communists in Relation to the Various Existing Opposition Parties") is the immediate consequence on the day. Or to put it another way, the point of the *Manifesto* is to warn workers off the various socialisms and communisms that Marx and Engels list – giving precise and satirical critiques in equal measure. But as a matter of strategy, Marx and Engels first outline the "real movement" through which the contemporary class structure has come into being, currently operates and will necessarily develop. Looked at that way, Marx's disavowal of system-building makes perfect sense, and so does his rhetoric.

Conclusions

Marx was a journalist and rhetoric was his *métier*. Almost all of his political activism was through this means. The biographical and

36. Marx, "Contribution to the Critique of Hegel's Philosophy of Law: Introduction," *CW* 3, p. 186–7.
37. *CW* 17, p. 90; emphasis in original.

bibliographical construction of him as a "theorist" (or worse, "philosopher") required considerable "bracketing off" of rhetoric as such, hence of large-scale sections in his works, and indeed whole works as such. It also required the concomitant construction of a canon and the invocation of a reading strategy through which to establish – repetitively – the identity and certainty of Marxism, or least to fix "standard" accounts of "Marx" the author in the libraries in a form fit for "reliable" reference.

Marx the man, the political animal and the writer was a more complex character, and arguably he is at least a useful supplement to – perhaps even antidote for – the rather tired accounts of Marx and his "theory" (or worse, "system"), and the even more enervated attempts to revive it. This article suggests a 180° turn in reading Marx – looking for the rhetoric, charting the scorn, enjoying the sarcasm – and just possibly, turning the same time-honored ways to do things with words to good use today.

The "Lesser Evil" as Argument and Tactic, from Marx to the Present*

Victor Wallis

Introduction

The concept of "lesser evil" is applicable, in principle, to any choice between alternatives, whether made by individuals or by organizations. It may refer to specific actions or to overall systems, and it has been invoked from every political direction. Within Marxist tradition, the concept has most commonly referred to decisions on whether to give momentary tactical support to one or another bourgeois political formation. But the essential argument for a "lesser evil" approach – with or without mention of those exact words – may emerge at widely varying levels of generality. It may be used with reference to basic institutional frameworks, pitting the democratic republic against some form of authoritarian rule. It may be used to argue for strategic retreat or compromise in the face of threats to a movement's (or a regime's) survival. Within a democratic republic, it may be used in advocating a united front with particular bourgeois parties against repression or in favor of progressive social policies. Or, in the specific context of electoral campaigns, it may be used to characterize the tactic of supporting one non-working-class candidate or party over another – a tactic which may or may not involve arguing that the favored candidate is to some degree "less bad."

*This article is revised and expanded from an entry originally published (in German translation, as "kleineres Übel") in the *Historisch-kritisches Wörterbuch des Marxismus*, vol. VII/1 (Hamburg: Argument, 2008). It is re-used here with the permission of HKWM editor Wolfgang Fritz Haug, to whom I am grateful for his encouragement. For primary-source citations, I have kept the HKWM format, using, in order of appearance, the following abbreviations: K= *Das Kapital* (Marx); NRhZ= *Neue Rheinische Zeitung* (newspaper edited by Marx); MEW = *Marx Engels Werke*; CW = *Collected Works* (Lenin). Dates of primary-source citations are given, where applicable, in day/month/year format. All italics within quotations are as in the original texts.

Socialism and Democracy, Vol.24, No.3, November 2010, pp.119–129
ISSN 0885-4300 print/ISSN 1745-2635 online
DOI: 10.1080/08854300.2010.513618

Common to all these choices is the underlying commitment to strive for the presumed "good," which in the long run is the society of "associated producers" (K III: ch. 48, sec. 3) and in the short run is the growth of an independent working-class movement or the consolidation of a revolutionary regime. Responses in every instance range from a *maximalist* position, which holds that the positive task of advancing the revolution eclipses in importance any possible concern with whether one expression of bourgeois power may be worse than another, to a *minimalist* one, which becomes so absorbed with responding to immediate threats that it loses sight of the movement's original goal. Maximalists sometimes use the derogatory expression "lesser evilism" in an attempt to discredit the idea of giving even limited and transitory support to any bourgeois formation. In fact, however, determinations of lesser evil (or least damage) are inherent in any decision requiring *defensive* calculations, as opposed to the unobstructed pursuit of one's positive goal. To avoid such calculations is impossible; the challenge, for a revolutionary party, is to keep them within appropriate bounds.

Outside of Marxist tradition and beyond the level of purely pragmatic calculations, however, the concept of lesser evil has in the past decade taken on a rather novel role as a purported ethical justification for capitalism in an epoch of intensified crisis – ecological as well as economic – and of untrammeled US global military intervention.

Marx/Engels and electoral calculations

The political debate over the lesser evil is as old as working-class politics. It originated with the project of constituting the working class as an independent political force. Marx and Engels were engaged in this project from its beginnings. From at least as early as 1847, much of their writing was directly linked to their organizational efforts at launching a communist movement against the backdrop of the Prussian monarchy (Nimtz 2000: 67ff, 93ff). The narrow range of electoral options quickly confronted them with a "lesser evil" scenario. Already in June 1848, the big bourgeoisie's alliance with feudal Reaction was clear to Marx and Engels (NRhZ, 14/6/1848; MEW 5: 65). Discussing the 22/1/1849 elections to the Prussian Constituent Assembly, however, Marx distinguished between the movement's electoral tactics and its longer-range organizing: "Where it is a struggle against the *existing government*, we ally ourselves even with our enemies ... Now, *after* the election, we again affirm our old relentless standpoint not only against the government but also against the official opposition" (NRhZ, 18/2/1849; MEW

6: 298). Underlying this approach was Marx's conviction that a democratic state, compared to any absolutist regime, had the advantage for the proletariat of not artificially blurring social antagonisms and, hence, of providing the setting "in which they come to a free fight and thereby to a solution" (NRhZ, 29/6/1848; MEW 5: 136). In this sense, the democratic state, about whose social grounding and ultimate allegiance Marx had no illusions, was indeed for him a "lesser evil."

From the moment that the institutional framework was no longer in question, however, Marx's emphasis would shift dramatically. Speaking in March 1850 on behalf of the Central Authority of the Communist League, Marx and Engels insisted "that everywhere workers' candidates are put up alongside the bourgeois-democratic candidates," and that the workers "must not allow themselves to be bribed by such arguments of the democrats as, for example, that by so doing they are splitting the democratic party and giving the reactionaries the possibility of victory" (MEW 7: 251). It should be noted, however, that in the setting to which they referred, the only danger they anticipated was "the presence of a few reactionaries in the representative body" (251). Within this framework of bourgeois parliamentarism but yet fully conscious of its conditional character, they would continue to stress the centrality of independent working-class organization (Draper 1978, Nimtz 2000). As for any eventuality in which the state might set limits to working-class advances, they would have no hesitation in strategizing – and acting – outside the parliamentary framework. Following the May 1849 shutdown of the *Neue Rheinische Zeitung,* Engels "went to fight with the insurrectionary forces" (Draper 1978: 240); in 1895, contemplating the real possibility of the working class attaining power through the institutions of the democratic republic, Engels nonetheless sought to remind his readers, despite censorship by the editors of *Die Neue Zeit*, that the decisive struggles might still require armed confrontations (MEW 22: 522). In this sense, although parliamentarism had initially emerged in Germany as a lesser evil compared to absolutism, street-fighting now came to be seen as a lesser evil – or at least, under certain conditions, as a practical necessity – in order to avoid the greater danger of parliamentary co-optation.

Lenin and bourgeois constitutionalism

Within the pre-revolutionary Russian setting, Lenin viewed bourgeois constitutionalism not as a viable option (let alone as a potentially preferable regime) but rather simply as a contrasting framework, whose implications for working-class organizing were vastly different from those of his own political surroundings. In *What Is to Be Done?* (1902), much of his discussion of organizational imperatives thus takes the form of drawing conclusions dictated by Russia's remoteness from that framework, i.e., by Russia's lack of "political liberty." The degree of tsarist repression was subject to change, however, dependent on the balance of class forces. When opportunities for legal agitation multiplied in 1907, Lenin insisted that the party should make use of them, so as not to become detached from its working-class base. In voting at that time for participation in the Duma (the weak parliamentary body allowed by the czar after 1905), Lenin aroused criticism from party comrades who saw this as an act of betrayal (Le Blanc 1993: 150).

Such criticism, of course, reflected a failure to distinguish between tactical or conjunctural decisions and long-term goal. Tactical decisions routinely involve compromise. To the extent that a succession of such decisions may alter the long-term outcome, the problem may be less one of betrayal than one of insufficiently acknowledging other forces that are at work. The assessment of those other forces must therefore be a key factor in judging the appropriateness of any tactical – or "lesser evil" – decision. A number of Lenin's decisions merit consideration with this in mind.

Lenin's essay "On Compromises," written less than eight weeks before the October 1917 Revolution, was prompted by a juncture similar to that of 1907. The advantage he sought was freedom of action for the Bolsheviks; the concession he proposed was that the Bolsheviks would support the continuation in power of a Menshevik/SR coalition (3/9/1917; CW 25: 307).[1] This concession was, under the circumstances, a "lesser evil" compared to the risk of having the Bolsheviks' agitation suppressed before they had built up sufficient support to be able to take power.

Once in a position of state power, the Bolsheviks faced a new set of threats, suggesting the need for compromises of various kinds. Lenin's proposal to sign an unfavorable peace agreement with Germany risked a split in the Bolshevik party, but in his deliberation with Trotsky on this decision, he asserted, in effect, "better a split in the party than the danger of a military defeat of the revolution" (Trotsky 1971a: 103; cf. Lenin, *"Left-Wing" Communism: An Infantile Disorder*, CW 31: 36). On the production front, Lenin clearly presented his calls for "iron discipline" and for reliance on bourgeois experts as being "a compromise" and "a step backward" ("The Immediate Tasks of the Soviet Government,"

1. For background on the various parties, see, e.g., Rabinowitch (2004).

4/1918, CW 27: 248f), but considered this approach less risky than the alternative, which he saw as dominated by "the element of petty bourgeois anarchy" and leading to "indiscipline, laxity and chaos" (CW 27: 265). He applied similar reasoning in formulating the New Economic Policy (NEP), which he put forward as a necessary measure to avoid the buildup of opposition in a country where the proletariat was vastly outnumbered by "the predominating peasantry" (Report to 10th Congress; 16/3/1921, CW 32: 265).

In all these cases, the choice made was, in immediate terms, a success, in the sense that the Bolsheviks' power-position was preserved. Such compromises may also have secondary effects, however, which become apparent over a longer period. These need to be kept in mind even if no definitive conclusion can be drawn as to the outcome of an alternative course of action. Such possible secondary effects highlight the importance of the particular conjuncture at which the original decision was taken. Among the specific decisions here mentioned, the military capitulation appears in retrospect as the least controversial, given the overwhelming popular opposition in Russia to continuation of the war. The other two decisions, even if driven by compelling considerations, may have had more complex ramifications. The NEP may have strengthened and emboldened sectors hostile to socialization and may have helped legitimize the eventual emergence of a privileged stratum. The imposition of harsh factory discipline certainly had the effect of blocking any possible evolution of incipient movements toward worker control, which, had they had an opportunity to flourish, might have counteracted the development of bureaucratic rigidities in the planning process.

"Lesser evil" choices may thus have costs that cannot initially be foreseen. A proper assessment of these costs, on the other hand, must take into account not only the directly affected society but also the impact of that society's presence on the world scene. In the Soviet case, the taking on of state power under less-than-optimal conditions surely helps explain – in combination with hostile foreign intervention – the emergence of a regime which would cast socialism in a negative light; but at the same time the mere existence of this regime, whatever its flaws, may have facilitated revolutionary advances elsewhere (Wallis 1990: 56ff).

Can compromise ward off the "greater evil"?

Lenin's fullest discussion of compromise is in *"Left-Wing" Communism...* (1920), where he draws examples both from the Bolshevik experience and from the politics of parliamentary regimes. In distinguishing acceptable from unacceptable forms of compromise, he explicitly uses the notion of "lesser evil" to describe the former: "One must distinguish between a man who has given up his money and fire-arms to bandits so as to lessen the evil they can do … and a man who gives his money and fire-arms to bandits so as to share in the loot" (CW 31: 38). His example here for the "lesser evil" compromise is the Brest-Litovsk Treaty; his counter-example of "treachery" is the 1914–20 role of parties of the Second International, in the support they gave to their governments' war policies, as "*accomplices* in *banditry*" (CW 31: 37).

Parliamentary struggles during the ensuing decades offered many instances in which the lesser-evil option would be debated, but usually without any prospect for the Left parties of coming to power. The most acute case of this type was the one posed by the rise of Nazism. Without going into detail about the intense debates that this elicited in Weimar Germany, we may note here that apart from the KPD's (Communist Party) maximalist stance of belittling the fascist threat (e.g., Ernst Thälmann's plenary speech of February 1932; Beetham 1983: 162) and the SPD's (Social Democratic Party) minimalist position of, in Rudolf Hilferding's words, "an absolute interest in the preservation of democracy" (speech to SPD conference of 1927; Beetham 1983: 253), there was the view that the Left parties, without in any way minimizing their critique of the bourgeois state, should at least join forces to confront the Nazis. As Trotsky described the choice between alternative bourgeois political forces (1931): "There are seven notes in the musical scale. The question as to which of these notes is 'better'… is a nonsensical question. But the musician must know when to strike and what notes to strike" (Trotsky 1971b: 136). The KPD/SPD split remained unresolved, however, and in the 1932 presidential election the only "electable" alternative to Hitler was Field Marshal von Hindenburg. This represented an extreme narrowing of the options, to the extent that the victorious "lesser evil" (Hindenburg) simply cleared the path for his adversary by then appointing him as Chancellor, thereby confirming the view that the choice, as offered, was no choice at all.

The "lesser evil" as a system-induced imperative: the US model

Considering electoral frameworks generally, the "lesser evil" logic is endemic to systems which lack proportional representation. It is only partly attenuated by runoff elections. It appears in undiluted form in situations of party "duopoly" with just a single round of voting. In the US case, it permeates all electoral calculations, including the nominating process, where, however, it also serves to transmit the power of the big-money contributors, who (with rare and purely individual exceptions) refuse to support progressive candidates but use the argument of "electability" to rationalize their choices.

The "electability" argument – illustrated in the Democrats' choice of John Kerry for president in 2004 and in their narrowing of the nomination contest to Obama vs. Hillary Clinton in 2008 – is integral to lesser-evilism. It is used exclusively against the Left. It presupposes the normality of an economically conservative platform and asserts that the best chance of defeating its Republican or right-wing version is not by offering a candidacy that would reject the conservative position but rather by offering one that shares, with only minor reservations, its central tenets. The assumption is that those tenets are what define the "mainstream" of the electorate (the electorate itself being relatively more prosperous than the approximately 50% of the adult population that does not vote), and that only by appealing to this mainstream is it possible to win. Within the US context, it is clear that the logic of lesser-evilism pulls the mainstream consensus steadily to the right. Thus, the more extreme the positions taken by Republican candidates and right-wing media personalities, the more the Democratic leadership will play to the voters' fears rather than mobilizing them for positive alternative programs.

A similar dynamic is repeated in the legislative process, as shown in the 2009–10 debate over healthcare. The Democratic leadership persistently silenced the advocates of an authentically universal healthcare system, permitting a steady weakening of the reform bill, allegedly in the hope of attracting Republican support which they did not need (in view of their substantial majorities in both chambers of Congress) and which they could on no account expect to obtain. Gradually, over the course of more than a year of narrowly circumscribed debate, those Democrats who initially insisted on at least a limited "public option" (a fully public system of health insurance having been ruled "off the table") were pressured and worn down to the point where they abandoned that demand and accepted a measure that, while adding a layer of subsidies and regulations, reaffirmed an augmented regime of private health insurance as a "lesser evil" compared to the previous arrangement in which the numbers of the totally uninsured had reached approximately 50 million.

It is important, by way of qualification, to note that the "lesser evil" approach is not always without political justification. As the long history of revolutionary organizing suggests, a timely retreat is preferable to an assured rout. In the US partisan framework, however, lesser-evilism reflects a virtual complicity between the two parties involved, comparable to the "good cop/bad cop" approach to interrogations. Thus, the electoral dynamic unfolds in a setting in which basic ideological assumptions are shared by the two parties and in which, despite any differences between their respective rhetorical stances (and their corresponding popular constituencies), major financial backers typically contribute not just to one of those parties but to both of them (Parenti 2002: 194–214; cf. Brenner 1988).

The resulting symbiosis has created a situation in which the Democrats as a party not only fail to challenge the Republicans ideologically, but also fail to assert their procedural rights in the face of corruption of the electoral process (Miller 2007). They thereby diminish even further the potential impact of any support they might attract. The end-result is that a vote for the "lesser evil" serves primarily as a legitimating mechanism, with little effect on policy. The social sectors that are thereby confirmed in power then become increasingly immune to any legal restraints, inasmuch as the instruments for holding them accountable have become inoperative.

Examples of lesser-evilism are by no means confined to the United States, even if that is where its effect in weakening the Left is most apparent. Another notable instance was the 2002 presidential election in France, when, in the first round of voting, the right-wing candidate Le Pen placed unexpectedly ahead of the center-left challenger Jospin. In the runoff contest between Le Pen and President Chirac, most of the Left supported Chirac, despite the latter's clearly conservative policy-positions. The opposite outcome at the runoff stage – reflecting the inherently limited appeal of the mainly negative approach implied by "lesser evil" – was seen in the 2005 election in Iran, where the less theocratic candidate Rafsanjani was defeated by Ahmadinejad. Thus, whether the "lesser evil" candidate wins or loses, the forces of the Left remain marginalized. A final example of this effect is the chronic situation in the US colonial territory of Puerto Rico, whose existing status, with its partial cultural autonomy, appears to most local citizens – including the many who resonate with calls for independence – as a lesser evil compared with complete absorption into the United States.

Lesser evil or greater good?

From the time of the Bolshevik Revolution until the collapse of the Soviet bloc, there were grounds for arguing that the socialist orbit was expanding. Its negative traits could be rationalized as transitional phenomena whose severity could be expected to diminish over time, and a socialist presence in the international arena could be seen as a bulwark against the most adverse manifestations of capitalism. It was in this spirit that Lukács could say, in 1968, "I have always thought that the worst form of socialism was better to live in than the best form of capitalism" (Lukács 1971: 58).

With the post-1989 "New World Order," however, lesser-evil discourse took on a new dimension. In the interests of capital, the dismantling of "existing socialism" had to be rendered permanent. As the polarizing tendencies of capitalism showed no signs of abating, its defenders shifted from extolling the system's virtues to proclaiming simply that, whatever might be capitalism's virtues or defects, "there is no alternative." More precisely, no disclosure about capitalism could possibly match, from this vantage point, the unmitigated evil of "communism." The widely diffused *Livre noir du Communisme* (Courtois et al. 1997) sought above all to put communism on the same moral level as Nazism, while at the same time insinuating, by its tendentious reckoning of casualties (Perrault 1997: 22f), that communism was even worse. The *Livre noir* in turn prompted a series of international conferences in 2000–01 culminating in an anthology entitled *The Lesser Evil: Moral Approaches to Genocide Practices* (Dubiel & Motzkin 2004: 2). The discussions here are more careful to acknowledge the complexities of comparing Nazism with communism, and they do not presume to judge either one as "worse" or "less bad" than the other. However, by reviving the unifying concept of totalitarianism, by implicitly linking "communism" with socialism while divorcing Nazism from capitalism, and by disregarding the historical and continuing record of mass atrocities and military interventions fueled by capitalism (Curtin 1969, Chomsky & Herman 1979, Stannard 1992, Blum 2003), the collection as a whole points to no other "lesser evil" than the institutions of liberal (bourgeois) democracy.

The justification of capitalism based on calling liberal democracy "the lesser evil" is raised to the level of doctrine by Ignatieff (2004). The "greater evil" now becomes terrorism rather than totalitarianism, but the argument is the same. If then a liberal democracy, defining its agenda as counter-terrorist, engages in practices of torture, these are by definition for Ignatieff (provided that certain procedural requirements have been observed) "lesser evils" (see Friel & Falk 2004: 151ff). Now, as before, the capitalist character of liberal-capitalist governments – and, hence, of their global priorities – goes simply unmentioned. "Terrorism" is so labeled only when directed against these governments (or their allies), never when carried out on their behalf (see Ray & Schaap 2003; Herman & Peterson 2010). The political rationalizations of liberal-capitalist governments are accepted at face value, and the possibility – dramatized in the post-1998 Venezuelan challenge to US hegemony – that what these governments might most fear is not the suppression of democracy but rather its more thoroughgoing implementation (Wallis 2006: 18) is not even considered.

Ironically, the current ideological flaunting of the "lesser evil" argument serves the interests of a political force (the US ruling class) which, in terms of its power, its sweep, its economic agenda, and its weapons of enforcement, can more plausibly be thought of as the world's greater evil – understanding the latter not in any cosmic or theological sense but strictly in terms of: (1) numbers of people harmed on a global scale, economically as well as militarily; (2) incidence of direct imposition via military occupation; (3) extreme character of the control techniques that are applied; and (4) systemic and non-negotiable character of the underlying priorities, namely those of capital. Thus, the United States is the country in which the power of capital is least restrained and in which, consequently, there is the highest level of obstruction to policies reflecting environmental and social service or working-class priorities. Not coincidentally, it is also, as we have seen, the country in which the "lesser evil" calculus most fully defines the limits of policy debates, and in which, as a result, the opportunities for positive electoral alternatives are most fully closed off.

Marx and Engels noted early in their trajectory that the ruling ideas of a society are the ideas of its ruling class. What this most recent twist of the lesser-evil argument reflects is the fact that a long-enshrined core "ruling idea" of capital – the conflation of capitalism with democracy – has lost all credibility. In other words, since "normal" capitalist politics has lost its democratic trappings, it can devise no other legitimizing rationale than the claim to be "less bad" than an alternative that it defines as one inherently committed to the imposition of terror. The hegemony of capital has thus suffered a decisive blow, and its ideologues have had to make a leap of intellectual desperation in order to argue that the system they uphold stands for any interests other than those of its owners.

References

Beetham, David. 1983. *Marxists in the Face of Fascism*. Manchester: Manchester University Press.

Blum, William. 2003. *Killing Hope: U.S. Military and CIA Interventions Since World War II*. Monroe, ME: Common Courage Press.

Brenner, Leni. 1988. *The Lesser Evil [The Democratic Party]*. Secaucus, NJ: Lyle Stuart.

Chomsky, Noam and Edward Herman. 1979. *The Washington Connection and Third World Fascism*. Boston: South End Press.

Cockburn, Alexander and Jeffrey St. Clair, eds. 2004. *Dime's Worth of Difference: Beyond the Lesser of Two Evils*. Oakland: AK Press.

Courtois, Stéphane, et al. 1997. *Le livre noir du Communisme: Crimes, terreur, répression*. Paris: R. Laffont.

Curtin, Philip D. 1969. *The Atlantic Slave Trade: A Census*. Madison: University of Wisconsin Press.

Draper, Hal. 1978. *Karl Marx's Theory of Revolution*, vol. II: *The Politics of Social Classes*. New York: Monthly Review Press.

Dubiel, Helmut and Gabriel Motzkin, eds. 2004. *The Lesser Evil: Moral Approaches to Genocide Practices*. London: Routledge.

Friel, Howard and Richard Falk. 2004. *The Record of the Paper: How the* New York Times *Misreports US Foreign Policy*. London: Verso.

Herman, Edward S. and David Peterson. 2010. *The Politics of Genocide*. New York: Monthly Review Press.

Ignatieff, Michael. 2004. *The Lesser Evil: Political Ethics in an Age of Terror*. Edinburgh: Edinburgh University Press.

Le Blanc, Paul. 1993. *Lenin and the Revolutionary Party*. Atlantic Highlands, NJ: Humanities Press.

Lukács, Georg. 1971. "Interview," *New Left Review*, no. 68 (July/August).

Miller, Mark Crispin. 2007. *Fooled Again: The* Real *Case for Electoral Reform*. New York: Basic Books.

Nimtz, August H., Jr. 2000. *Marx and Engels: Their Contribution to the Democratic Breakthrough*. Albany: SUNY Press.

Parenti, Michael. 2002. *Democracy for the Few*, 7th ed. Boston: St. Martin's Press.

Perrault, Gilles. 1997. "Communisme, les falsifications d'un 'livre noir'," *Le Monde diplomatique* (December).

Rabinowitch, Alexander. 2004. *The Bolsheviks Come to Power: The Revolution of 1917 in Petrograd*. Chicago: Haymarket Books.

Ray, Ellen and William H. Schaap, eds. 2003. *Covert Action: The Roots of Terrorism*. Melbourne: Ocean Press.

Stannard, David E. 1992. *American Holocaust: Columbus, Christianity, and the Conquest of the Americas*. New York: Oxford University Press.

Trotsky, Leon. 1971a. *Lenin: Notes for a Biographer*, trans. Tamara Deutscher. New York: Capricorn Books.

Trotsky, Leon. 1971b. "For a Workers' United Front Against Fascism", (8 Dec. 1931), in L. Trotsky, *The Struggle Against Fascism in Germany*. New York: Pathfinder Press.

Wallis, Victor. 1990. "Marxism in the Age of Gorbachev," *Socialism and Democracy*, no. 11 (September).

Wallis, Victor. 2006. "Socialism and Democracy during the First 20 Years of *Socialism and Democracy*," *Socialism and Democracy*, no. 40 (March).

In Capitalist Crisis, Rediscovering Marx

Rick Wolff

The rise, fall, and return of Marxian analyses

Marxian analyses are now resurfacing in public dialogues about economy and society. Thirty years of systematic and often successful anti-Marxism agitation are fading in politics, the media, academia, and beyond. A new generation discovers and wrestles with the diverse richness of that tradition's insights. Capitalist economic crises contributed to Marx's original insights and to their growing reception across the 19th and 20th centuries. Yet another crisis now renews broad social interest in Marxism. While the intensity of capitalism's dysfunction in its recurring crises motivates that interest, the logic of Marxian analysis makes the capitalist system itself, in or out of crisis, the object of criticism.

In the century before the 1970s, the victims of capitalism's recurring crises and its critics increasingly found theoretical and strategic resources in Marx's and other Marxists' works. That helped the Marxist tradition of social analysis spread widely across the world. As it interacted with many varied social contexts through changing times, the tradition developed multiple, different – and sometimes contested – interpretations or versions of Marxist social theory. Marxism accumulated diverse critical analyses of capitalism, varied critical engagements with theories that supported capitalism, and complex connections to an array of political movements and organizations. It gathered and debated the theoretical and practical lessons drawn from the experiences of social movements more or less inspired by Marxism. Even during periods when dogmatism promoted one interpretation (or "tendency") within Marxism as "the" genuine Marxism and marginalized or suppressed other interpretations, the latter survived. At the same time, new tendencies arose. Marxism continues as a cumulatively enriched (albeit diverse and contested) resource for theorists and activists seeking social change beyond capitalism.

Capitalism's defenders have variously sought to kill, repress, ignore, or otherwise marginalize Marxism and Marxists. Their efforts

Socialism and Democracy, Vol.24, No.3, November 2010, pp.130–146
ISSN 0885-4300 print/ISSN 1745-2635 online
DOI: 10.1080/08854300.2010.513619

often succeeded in slowing or temporarily reversing Marxism's advances in the century before the 1970s. Unevenly yet relentlessly, the Marxist tradition grew to encompass labor unions, political parties, newspapers, academic associations and research institutes, local, regional and national governing regimes, and internationals. It also generated internal differences, debates, and conflicts, mostly peaceful but sometimes violent, among its constituent tendencies.

However, the 1970s changed the conditions of and the social prospects for Marxism. Capitalism had by then recovered significantly from the damage to its institutions and public support caused by the Great Depression of the 1930s. The 1970s saw sharply intensified business and conservative counterattacks against the reforms, regulations, and other Depression-era state interventions imposed upon private capitalists. The US government cooperated by enhancing the demonization of all things Marxist, especially after Reagan became president. Well-funded crusades denounced state, labor union, or popular interventions limiting private capitalism as Marxist, "anti-American," dictatorial, and counterproductive. The deepening internal contradictions of the "actually existing socialisms" that officially celebrated Marx and Marxism facilitated those crusades. Marx, Marxism, and communism were conflated into synonyms - a conflation promoted by both the USA and the USSR albeit for different reasons.

A resurgent post-war capitalism celebrated its renewed strength and the weaknesses of its enemies, both foreign and domestic. In the US, the New Deal, already compromised from 1945 to the 1970s, was afterwards largely and systematically reversed. Unions' membership and social influence declined. Together with shifting labor market conditions, unions' weaknesses put a permanent end in the 1970s to the 100-year period of rising US real wages. Economics, politics, and culture shifted rightward, bringing a neoliberal era committed to privatizing means of production and deregulating markets. A reinforced individualism focused on getting rich quick while also denigrating and deriding most collective social efforts and values.

In the 1970s, a new set of global investment opportunities opened up for capitalist enterprises. Technological changes inside enterprises (computers), in transportation (jet aviation) and in telecommunication (the internet) greatly enhanced global coordination within and among capitalist corporations. Producing, installing, maintaining, and refining those technological changes became extremely profitable investment opportunities as well. Most important was combining global capitalism with vast new sources of relatively cheap labor (both located in and immigrating from the former "second" and "third" worlds). *Technological changes driving up the productivity of labor combined with new supplies of labor power to keep real wages from rising.* That made capitalist surpluses soar. The 30 years before 2008 thus saw one of the greatest profit booms in capitalist history.

Capitalism's admirers in business, politics, media, and the academy celebrated. Labor, socialism, and Marxism weakened and shrank, unevenly but nearly everywhere. Capitalism's apologists insisted yet again that capitalism had "overcome its crisis tendencies." Alan Greenspan, the US Federal Reserve's chairman, said in the late 1990s that we "now live in a new economy." Once the USSR had imploded, Marxism's enemies changed their attacks. Before 1989, they had portrayed it as an erroneous theory informing a failed and also treasonous practice. After 1989 they treated it more as a fading historic relic deserving no modern person's serious attention. Capitalism had won the struggle with socialism. "There is no alternative" to capitalism, and the US is its appropriate superpower champion.

By means of such adjusted anti-Marxist rationales, Marxist analyses continued to be excluded from the mass media and Marxists from academic and political positions. They were not needed; history had rendered them anachronistic. The world had moved on. Not a few Marxists found it difficult to sustain their beliefs in so changed an environment; they therefore modified their positions or abandoned Marxism altogether.

Once Greenspan's "new economy" had collapsed in 2008, exposed as the same old crisis-prone capitalism, Marx and Marxism were rediscovered yet again. The Marxian tradition was found to be helpful in understanding the crisis's causes and costs and in finding solutions that entailed alternatives to capitalism. The rest of this paper illustrates that helpfulness.

Those newly encountering Marxism, like many familiar with the tradition, were both attracted and troubled by its richness and diversity. Some were sufficiently distressed by the multiplicity of contending tendencies that they fixed upon one tendency as if it were Marxism per se and either ignored other tendencies or read them out of Marxism; such theoretical sectarianism has been a recurring problem. Others embraced Marxism's richness and engaged the debate among its internal tendencies. They supported, extended, and applied one or a subset of those tendencies and debated their reasons for doing so with advocates of alternative tendencies. They conceived their project as building a complex, diverse tradition struggling to move society beyond capitalism.

In that spirit, let me make clear that I am using here a particular interpretation of Marxian theory to provide a unique explanation of the current capitalist crisis's multiple causes with emphasis on the US. On the basis of this interpretation, I offer arguments for a Marxist response to capitalist crises. My intervention, together with those of other Marxists, demonstrates again the productive insights made possible through Marxism's critiques of capitalism. These interventions feed and foster today's rediscoveries of Marxism's indispensable resources for superseding the instabilities, social costs, and limitations of the capitalist system.

Capitalism as an oscillating system

Capitalist economies everywhere display a recurring pattern of oscillation. Periods of relatively limited state interventions in markets and private property repeatedly encounter crises that they manage more or less well. Eventually, however, a crisis arrives that exceeds their management capacities. Then, transition occurs to a period with relatively more state economic interventions. This latter period then similarly encounters and manages some lesser crises before it too confronts one that it cannot contain. Then a reverse transition generates a period of relatively less state economic intervention. What remains the same across both periods of this oscillation is the capitalist structure of production inside enterprises. There, a small group of people oversees the production and sale of commodities produced by a large group of hired laborers. That small group appropriates and distributes the surplus - the excess of the value added by workers over their wages - embodied in those commodities.

We shall use the names "private" and "state" to differentiate these oscillating periods or forms of capitalist economy. Thus, for example, the 1929 crisis of a private capitalism in the US ushered in a state capitalism, Roosevelt's New Deal. Eventually, in the 1970s, that state capitalism encountered a crisis serious enough to provoke a transition back to private capitalism. When the latter experienced a meltdown in 2008, that crisis provoked yet another move back toward a state capitalism. Comparable oscillations characterize all capitalisms.

Two different and contending mainstream (i.e., non-Marxian) theories have alternatively explained capitalism's repeated crises over the last century. For each crisis, those different theories proposed correspondingly different solutions. Today's crisis is no exception. Ideological hegemony has oscillated between those two theories just as capitalism has oscillated between its two forms.

One theory – now called "Keynesian economics" – claims that relatively unregulated private enterprises and free markets have structural limits and imperfections that periodically push capitalist economies into inflations, recessions, or even depressions. Without intervention from outside, private capitalism may remain depressed or inflated long enough to generate the mass opposition that could threaten capitalism itself. Keynesian economics identifies those key mechanisms that produce crises in private capitalisms and recommends various state interventions (regulations and monetary and fiscal policies) to reduce their depth, duration, and frequency.

The other mainstream theory is associated by its devotees with Adam Smith, the classical "founder of modern economics." It celebrates private capitalism (free markets plus private property) as the economic system that generates the maximum possible wealth and thereby social stability. In its evolved "neoclassical" form, this mainstream theory emphasizes how and why private capitalism yields the best ("optimum") of all possible economic outcomes. When non-optimal outcomes occur, neoclassical economists usually argue that their causes are either external (e.g., state) interventions into or internal violations of private capitalism's rules of unfettered individual pursuit of self-interest, competition, etc. Thus, the best solution for non-optimal outcomes is to re-establish a properly rule-driven private capitalism free of external interference.

The neoclassical economists denounce Keynesian-inspired state interventions as inevitably yielding regulators' mistakes, politically manipulated markets, and such resulting inefficiencies as inflation, stagnation, and stagflation. State officials cannot, they argue, efficiently replace, let alone improve upon, the unregulated ("free") market mechanism. Neoclassical economists insist that free markets accommodate the infinity of different demands and supplies and communicate the infinity of information about them more efficiently than any state could. On the other side, the Keynesians mock the neoclassical economists for their opposition to state interventions that are essential to support the capitalism those same economists champion.

From the 1970s to 2008, as private capitalists campaigned against national and international state interventions that constricted their profitability, neoclassical economists renewed and extended their theory under the rubric of a "neo-liberalism." They overthrew the previous domination of Keynesianism in government economic policy and academia that emerged from the Great Depression of the 1930s. Neoclassical economists had always attacked the Keynesian economics of FDR's New Deal for seriously distorting and slowing economic growth and promoting social conflict (sometimes dubbed "class war"). They sought to reinstitute the neoclassical utopia: private property and competitive markets lifting the incomes of both labor and capital and thereby avoiding class conflicts by means of growth.

From the 1970s to 2008, market deregulation and privatization became the official and prevailing principles of business, politics, journalism, and academia. Neoclassical economics became once again, as before the Great Depression, the "correct" modern economics. It banished Keynesian economics as a theoretical mistake. Unrepentant Keynesians found their professional advances blocked. *Such extreme intolerance and hostilities between these mainstream theoretical schools replicated some of the ways both of them had jointly suppressed Marxian economics and economists since the late 1940s.*

From the 1970s to 2008, as productivity gains combined with stagnant real wages, corporate profits soared. Because this occurred together with neoliberal policy shifts, neoclassical economists credited the latter as the cause of the boom of the 1980s and 1990s. As the years passed, however, the relatively privatized economy also exhibited increasingly unequal income and wealth distributions and the associated explosion of debt and risky new credit instruments. Eventually, economic bubbles in stock, real estate, and credit markets burst, as had been darkly predicted by Keynesian and Marxian critics.

The new millennium opened with a stock market crash in the spring of 2000. A few years later, the rapid decline of interest rates (intended to limit the recessionary consequences of that crash) helped to propel a real estate bubble that collapsed into a liquidity-cum-credit crisis. Today a deep recession threatens to slide into a depression of major proportions. Neoclassical economists are in retreat as Keynesians resurface from ideological exile while conversions from the former to the latter also occur.

The Keynesian message remains what it always was: state intervention must save capitalism from its private form. That has become, again, today's wisdom. Faced with the current crisis, those who remain neoclassical economists have become advocates of yesterday's failed paradigm. However, if the Keynesian interventions begun by Bush and enlarged by Obama usher in a state interventionist form of capitalism for a while, capitalist crises will recur as they always have. Those crises will then again set the stage for yet another possible oscillation back to a private form of capitalism and to the associated hegemony of neoclassical economic theory.

Both sides share a profound conservatism vis-à-vis capitalism, despite their differences on state intervention. Each presumes the absolute necessity of (and never questions) the capitalist structure of production: a small group of employers – typically boards of directors chosen by major shareholders – that hires and controls, through its managerial staff, a different and much larger group (workers) who produce surpluses appropriated by the employers. The oscillations between the two forms of capitalism and between the two mainstream theories prevent crises *in* capitalism from becoming crises *of* capitalism, wherein the capitalist production system itself is thrown into question. Oscillation between the two theories shapes and contains public debate when capitalist crises cause serious social suffering. It keeps the range of discussable solutions to more or less regulation, more or less monetary or fiscal policies, and so on. That range keeps the public from imagining, let alone considering, the Marxian alternative solution, namely transition out of either form of capitalism into a different system.

A Marxian alternative

Yet after repeated oscillations between neoclassical and Keynesian theories, the promises of both sides that their solutions would "prevent future crises" ring increasingly hollow. The scope and duration of the current crisis therefore tarnishes not only neoclassical theory. Even as Keynesians rush in to fill the void created when this crisis undercut neoclassical theory's hegemony, they face an accumulated skepticism. Space opens for a rediscovery and consideration of Marxism. As Marxism produces distinctive explanations for the crisis and non-capitalist solutions, that space and its attractiveness expand.

The particular Marxian economic theory we deploy – and its application to the current capitalist crisis – is presented in detail elsewhere.[1] We will use it summarily here to explain the causes of the current crisis and to offer a new solution. Both the explanation and the solution differ radically from the neoclassical and Keynesian alternatives. They exemplify the fruits of applying Marxist theories to contemporary issues.

Today's crisis has deep roots in US capitalism's previous 125 years. From the 1870s to the 1970s, two key economic trends shaped the system: average real wages rose by about 1.3% per year while workers' average productivity rose by just under 2% per year. For that century, workers

1. For the basic theory, see Stephen Resnick and Richard Wolff, *Knowledge and Class: A Marxian Critique of Political Economy* (Chicago: University of Chicago Press, 1987), Chapter 3; Stephen Resnick and Richard Wolff, *New Departures in Marxian Theory* (New York: Routledge, 2006). For the theory's application to the current crisis, see Wolff, *Capitalism Hits the Fan: The Global Economic Meltdown and What to Do About It* (Northampton, MA: Olive Branch Press, 2010).

enjoyed a rising standard of living purchased chiefly with rising real wages. Capitalist employers simultaneously appropriated a rising *surplus* (because value added to output per worker *rose faster* than wages paid per worker). The social gap between workers and capitalists thus grew. Yet it posed no political problem where and when workers were satisfied with rising real wages and not troubled by that rising gap.

The century before the 1970s was thus largely a sustained success for US capitalism. Capital's steadily rising surpluses were distributed effectively to enhance the conditions for their further growth. Those surpluses helped to pay for technical change, for taxes to finance infrastructure development and public education, for mergers and acquisitions to gain economies of scale, etc. Workers became focused on the rising consumption made possible by their rising wages. They self-identified increasingly as consumers more than as workers. Consumerism became a powerful ideological and therefore social force. Unions accommodated that force by aiming chiefly to facilitate more consumption through better pay rather than to make basic social change. The exceptional "success" of US capitalism thus reflected but also depended on the continued growth of real wages combined with a faster growth of productivity.

However, that success had its costs. As the surpluses appropriated by capitalists rose faster than wages, the consequently growing economic disparity financed widening political and cultural gaps. Over the century before the 1970s, politics settled ever more deeply into an institutionalized, *merely formal* electoral democracy of money-driven elections and bureaucracies where capitalists' interests prevailed. Likewise cultural divides increasingly distanced the growing mass of workers from an elite of multinational corporate capitalists, their larger shareholders, and their better-paid, more or less "professional," dependents.

The dangers of deepening social divisions were postponed by the combination of rising personal consumption and a culture that celebrated it. The qualities and quantities of consumption became the measures of one's personal achievements and worth. They likewise functioned as compensation for increasingly demanding work (the "other" side of rising productivity). The birth and remarkable growth of modern advertising both resulted from and reinforced that culture. It challenged the religious self-image of US culture sufficiently to provoke endless clerical repetitions of sermons that bemoaned and denounced "mass obsession with material rather than spiritual values." Yet the rise of mass consumerism persisted. It had become the needed social glue binding workers and capitalists across the growing social gaps between them.

Starting in the mid 1970s, the long-running success formula of US capitalism stopped functioning. Real wages in the US stopped rising while labor productivity continued to rise (see chart below). The surpluses that capitalist employers appropriated consequently soared because their workers no longer shared in the rewards of their productivity gains. The social divide between producers and appropriators of the surplus surged as well.

Capitalist employers no longer had to pay rising wages for four major reasons. First, the computer revolution started displacing millions of US workers in the 1970s. Second, US corporations responded to growing European and Japanese competition by increasingly shifting production out of the US to lower-wage production sites. These developments slowed and further changed the composition (from manufacturing to services) of the demand for workers inside the US. Third and fourth, the mass movement of women from households into paid labor positions plus growing immigration increased the number of job-seekers. These changing demands and supplies in the labor market enabled employers to stop raising real wages.

Most importantly, the demise of rising real wages ended an era. The impact of that ending on the US cannot be overstated. A capitalism that had come to define, celebrate, and defend itself by reference to rising consumption afforded by rising wages could no longer do so. The impact was all the greater because the meaning and implications of the change were not even recognized – let alone debated. Workers experienced the change as a personal and individual matter rather than as a social issue of historic scope.

The post-1970s explosion of surplus value accruing to employers transformed US capitalism in multiple ways. Wealth poured into capitalists' financial accounts. It financed a stunning further expansion of corporate wealth, power, and social influence. Corporate boards of directors distributed the exploding surpluses partly to themselves (as fast-rising top managerial salaries, benefits, and bonuses). They justified doing so by attributing the enhanced profitability of their enterprises not to the end of rising wages but to their own genius (as if they had suddenly become "much more entrepreneurial"). Corporate boards distributed another part to lower-level managers (as their remuneration and operating budgets), bankers (interest and fees), shareowners (dividends), lawyers and advertisers, etc. These groups thus also prospered at one remove from the surplus trough, while the vast mass of workers with flat real wages found life increasingly difficult.

Those workers' families faced a choice. They might have foregone rising consumption since they no longer earned the rising wages to

Figure 1. Indexes of Output and Real Wage per Hour, Manufacturing, 1890 to 2007,
Index 1890=100

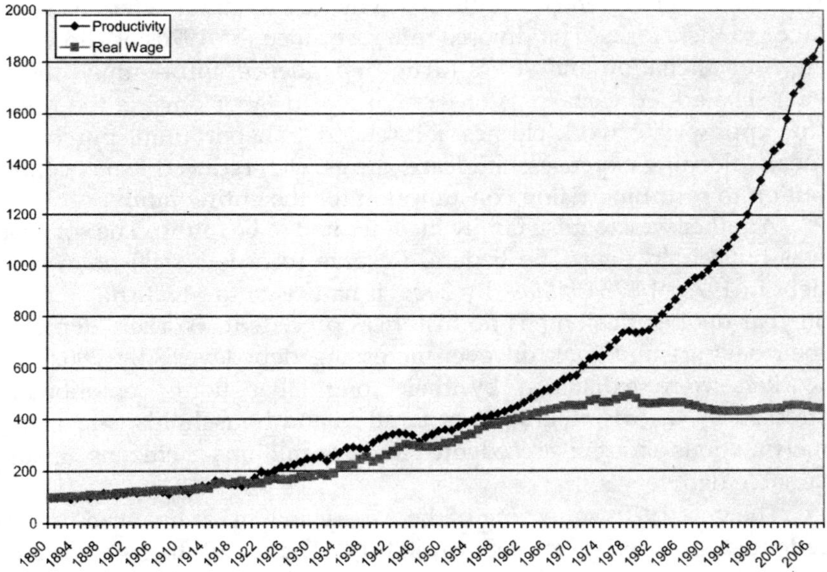

Sources: US Department of Labor, Bureau of Labor Statistics; US Department of Commerce, Bureau of the Census, *Historical Statistics of the United States*. Graph by Jason Ricciuti-Borenstein.

afford it. They did not do that. Rising consumption was the realization of lifelong personal hopes, the sign of social success, the reward earned by hard work, and the promise to one's children that *had* to be kept. When their wages no longer rose, workers responded by finding two other ways nevertheless to continue raising their consumption.

First, with real hourly wages stagnant, workers' households sent more of their members to do more hours of paid labor. Husbands did more work while teenagers and retired people took at least part-time jobs. Most importantly, millions of housewives and mothers entered the paid labor markets. These responses helped add to family incomes, yet by also increasing the supply of job-seekers, they further undermined wages generally.

Increased paid labor by more members of workers' families also imposed additional personal and social costs on workers' households. Women increasingly held two fulltime jobs, one outside the household and one inside, since they continued to do most of the housework. The added stress of this double shift altered and strained household relationships. The emotional supports that integrated and sustained the institution of the family - performed so disproportionately by women - were often compromised when they added external wage-labor to their tasks. The divorce rate rose since the 1970s as did other signs of alienation and stress (drug dependence, intra-family abuse, etc.). The added cash costs of women's paid labor outside the home (for appropriate work clothes, job-related transportation, purchased meals, cleaning expenses, childcare, drugs, etc.) reduced its *net* contribution to resuming rising consumption for the entire family.

Another way to raise family incomes had to be found. The solution was household debt. The Federal Reserve records a total household debt in 1975 of $734 *billion*. By 2006, it had risen to $12.8 *trillion*. This 30-year debt explosion has no historical precedent. Workers depleted their savings and took on ever-increasing debt levels. By 2007, US workers were exhausted by their long labor hours, emotionally stressed by the disintegration of families and households, and extremely anxious about unprecedented and, for millions of citizens, unsustainable debt levels.

The post-1970s squeezing of the American worker financed unprecedented prosperity for US capitalists. They and their associates enjoyed a new "gilded" age. Extreme personal wealth among them became the object of media adulation that cultivated mass envy. The US at the end of the 20th century replicated for a new group of capitalists what Rockefeller, Carnegie and their ilk had achieved at the end of the previous century. Corporate boards of directors could also spend lavishly on computerization, research and development, and costly shifts of production facilities abroad. They generously lubricated politicians to better control government at all levels, just as flat wages and household turmoil turned workers away from civic affairs to concentrate on jobs and families. Capitalists thus could and did make government much more responsive to them in enhancing the conditions and profitable outlets (lower tax burdens, technical change, immigration, job exports, etc.) for their exploding surpluses. Workers felt ever more alienated from politics and resentful of politicians.

Exploding wealth concentrated in relatively few hands fueled rapid growth in enterprises specialized in managing such wealth by finding profitable investments for it. Investment banks, hedge funds, and so on pandered to and competed for "high net worth individuals." They discovered, invented and marketed new financial instruments as outlets for investment. As recurred so often in capitalism's history, when profits soared, competitive wealth management slid seamlessly into speculation fueled by the euphoria of exploding riches at the top. The search for ever higher returns drove wealth managers and owners to take ever bigger financial risks. To a point, this process was self-validating and self-reinforcing.

Symptomatic of (and also contributing to) the deepening divisions in US society, one major financial speculation undertaken with corporate surpluses involved lending them at high interest rates to working-class families. As noted, the latter were eager borrowers to sustain their "American dream" of rising consumption after their wages had stopped rising. The so-called "sub-prime" loans – made to those working-class families at the greatest risk of becoming unable to service them – eventually punished the lenders when those borrowers defaulted. Workers' families could no longer work more, earn more, or borrow more to support outstanding loans. The financial deals among banks, hedge funds, insurers – a house of cards dependent on mass consumer debt – crashed. The stagnant real wages that had enabled the capitalists' boom came back finally to burst the capitalists' investment bubble. Marx would not have missed the irony. People rediscovering Marxist analysis today are intrigued by the insight as well as the irony.

Contradiction and crisis

In the Marxian idiom, the clashing interests of workers and capitalists (i.e. class structures and struggles) were key influences upon the real wage stagnation after the 1970s that launched the trajectory to crisis. Likewise, the clashing interests among capitalists (i.e. competition) drove their search for ever more and newer profitable investments for their expanding surpluses. They took on ever more risk. Financial innovation morphed into dangerous speculation that launched another trajectory toward crisis.

Capitalists exulted after the 1970s as the system delivered wealth to them on an unprecedented scale. They had, although without acknowledging the fact, substituted rising loans to their workers in place of the rising real wages paid over the previous century. This was little short of a capitalist fantasy come true. However, they preferred to believe instead that the entrepreneur-led, efficiency-driven mechanisms of private enterprise and free markets accounted for their good fortune. To them and their ideological supporters, their wealth proved that private, unregulated capitalism was superior to any conceivable alternative system. While the good times for capitalists rolled, the politicians, media spokespersons, and academics that they increasingly funded affirmed such beliefs only too eagerly.

Marxian theory offers the following basic theses about the roots of today's crisis: (1) that the end of rising real wages was the hard reality underlying a debt-dependent prosperity since the 1970s, and (2) that the capitalists' gains were the workers' losses. In the long post-1970s neoliberal reaction to the 1960s, such theses were fundamentally unacceptable and therefore generally ignored. Only when mass worker exhaustion, stress and debt, coupled with capitalists' poor investments and financial speculations, drove the system to collapse did capitalist triumphalism crumble. The return to Marxian analysis was partly an effect and is also a further cause of that crumbling.

A Marxian solution

Stagnating (if not falling) wages alongside rising productivity are always desiderata of capitalists in their endless struggles with their productive laborers. If and when conditions permit, capitalist corporations will seek to realize those desiderata. When they do, the results have repeatedly been growing inequality of wealth and income, financial speculation, booms, bubbles, and their bursting into crises. So it is yet again today.

The neoclassical economists and their allies insist, as usual, that the causes of today's crisis were ignorant, misguided, or corrupt governmental intrusions into private capitalism. Their solution is to return to as pure a private capitalism as possible as soon as possible. Unfortunately for them, it was major private US capitalists who led the way this time toward massive governmental support and intervention to counter a crisis. Thus, such neoclassical arguments since 2008 got far less of the widespread uncritical support that had become customary over the last quarter-century. Those arguments struck ever more people as disconnected from the reality of a capitalist system mired in a costly and socially painful crisis.

Moderately Keynesian economists and their allies came to power with Obama.[2] They have begun, against an entrenched neoclassical "mainstream" establishment, to regain some of the social influence

2. "Moderate" because they had been cowed and intimidated by the post-1970s hegemony of the neoclassical economists. Much less aggressive and social democratic than the earlier Keynesians from FDR's to Lyndon Johnson's times, these moderates showed their hesitant "centrism" as advisers first to the Clinton administration and then again to Obama's. Unlike FDR and Johnson, they did not include massive programs for average workers (e.g., government jobs) in their Keynesianism.

they had enjoyed before the 1970s. They argue that government deregulation and non-intervention since the 1970s were major causes of the crisis, and that a hefty dose of re-regulation and intervention is the solution. Yet they too, like their neoclassical counterparts, confront serious doubts. Skepticism about the likely efficacy of Keynesian state interventions now stems not only from a politically alienated public's deep suspicion of government, but also from the actual history of the Keynesian response to the last great capitalist crisis in the 1930s.

FDR imposed a mass of regulations, spending programs, and taxes upon US capitalism in the 1930s. He intended thereby to end the Great Depression. In fact, that intent was not realized; his economic policies never solved unemployment. Very different policies - preparation for war and then war itself - finally ended the mass unemployment. New Deal economic regulations, expenditures, and taxes only partly ameliorated the social costs and pains of the Great Depression. FDR also promised that his state interventions would prevent future depressions. Yet, the US economy experienced a dozen economic recessions after the 1930s culminating in today's crisis (frequently referred to as the Great Recession).

Marxism offers a unique explanation for the limits and failures of Keynesian policies. It proposes a corresponding alternative to them as well as to the neoclassical advocacy of a return to private capitalism. The growing attention to Marxian analyses and proposals reflects their status as serious alternatives to what both mainstream schools of economics are offering.

New Deal regulations, expenditures, and taxes often constrained the ways and means for capitalists to pursue their goals. However, those state interventions in the US economy never basically changed the capitalist class structure of production. That is, inside capitalist enterprises, the employers always remained in charge. They decided what to produce, where and how. They appropriated the surpluses and distributed them. Their employees lived with the consequences of the employers' decisions, but they neither participated in reaching them nor exercised significant control over them. This structure of production existed even inside the state enterprises that were established at that time (e.g., Tennessee Valley Authority).

The employers of private capitalist enterprises - mostly organized as corporate boards of directors selected by major shareholders - faced competition from other enterprises and demands from their shareholders, government tax collectors, creditors, managers, suppliers, etc. Those pressures could be better contained or managed the more surpluses employers could appropriate and devote to those tasks. Thus, corporate boards had every incentive to evade, weaken or undo the New Deal state impositions that impinged upon their surplus appropriation – or, as they put it, upon their profits and the freedom to pursue their growth. Moreover, because they appropriated the surpluses generated inside the enterprises, corporate boards disposed of the resources needed to evade, weaken, or undo the New Deal. In fact, capitalists responded to those incentives in just those way starting in the 1930s, accelerating after war's end in 1945, and soaring in just those ways, especially after the 1970s under Reagan, Bush 1, Clinton, and Bush 2.

Given this history, Obama's current reliance on Keynesian policies poses two inescapable questions. First, why reinstitute such state interventions when they failed before? Second, since corporations accumulated great expertise in controlling, circumventing or undoing state interventions, will they not accomplish those same results faster and more effectively this time? Those who ask such questions and consequently lose confidence in Keynesian anti-crisis policies sooner or later encounter Marxism's alternative analyses and proposals.

The Marxian response to such repeated crises would be neither an oscillation toward private capitalism (the neoclassical solution) nor one toward state capitalism (the Keynesian solution). It would *not* favor one form of capitalism over another. The Marxian alternative solution to capitalist crises would be to change the system, to move society beyond capitalism on the grounds that we can and should do better. Because traditional visions as well as "actually existing" versions of socialism were overwhelmingly and often exclusively focused on its macro-dimensions, our argument here will instead focus on the micro-level. That means we will sketch the sort of transformation inside enterprises that would mark a transition from capitalist into non-capitalist organizations of the production, appropriation, and distribution of the surpluses.

The goal would be to put workers inside each enterprise in the collective position of receiving the surpluses they produce in that enterprise. That would, of course, position them also as the distributors of those surpluses. The surplus-producing workers in each enterprise would, in effect, become their own collective board of directors. They would replace traditional corporate boards chosen by and responsible to major shareholders. This would eliminate the capitalist enterprise's built-in confrontation between workers and capitalists. Workers who have become their own board of directors would systematically alter the what, where and how of production and likewise the distribution of enterprises' surpluses. Had this change been in effect in the 1970s, real wages would not likely have stopped rising, nor would the export of jobs have soared, nor would so many health-endangering new technologies have been installed at worksites. And these are but some illustrative examples.

Such a change out of capitalism could be a major first step in the democratization of the economy generally. Economic democracy would require first that in each enterprise, productive employees would collectively and equally make such decisions. Subsequent steps would extend that economic democracy by integrating it with the democratic organization of residential communities (local, regional, etc.) interdependent with each enterprise. Workers and residents would then share democratic power over the products and the surpluses produced in and distributed by each enterprise as well as over public institutions, rules of behavior, etc.

Such a Marxian policy would aim to eliminate capitalism at the micro, individual enterprise level by fundamentally changing its class structure. As the "other" of capitalism, traditional socialism stressed the macro-level dimensions of superseding capitalism – e.g., changes in the public/private mix of ownership of productive property and changes in the mix of market and planned distributions of resources and products. Traditional socialism neglected its micro-dimensions. In contrast, the vision here of a 21st-century socialism presumes that, to succeed, those macro-level policies must henceforth be grounded on an enterprise/micro level transformation where workers become collectively the appropriators and distributors of the surpluses they produce.

Changing the class structure in this way will not eliminate contradictions or even crises arising in an economy. Crises occurred in pre-capitalist societies and they likely will in post-capitalist societies as well. However, crises occur differently, are understood differently, and provoke different responses depending on the different class structures comprising their contexts. And these differences matter. To take a particular example, in a post-capitalist class structure of the sort sketched above, crises will less likely emerge, as the current one did, from stagnating real wages. Had US workers collectively comprised their own boards of directors, the conditions of the 1970s would not likely have led them to stop raising their own real wages. To make the more important general case: the extension of democracy entailed by a post-capitalist transformation promises more equitable economic rules, regulations, adjudications of disputes, distribution of economic benefits and of costs than what exists today. Similar promises and goals lay behind movements for political democracy since before the French Revolution. Today they drive the movement for an economic democracy whose absence has so long hobbled political democracy, keeping it more formal than substantive.

The goal of a new 21st-century Marxism is finally to make the latter real by grounding it in economic democracy at the worksite. The sustained capitalist crisis that now imposes huge social costs globally also challenges the repeatedly oscillating neoclassical and Keynesian paradigms. That opens space for and drives the rediscovery of Marxism and its critique of capitalism at both the macro and micro levels. The alternative theoretical and practical possibilities that tradition offers are again becoming part of the international debates over social change.

Marx in Hispanic America

Francisco T. Sobrino

When we speak about reception, we should keep in mind what Walter Benjamin considered in his studies of it. He sought to replace the "old, dogmatic and naive" idea of reception with a "new and critical" one.[1] The former stressed the influence of a certain work on its contemporaries. The latter stresses the historical constellation between texts from the past and the prevailing interests and preoccupations of the present.[2] In the case of Karl Marx, a question then arises: What makes Marx's texts a challenging legacy for us in Latin America today?

In the 1980s and 1990s, neoliberalism prevailed in most of the region. The Latin American left appeared to be exhausted, doomed as it was by the End of History. But the neoliberal wave with its vicious pro-market reforms failed to extinguish social resistance. Resistance in fact grew. Not only workers, but also indigenous people, small peasants, the unemployed, and women joined its ranks. In the late 20th century, neoliberal policies began to wither, as the resulting crisis devastated the population and triggered unrest, revolts and government collapse. As a result, the new century witnessed an unforeseen landscape, with its so-called "left turn of Latin America." New administrations in Argentina, Bolivia, Brazil, Ecuador, Nicaragua, Paraguay, Uruguay and Venezuela share, despite obvious distinctions, a common critical view of neoliberal policies. This move, as well as the eruption and development of the current world economic crisis, has affected the intellectual arena in various ways. At the same time, the traditional reading of Marxian texts was enriched by new theoretical contributions, partially due to the different social agents getting involved in current developments.

We shall survey the various countries in alphabetical order, but we must first briefly mention **Spain**, given the significance of Spanish

1. Walter Benjamin, "Historia y coleccionismo: Eduard Fuchs." In *Discursos interrumpidos I* (Madrid: Taurus, 1987), p. 9. Quoted by Miguel Vedda in "Crisis y crítica. Notas sobre la actualidad de Walter Benjamin," *Herramienta*, no. 43, March 2010: 8.
2. See Vedda, "Crisis y crítica."

Socialism and Democracy, Vol.24, No.3, November 2010, pp.147–154
ISSN 0885-4300 print/ISSN 1745-2635 online
DOI: 10.1080/08854300.2010.513625

translators and scholars in the publication of Marx-Engels *Collected Works* in our language. New editions of the *Werke* by the Fondo de Cultura Económica de México (edited by Wenceslao Roces) and Manuel Sacristan's version in Grijalbo España (called *OME*: *Obras de Marx-Engels*) are currently interrupted, because of the respective directors' deaths – Roces in 1992, Sacristan in 1985. Today, in the Spanish-speaking world there are no critical, philologically grounded Spanish editions of Marx-Engels works in progress. The Spanish version of *Capital* by Pedro Scaron,[3] despite having corrected a number of widely known mistakes from Roces' translation,[4] is considered by some researchers as only "partially critical," because Scaron did not take into account, for example, the French edition of *Capital* which had been corrected and modified by Marx, who viewed it as an "independent" work from the original German edition, with a scientific value of its own.

In **Argentina,** after the *coup d'état* of 1976 a brutal dictatorship was imposed that lasted until 1983, repressing any resistance and trying to wipe out any traces of Marxism and, for that matter, any other body of critical ideas. With the restoration of democratic regimes and the return of many exiled intellectuals, there was a revival of cultural activities. The emerging intelligentsia was heavily influenced by European and North American trends: postmodernism, post-structuralism, post-Marxism and the like. Few scholars and researchers remained devoted to Marx's ideas. José Sazbón stood out among them. Some of his last essays (he died in 2008) were published in his book *Historia y representación*.[5] The interest in Marx began to grow again in the late 20th century, embodied in a growing minority of young scholars and researchers. New translations of Marx-Engels works have appeared: *Escritos sobre literatura* (Marx-Engels),[6] *Manuscritos económico-filosóficos de 1844*[7] and *El manifiesto comunista*.[8] These books are direct new translations from German by Miguel Vedda and a team of translators, and include critical notes about each text.

Nicolás González Varela, an Argentine scholar residing in Spain since 2002, recently translated Marx's notebooks on Spinoza, of which he has written a study soon to be published in Barcelona.[9]

3. México: Siglo XXI, 1983.
4. México: Fondo de Cultura Económica, 1968.
5. Buenos Aires: Universidad de Quilmes, 2002.
6. Buenos Aires: Colihue, 2003.
7. Buenos Aires: Colihue, 2004.
8. Buenos Aires: Herramienta, 2008.
9. *Cuaderno Spinoza* (Barcelona: Montesinos, 2010).

Nestor Kohan, another young author devoted to Marxian thought, has written several books on Marx and his work,[10] stressing his relevance for our days. Oscar del Barco has republished his *El otro Marx*.[11] Independent Marxist journals have appeared (and, regrettably in some cases, also disappeared) in the last two decades: *El rodaballo, Herramienta, Cuadernos del sur, Doxa, Razón y Revolución, Periferias,* and *El nuevo topo. Herramienta* also publishes Marxist books and is currently sponsoring a seminar on Marxism at the University of Buenos Aires. Some leftist parties and groups have also published theoretical-political Marxist journals: *Cuadernos Marxistas, Socialismo o barbarie, Socialismo libertario, Lucha de clases, En defensa del Marxismo, Tesis 11.* Both the Instituto del Pensamiento Socialista "Karl Marx" and the Centro de Documentación e Investigación de la Cultura de Izquierdas are academic and archival institutions, engaged in the dissemination of Marx's ideas, teaching, researching and preserving Marxist publications and books.

Regarding **Bolivia** some background remarks are necessary. In 1946 the Bolivian labor movement adopted the Theses of Pulacayo, a political platform based on Trotsky's conception of permanent revolution. Armed miners paraded through the streets of La Paz in the 1950s. All this nurtured the legend of a deeply committed Marxist revolutionary working class. Nonetheless, in the early 21st century, the socialist views of most of the Bolivian population (as well as of the Bolivian government and intelligentsia) are shaped much more by indigenism than by the ideas of Marx. Early Marxism in Bolivia was rooted in the modern sector of the working class - miners and industrial workers - and was greatly influenced by the rationality of capitalist modernization. Dogmatic manuals with their reductionist views were adopted by the various Marxist parties, which thus denigrated the overwhelming Indian and peasant population of the country, ignoring what Marx himself had written on that topic.[12]

The later decline of Bolivian mining, and hence of the trade unions, coincided with the rise of Indian and social movements, which were nearly totally alien to these Marxist groups and intellectuals.[13] At the

10. *Marx en su (tercer) mundo* (Buenos Aires: Biblos, 1998) and (Havana: Juan Marinello, 2003); *Nuestro Marx*, www.lahaine.org/index.php?p=42629.
11. Buenos Aires: Caserola, 2008.
12. For instance, Karl Marx, *Escritos sobre Rusia II. El porvenir de la comuna rural rusa* (México: PyP, 1980); *Los apuntes etnológicos de Karl Marx* (Madrid: Pablo Iglesias-Siglo XXI, 1988).
13. Álvaro García Linera, "Indianismo y Marxismo .El desencuentro de dos razones revolucionarias," *Barataria. Revista del Juguete Rabioso*, N° 2, La Paz (2005).

same time, a new generation of critical Marxists emerged, reflecting a more appropriate view of the indigenous and communal subject.[14] This new trend seeks to reconcile indigenism with Marxism, in order to link domestic with universal knowledge production. Among the books embodying this critical Marxist current are *El fantasma insomne: Pensando el presente desde* El manifiesto comunista [The awakened specter: Viewing the present through the *Communist Manifesto*],[15] *De demonios escondidos* [hidden demons] *y momentos de revolución: Marx y la revolución social en las extremidades del cuerpo capitalista*,[16] and *La potencia plebeya*.[17]

In **Chile,** General Pinochet's coup (1973) and subsequent repressive dictatorship dealt a heavy blow to academic and intellectual life. Despite the subsequent democratic restoration, study of Marx and of Marxist theory has been severely diminished. An exception is Jorge Larraín's *El concepto de ideología – Carlos Marx*.[18] The Centro de Estudios Nacionales de Desarrollo Alternativo (CENDA) organizes seminars on Marxist economic and social issues. There are some seminars devoted to Marxian ideas: a "Hegel-Marx Permanent Seminar" in the University of Chile and a "Marx Vive" International Seminar in the Arcis University.

Of all Latin American countries, **Colombia** is perhaps the one where the intelligentsia and the academic world have moved furthest to the right since 1989. The only exception was a commemoration of the 150th anniversary of the *Communist Manifesto,* organized by Jairo Estrada, a professor in Colombia's National University, and entitled (as in Chile) "Marx Vive." Six follow-up meetings have been held in subsequent years. There have been no domestic editions of Marx's works, except the *Manifesto,* in the last decade. According to a Colombian Marxist author, the most important shortcoming of Colombian leftists today is that "nobody reads nor studies, because they are only devoted to electoral participation, hence their theoretical orphanhood."[19]

---

14. Luis Tapia, *La condición multisocietal* (La Paz: CIDES-UMSA, 2002); Raúl Prada, *Largo octubre* (La Paz: Plural, 2004); varios autores, *Tiempos de rebelión* (La Paz: La Comuna, 2001); varios autores, *Memorias de octubre* (La Paz: La Comuna, 2004).
15. Raquel Gutierrez, Raúl Prada, Álvaro García Linera and Luis Tapia, *El fantasma insomne: Pensando el presente desde* El manifiesto comunista (La Paz: Editorial Muela del Diablo, 1999).
16. La Paz: Álvaro García Linera, Editorial O. R., 1991.
17. Buenos Aires: Álvaro García Linera, CLACSO-Prometeo, 2008.
18. Santiago de Chile: Lom, 2007.
19. A remark by Renan Vega Cantor, who wrote and edited *Marx y el Siglo XXI* (2 vol.) (Bogotá: Editorial Pensamiento Crítico, 1998–1999), and was awarded the "Premio Libertador al Pensamiento Crítico 2007" in Venezuela, for his book: *Un mundo*

Cuba is of course a special case, given the firmly established revolutionary commitment of its ruling party. Two major journals reflect the range of thought and debate among Cuba's leading intellectuals. One is *Marx Ahora,* edited by Isabel Monal;[20] the other is *Temas,* edited by Rafael Hernández. The former is, as its name suggests, the more explicitly focused on Marx, but the latter is significant as an expression of the scope of critical discussion currently taking place in Cuba, which has broadened significantly over the past decade.[21] Both in these journals and in its book-publishing, Cuba has served also, for several decades, as a forum for Marxist writing from all over Latin America.

Of course, some Marxian texts are mandatory in Cuban universities, but their reception is mixed. While a segment of Cuban opinion, under the guise of being apolitical, has an implicit pro-capitalist orientation, the major part of the intellectual spectrum ranges from those who identify closely with the state and its institutions to those who, although strongly critical of the state, adhere firmly to socialist and democratic principles.[22]

Two factors have remarkably increased the number of Marx's readers in **Ecuador**: the generalized capitalist world crisis and ensuing search for answers, as well as a new interest in socialism since President Rafael Correa avowed his affinity with "21st-century socialism," following his Venezuelan colleague Hugo Chávez. Nevertheless, no book on Marx has been published in these last ten years, and there are no domestic publications of the *Collected Works* of Marx-Engels, perhaps due to the limited dimensions of the domestic publishing industry. *Espacios,* edited by Francisco Hidalgo, is the most important Marxist journal. Interestingly enough, in 2004 a bilingual version of the *Communist Manifesto,* in Spanish and in Quechua was published by the PCMLE (Ecuador's Marxist Leninist Communist Party). This is probably the first translation of this famous text into the most important indigenous language of South America (spoken also in Peru, Bolivia, Chile, and Argentina).

---

incierto [an uncertain world], *un mundo para aprender y enseñar. Las transformaciones mundiales y su incidencia en la enseñanza de las Ciencias Sociales.*

20. Available at www.nodo50.org/cubasigloXXI/index.htm.

21. For a sampling in English of some of these views, see the collectively edited special issue of *Socialism and Democracy* (no. 52, March 2010) entitled *Cuban Perspectives on Cuban Socialism.*

22. See Chaguaceda, Armando, "Intelectuales públicos y política en Cuba: continuidades y emergencias," (2010), available at www.herramienta.com.ar/herramienta-web-5/intelectuales-publicos-y-politica-en-cuba-continuidades-y-emergencias.

In **Mexico**, a number of researchers and scholars, such as Miguel Angel Porrua. Adolfo Sánchez Vázquez,[23] Jorge Veraza,[24] Pedro López Díaz,[25] the late Ecuadoran-born Bolívar Echeverría (who edited and translated the *1861-1863 Manuscripts*),[26] and others, have recently written books on Marx's ideas and influence in the Latin American context. Marxist journals include: *Dialéctica* (edited by Gabriel Vargas Lozano), *Bajo el volcán* (edited by John Holloway, Sergio Tischler and Carlos Figueroa Ibarra) and *Memoria* (edited by Héctor Díaz-Polanco). One may mention here Eugene Gogol, a US researcher on Hegel's and Marx's ideas on Latin America, who resides mostly in Mexico. Gogol published the Spanish version of his work, *El concepto del otro en la liberación latinoamericana*.[27] Enrique Dussel, an Argentine-born philosopher, resident in Mexico since the 1970s, has written well-known works on Marx,[28] including one suggesting that Marx wrote four drafts of *Capital*.[29] A devotee of "philosophy of liberation," Dussel continues to write on Marx and his works. His essays from 2007, "Las 'Kategorias' en Marx" and "Descubrimiento definitivo de la categoría de 'plusvalor'" [on surplus value] are available on the Internet.[30]

Peru's José Carlos Mariátegui, described by Michael Löwy as "the true founder of Latin American Marxism,"[31] wrote in 1928, "We do not want socialism in Latin America to be an imitation or a copy. It must be a heroic creation. We must inspire Indo-American socialism with our own reality, our own language. That is a mission worthy of a new generation."[32] His warning went largely unheard, for at that time the Latin American communist movement was strongly influenced by Stalinism. But nowadays his perspective is widely shared by Marxist intellectuals

---

23. *De Marx al marxismo en América Latina* (México: Itaca, 1999).
24. *Leer el capital hoy* (México: Itaca, 2007).
25. *Capitalismo y crisis. La visión de Karl Marx* (México: Itaca, 2006). This book is grounded in a close, albeit biased, reading of the *Grundrisse*.
26. *La tecnología del* Capital (México: Itaca, 2005). Bolívar Echeverría has also earned the "Premio Simón Bolívar al Pensamiento Crítico 2007."
27. *El concepto del otro en la liberación latinoamericana* (México: Juan Pablos, 2004) and (Buenos Aires: Herramienta, 2007).
28. *La producción teórica de Marx* (Mêxico: Siglo XXI, 1985), *Hacia un Marx desconocido* ((México: Siglo XXI, 1988), and *El último Marx* (México: Siglo XXI, 1990).
29. See his essay "The four drafts of *Capital*: towards a new Interpretation of the Dialectical Thought of Marx," *Rethinking Marxism*, 13, No. 1 (2001): 10–26.
30. See www.enriquedussel.org/articulos.html.
31. *The Marxism of Che Guevara: philosophy, economics, revolutionary warfare*, 2nd ed. (Lanham, MD: Rowman & Littlefield, 2007), p. 119.
32. Quoted by Löwy, *ibid.*

throughout the continent. Despite the undeniable and persistent influence of Mariátegui in his home country, Peru was also hard hit by developments in the 1980s and 1990s, weakening the domestic Marxist intelligentsia. Very few scholars now identify with Marxism. Notable among them is Aníbal Quijano, who coined the concept of "coloniality of power" to denote the structures of power, control, and hegemony that have emerged during the modern era, the era of colonialism, which stretches from the conquest of the Americas to the present. We should also mention Guillermo Rochabrún, who recently wrote *Batallas por la teoría. En torno a Marx y el Perú.*[33]

In **Puerto Rico**, because of its intellectual and cultural isolation, the one notable researcher on Marx is Georg Fromm, who has written "Hegel y el joven Marx: Análisis del trabajo enajenado" [on alienated labor];[34] "Hegel y el joven Marx: 'El hombre como ser natural *humano*'" [on man as a natural being];[35] and "Empirismo, Ciencia y Filosofía en *La ideología alemana*."[36]

In **Venezuela,** as a consequence of the Chávez administration's campaigns,[37] the publication of Marxist and Marx-Engels books quadrupled between 2004 and 2010. Twenty percent of this production was by private publishing houses: Vadell Hnos, Alfadil Editores and Ediciones B. The remaining 80% was published by the Venezuelan State. Of more than 72 million books published in these last six years, nearly 20% are works of Marx or Marxist authors. There are cultural and academic think tanks dedicated to spreading such works, such as the CIM (*Centro Internacional Miranda*).

Let us now consider again the overall panorama in Latin America. Since the early diffusion of Marx's books and pamphlets in the late 19th century, the reception of his work has developed through various stages. As we have seen, this reception has been uneven in the different countries. The one commonality is what we might call a *Latin American* reading of Marx's ideas – a reading characterized by heterodoxy, anti-imperialism, cultural concerns, voluntarism, self-criticism vis-à-vis Stalinist dogmas, and rejection of Eurocentrism; in short, in Mariategui's already quoted words, "neither an imitation nor a copy." As Omar Acha and Débora D'Antonio affirm, "former polarities are now being

33. Lima: Instituto de Estudios Peruanos, 2007.
34. *Diálogos*, 84 (2004), 133–155.
35. *Diálogos*, 85 (2005), 7–27.
36. *Diálogos*, 86 (2005), 63–93.
37. President Chávez, in his televised talk show, advises: "Read, read and read, this is every day's slogan." Among the books he recommends are the *Communist Manifesto* and other Marx-Engels works.

rethought: reform/revolution, national/international, class/race or class/gender, democratic/revolutionary, state/civil society, and so on.... No local experience (like the current ones of Bolivia and Venezuela) aspires to prevail as a continental model."[38] Nonetheless, such experiences have an effect on the rest of the continent, thus helping to shape the general Latin American reception of Marx's ideas.

38. "Cartografía y perspectivas del 'marxismo latinoamericano'," in *A Contra Corriente*, Vol. 7, No. 2 (Winter 2010): 210–256, www.ncsu.edu/project/acontracorriente.

Marx in Brazil

Armando Boito and Luiz Eduardo Motta

Interest in the work of Karl Marx is growing in Brazil as it is internationally. But the reception of Marx in Brazil is clearly marked by the country's own traits and by its ideological conjuncture over the past two decades.

The new international interest Marx's work dates from the 1990s, when the neoliberal capitalist model came under attack. Key moments were, in Europe, the general strike that paralyzed France in late 1995, and, in Latin America, the election of Hugo Chávez as president of Venezuela in 1998. Meanwhile, 1998 also witnessed worldwide celebrations of the 150th anniversary of the *Communist Manifesto*, in which the supposed "death of Marxism" was massively rejected.

In Brazil in 2001, countless cities celebrated the 130th anniversary of the Paris Commune. Those meetings exemplified two key aspects of the current interest in Marx: on the one hand, a convergence between political and intellectual activists seeking to revive Marxism, but on the other, a clear predominance of intellectuals and their dependence, for this project of revival, upon the cultural institutions of the capitalist state, specifically the universities. This basic trait is shown in the founding of numerous Marxist research centers in several universities, as well as in journals and other publications that emerged since the 1990s, and in the cultural and scientific conferences that featured major roles for Marxists across all the academic disciplines.

In 1996, the Center of Marxist Studies (Cemarx) was founded at the State University of Campinas (Unicamp). Several similar centers were subsequently created in other public universities, including the Fluminense Federal University, the State University of Southwest Bahia, State University of São Paulo, and also in Rio Grande do Sul. The Cemarx organized in 1999 at Unicamp the first International Colloquium of Marx and Engels. Since then, this colloquium has been held biennially, bringing together on each occasion hundreds of researchers from all over Brazil. Since 2000, there have been regular regional and national Marxist meetings (annual or biennial)

Socialism and Democracy, Vol.24, No.3, November 2010, pp.155–159

ISSN 0885-4300 print/ISSN 1745-2635 online

DOI: 10.1080/08854300.2010.513620

of a thematically specialized character, such as the conference of Marxist researchers on education, the conference of researchers on social movements in Latin America at Londrina, the socialist studies conference at São Paulo State University in Marília, and the colloquium on Marx at the University of São Paulo. Total participation in such meetings numbers in the thousands. Also worth noting is the participation of Marxist researchers in the largest national associations of sociology, history, philosophy and economics – Anpocs, Anpuh, Anpof, SEP – within each of which Marxist groups have been formed.

In respect to publications, there were some journals linked to the Brazilian Communist Party that were published before the coup d'état of 1964, such as *Problemas, Brasiliense,* and *Estudos Sociais.* As an initial expression of non-official Marxism, generally from authors identified with so-called Western Marxism, there was the *Revista Civilização Brasileira* (published from 1965 to 1968), founded by Enio Silveira (owner of the publishing house Civilização Brasileira and a member of the Brazilian Communist Party) and Moacir Félix. Its authors included Georg Lukács, Adam Schaff, Jean-Paul Sartre, Herbert Marcuse, Antonio Gramsci, Louis Althusser, as well as Brazilian intellectuals such as Nelson Werneck Sodré, José Arthur Giannotti, Fernando Henrique Cardoso and Theotônio dos Santos. Despite its circulation of 10,000, however, it did not survive the intensified repression that began in 1969.

Other journals, such as *Princípios* (Principles) and *Novos Rumos* (New Directions), which were organically linked to Marxist parties like the Communist Party of Brazil (PC do B) and the Brazilian Communist Party (PCB), respectively, are still being published. Nevertheless, *Teoria & Política,* released in 1980 by scholars with a Marxist-Leninist tendency, ceased publication in the 1990s, as did *Presença,* created by intellectuals affiliated with the PCB and attuned to the Eurocommunist perspective. Although such party-connected journals enjoy the active participation of intellectuals linked to universities, their support depends on the relevant political organizations.

The new generation of Marxist journals that appeared in the 1990s were distinguished by their ties to public universities. The pioneer publication of this new generation – the semiannual *Crítica Marxista,* launched in 1994 – was created by the same group of intellectuals that founded the Cemarx at Unicamp. Its founders were mostly professors at Unicamp and did not belong to any political parties. During the following years, other publications appeared: *Outubro* (October), *Margem Esquerda* (Left Margin), *História e Luta de Classes*

(History and Class Struggle), *Marxismo Vivo* (Living Marxism), *Novos Temas* (New Themes), *Antítese* (Antithesis) and others.[1]

Those journals bring together intellectuals affiliated with or close to various Marxist currents - Antonio Gramsci, Georg Lukács, Louis Althusser, the Frankfurt School, E.P. Thompson and others. Each has certain distinct characteristics. Some, such as *Crítica Marxista,* focus on theoretical texts or on structural analysis of capitalist economy and society, while others, like *Margem Esquerda* and *Outubro,* are more open to conjunctural themes. In all of them, nonetheless, it is possible to emphasize two important traits. First is the already noted dependence of universities on the Brazilian state. The founders of these journals are mostly university professors, and their audience is also, fundamentally, the university public. This is true even for journals like *Outubro,* which is linked to the United Socialist Workers Party (PSTU), and *Novos Rumos,* which has indirect ties with the Brazilian Communist Party (PCB). Secondly, these journals do not focus much on Marx's own work. Their theoretical discussions focus instead on the work of Marx's successors, and on the issues that have occasioned divisions among them through the course of the 20th century.

These considerations account for what is distinctive about the current period of Brazilian Marxism. In the 1930s and 1940s, by contrast, the spread of Marxism was associated with cultural events linked to the PCB, rather than with universities. Marxism did not get into the universities until the end of the 1950s, beginning with meetings of the well-known study group of *Capital,* organized by José Arthur Giannotti. Aside from occurring largely outside the university, Marxist theoretical production was focused on the work of Marx himself. As for historical, economic, and social analysis, this was the period in which Brazilian Marxists, unlike their present-day counterparts, devoted themselves to analyzing the nature of Brazilian society - slavery, feudalism, capitalism - and the process of bourgeois revolution in Brazil. Key authors include: Caio Prado Jr., Nelson Werneck Sodré, Florestan Fernandes, Luiz Pereira, Jacob Gorender, Roberto Schwarz, José Arthur Giannotti, and Ruy Fausto.

Getting back to the current time, the publication of Marx's work has also been revived. Earlier Brazilian translations of Marx and Engels were few and of poor quality. Many were done from other translations and not from the original texts. The first complete

1. Two other important Marxist journals - *Práxis,* edited by a national intellectual organization, and *Praga,* close to the group of Marxists at the University of São Paulo - emerged in the 1990s, but are no longer published.

edition of *Capital* directly translated from German came out only in 1960, thanks to the publishing house *Civilização Brasileira;* a new translation was issued in 1986 by the publishing house *Abril*. The *Communist Manifesto* appears not to have come out until 1945, published by Editora Horizonte in Rio de Janeiro, and also in an edition published by Edições Populares, with D. Riazanov's historical introduction and with a number of appended documents, including the *Statutes of the Communist League* and a critical comparative study of the I, II and III Internationals. After that, the *Manifesto* was reissued in many editions.

Nowadays, two major publishers of Marx's texts are Boitempo and Expressão Popular. Boitempo has privileged the work of the young Marx (*Crítica da Filosofia do Direito de Hegel, A Questão Judaica, A Sagrada Família, Manuscritos Econômicos-Filosóficos*) and his pieces from the later 1840s (*Ideologia Alemã, Miséria da Filosofia, Manifesto Comunista*). Expressão Popular (which is linked to the Landless Workers Movement, MST), does not specialize in any phase of Marx's works, but publishes popular editions of works spanning his whole career.

In these last 15 years of Marx-revival in Brazil, some 30 books have appeared that deal directly with the work of Marx, largely emanating from academic studies and, in particular, from philosophy faculties. Works by previously mentioned Marxist writers from an earlier period have also been republished. Notable among those publications are: Francisco Teixeira, *Pensando com Marx: uma leitura crítico-comentada de O Capital*,[2] Carlos Henrique Escobar, *Marx, filósofo da potência*,[3] Jorge Grespan, *O negativo do Capital. O conceito de crise na crítica de Marx à economia política*,[4] Marcio Bilharinho Naves, *Marx – ciência e revolução*,[5] Jesus Raniere, *A câmara escura. Alienação e estranhamento em Marx*,[6] Ruy Fausto, *Marx: Lógica &Política – Tomo III Investigação para uma reenstituição do sentido da dialética*,[7] Celso Frederico, *O jovem*

2. Francisco Teixeira, *Pensando com Marx: uma leitura crítico-comentada de O Capital* (São Paulo: Ensaio, 1995).
3. Carlos Henrique Escobar, *Marx, filósofo da potência* (Rio de Janeiro, Editora Taurus, 1996).
4. Jorge Crespan, *O negativo do Capital. O conceito de crise na crítica de Marx à economia política* (São Paulo: HUCITEC, 1998).
5. Marcio Bilharinho Naves, *Marx – ciência e revolução* (São Paulo/Campinas, Ed. Moderna/Editora da Unicamp, 2000).
6. Jesus Raniere, *A câmara oscura. Alienação e estranhamento em Marx* (São Paulo: Boitempo editorial, 2001).
7. Ruy Fausto, *Marx: Lógica & Política – Tomo III (Investigação para uma reenstituição do sentido da dialética* (São Paulo: Editora 34, 2002).

Marx: 1843–1844 – As origens da ontologia do ser social,[8] Jose Chasin, *Marx: estatuto ontológico e resolução metodológica*,[9] Hector Benoit and Jadir Antunes, *Crise: o movimento dialético do conceito de crise em O capital de Marx*,[10] and the selection organized by Armando Boito, Caio Navarro de Toledo, Jesus Raniere and Patrícia Tropia, *A obra teórica de Marx – atualidade, problemas e interpretações*,[11] which published the works showed at the I Colloquium Marx-Engels of 1999. The republication of works of Marxist authors such as Caio Prado Jr., Nelson Werneck Sodré and Florestan Fernandes is further evidence of the revitalization of Marxism.

The growth of Marxism inside the universities can be explained by the current and recent situation of Brazilian society. Brazil, even allowing for its dimensions, has a very large university system, with hundreds of postgraduate courses financed by the state and with tens of thousands of professors and researchers. Although many university students come from working-class backgrounds, Brazil does not have a strong tradition of massive party organization of the working class. The PCB came close to such an achievement in the 1940s and 1950s, but was then forced underground. The Workers' Party (PT) also might have become a mass working-class party, but since its creation, its major tendency was indifferent or even hostile to Marxism. An important question for further study is, to what extent the academic framework of Brazil's Marxist revival has shaped its characteristics.

8. Celso Frederico, *O jovem Marx: 1843–1844 – As origens da ontologia do ser social* (São Paulo: Ed. Expressão Popular, 2009).
9. Jose Chasin, *Marx: estatuto ontológico e resolução metodológica* (São Paulo: Boitempo, 2009).
10. Hector Benoit and Jadir Antunes, *Crise: o movimento dialético do conceito de crise em O capital de Marx* (São Paulo: Tykhe, 2009).
11. Armando Boito, Caio Navarro de Toledo, Jesus Raniere and Patrícia Tropia, *A obra teórica de Marx – atualidade, problemas e interpretações* (São Paulo: Editora Xamã, 2000).

Marx in the Anglophone World

Paul Blackledge

The twenty-first century opened on a pessimistic note from some older voices within Anglophone Marxism. Perry Anderson relaunched *New Left Review* in 2000 with the claim that there no longer existed any "collective agency able to match the power of capital",[1] while in *Marx's Revenge*[2] Meghnad Desai argued that though capitalism is "the only game in town", because Marx had outlined the most sophisticated account of its crisis-prone nature his work remained relevant to debates on the merits of its various forms. If Anderson's and Desai's pessimism dovetailed with the zeitgeist, counter-trends opened a space for more radical perspectives. Thus journals as diverse as *Capital & Class, Capitalism Nature Socialism, Critique, International Socialism, Historical Materialism, Monthly Review, New Politics, Rethinking Marxism, Science & Society*, and *Socialism and Democracy* continued to cater in differing degrees to academic and activist audiences from perspectives rooted in Marx's legacy.

All these journals benefited enormously from the completion of the English-language edition of *Marx and Engels Collected Works*. Although criticised in comparison with the German MEGA^2, which has the benefit not only of being in German but also of including the various drafts of *Capital* and Marx's excerpt notebooks, the more limited 50 volumes of MECW is nevertheless a fantastically important resource which brings together all of Marx and Engels' early works (vols. 1-3), their published and unpublished general works (vols. 4-27), their letters (vols. 38-50), and Marx's major economic writings (vols. 28–37).[3] For those wanting a more manageable introduction to Marx's politics, Verso's new edition of the three volumes of his political writings is an invaluable resource,[4] while Jim Ledbetter's recent collection

1. Perry Anderson, 'Renewals', *New Left Review* II/1(2000), p. 13.
2. London: Verso, 2002.
3. London: Lawrence and Wishart; New York: International Publishers; Moscow: Progress Publishers, 1975–2004.
4. London: Verso, 2010.

Socialism and Democracy, Vol.24, No.3, November 2010, pp.160–168
ISSN 0885-4300 print/ISSN 1745-2635 online
DOI: 10.1080/08854300.2010.513631

of his journalism for the *New York Tribune* illuminates both the breadth and depth of his work and the continuing relevance of many of his insights.[5]

Alongside these new editions of Marx and Engels' writings, the last decade has been marked by an embarrassment of riches of book-length studies of Marx and his relevance to contemporary debates. The new millennium opened with the publication of two powerful counters to the myth that Marx had little of interest to contribute to the growing environmentalist movement. In his *Marx and Nature*,[6] Paul Burkett demolishes Leszek Kolakowski's oft-repeated claim that Marx was a "Promethean" thinker with little or no interest in the natural conditions of human existence. Burkett shows, first, that Marx provided the essential conceptual tools whereby to understand the historical specificity of modern (capitalist) relations between humanity and the natural world; second, that value theory informs a conception of crisis which encompasses the environmental alongside the economic and political; and, third, that these insights suggest a revolutionary strategy which is at once both socialist and environmentalist. John Bellamy Foster complements these arguments in his *Marx's Ecology*.[7] Against a certain type of Romantic anti-scientific and anti-materialistic environmentalism, Foster shows how materialism and science, as mediated most importantly through Darwin and Marx, provide the necessary framework from which ecological ways of thinking emerged. Marx's importance to this tradition is rooted, in part, in his doctoral research into the work of Epicurus. This Greek background informs Marx's conceptualisation of alienation as including a "metabolic rift" between nature and humanity. Like Burkett, Foster explores how Marx, thus understood, contributes fundamental resources necessary to conceptualise the specifically capitalist nature of the contemporary environmental crisis.

Burkett noted the influence of Hal Draper's magisterial *Karl Marx's Theory of Revolution*[8] to his attempt to rescue Marx from the mythmakers. Draper was a similarly strong influence on August Nimtz's devastating counter to the slander that Marx and Engels were elitist anti-democrats. In *Marx and Engels: Their Contribution to the Democratic Breakthrough*,[9] Nimtz shows not only that Marx and Engels were, first and foremost, political activists who were leading protagonists in the

5. London: Penguin, 2007.
6. New York: St. Martin's Press, 1999.
7. New York: Monthly Review Press, 2000.
8. New York: Monthly Review Press, 1977–1990.
9. Albany, NY: SUNY Press, 2000.

democratic movements from the 1840s onwards, but also that this activity informed their fundamental contribution to democratic theory: their insistence on the growing convergence of the movement for democracy and the self-organisation of the working class and its allies. Three years later Nimtz extended the arguments of one of the chapters of this book into another full length study: *Marx, Tocqueville, and Race in America.*[10] Whereas mainstream American political science tended to afford Tocqueville a premier position amongst nineteenth-century commentators on the social underpinnings of the US political system, Nimtz argues that Marx and Engels had a far clearer conception of American democracy in this period because they understood, as he did not, the importance of racism and slavery to American life, and the need for a real democratic movement to challenge and overthrow these institutions.

Draper died in 1990, just prior to the completion of the fourth volume of his *Karl Marx's Theory of Revolution.* It might have been supposed that, but for the odd minor piece, this would be the last of his works to see the light of day. Fortunately, Ernie Haberkern at the Center for Socialist History continued to work on two further volumes of Draper's study, the first of which was published in 2005. Subtitled *Volume V: War and Revolution,*[11] this new volume seeks to untangle Marx and Engels' comments on the politics of war from the distortions of friends and foes alike. Haberkern pieced together and added to Draper's detailed reconstructions of Marx and Engels' analyses of various conflicts from the 1840s to the 1890s with a view to exploding the myth that the pro-war positions of some leftists in 1914 had roots in their work. In a period marked by a new generation of liberal apologists for imperialism, Haberkern and Draper's book could not be more apt.

Interestingly, John Bellamy Foster commented that the process by which he came to recognise the importance of Marx's materialism to ecological thinking was hampered by his education as a Hegelian Marxist. If his engagement with the *Monthly Review* tradition introduced him to an intellectually powerful and creative materialism, others re-engaged with Hegel with the intention of rescuing Marx from the opposite error: the prison house of Soviet "Diamat" [dialectical materialism]. Chris Arthur's *The New Dialectic and Marx's Capital*[12] was intended to contribute to this process not merely by distancing Marx

10. Lanham, MD: Lexington Books, 2003.
11. New York: Monthly Review Press, 2005.
12. Leiden: Brill, 2002.

from the distortion of his ideas by the Stalinists, but more importantly by moving the debate about Marx's relation to Hegel on to discuss the methodological homologies between Hegel's *Logic* and Marx's *Capital*. Of central importance to Arthur's project was an attempt to reconstruct the value form in Hegelian terms as the essence of the capitalist mode of production. Arthur was also involved in a collective engagement with similar debates as one of the contributing editors to three important collections, relating, in turn, to volumes II, III, and I of *Capital* respectively: *The Circulation of Capital*;[13] *The Culmination of Capital*;[14] and *The Constitution of Capital*.[15] These volumes explore and extend Marx's historically specific conception of the capitalist social form through detailed Hegelian-Marxist readings of his value theory.

Parallel concerns informed the core chapters of Andrew Chitty and Martin McIvor's excellent collection *Karl Marx and Contemporary Philosophy*.[16] Beyond these issues, the Anglo-American writers brought together by two of the organisers of London's Marx and Philosophy Society interrogate themes as diverse as Marx's inheritance from both German idealism and Aristotle, his interpretation by twentieth-century Marxists, and his relevance to contemporary debates within both political philosophy and feminism.

Alfredo Saad-Filho produced a more detailed discussion of Marx's value theory in his *The Value of Marx: Political Economy for Contemporary Capitalism*.[17] Saad-Filho's reconstruction of Marx's critique of political economy shows, first, its relevance to any serious attempt to grasp the inner workings of the capitalist mode of production, and second, its ability to comprehend contemporary developments in this history of capitalism. He also shows how recent Marxists' work on value theory has deepened Marx's insights. Saad-Filho was far from alone in exploring these concerns. Not only has this issue been a recurring theme of the journal *Capital & Class*, with important contributions from writers such as Ben Fine and Alan Freeman; it has also been taken up in Andrew Kliman's book-length study of the transformation problem: *Reclaiming Marx's "Capital": A Refutation of the Myth of Inconsistency*.[18] The inconsistency referred to in the subtitle of Kliman's book is the famous "error" in Marx's attempt to derive prices from values.

13. London: Palgrave, 1998.
14. London: Palgrave, 2002.
15. London: Palgrave, 2004.
16. London: Palgrave, 2009.
17. London: Routledge, 2002.
18. Lanham, MD: Lexington Books, 2007.

Kliman's powerful and coherent counter to this oft-repeated claim provides a conceptual defence of Marx's system which acts as a necessary prerequisite for further empirical work by Marxists.

Kliman's and Saad-Filho's books essentially defend powerful reinterpretations of aspects of the conceptual infrastructure of Marx's *Capital*. David Harvey's *A Companion to Marx's Capital*,[19] by contrast, was intended merely as an introduction to Marx's ideas. Written up from Harvey's enormously popular introductory course on *Capital* – millions downloaded videos of these lectures in the months prior to the publication of the book – this was one of a number of first-rate textbooks published on Marx over the last decade. Alongside welcome new editions of Alex Callinicos' *The Revolutionary Ideas of Karl Marx*,[20] Ben Fine and Alfredo Saad-Filho's *Marx's Capital*[21] and Allen Wood's *Karl Marx*,[22] Andrew Collier penned an excellent introduction to Marx's oeuvre,[23] while Peter Osborne produced an admirably clear guide to the more philosophical aspects of his work: *How to Read Marx*.[24]

Complementing Saad-Filho's and Kilman's conceptual works, Chris Harman and David Harvey built upon Marx's critique of political economy in their powerful analyses of the current crisis. Harvey's *The Enigma of Capital*[25] deploys concepts derived from Marx to make sense of the current crisis as a basis for locating those social forces able to challenge the rule of capital. Harman's *Zombie Capitalism: Global Crisis and the Relevance of Marx*,[26] which extended the arguments of a number of important essays from *International Socialism*, has a similarly strategic orientation. He combines a reconstruction of Marx's system with a model of capitalism's historical evolution. Upon this foundation he explores the dual nature of the contemporary crisis – environmental and economic – as aspects of a broader system of alienation. The book ends with a reconstruction and defence of Marx's conception of the proletariat as the universal class through whose struggles a democratic solution to the crisis of capitalism becomes a historical potentiality.

Harman's attempt to marry Marx's critique of political economy with his strategic orientation towards the working class coheres with

19. London: Verso, 2010.
20. London: Bookmarks, 2010.
21. London: Pluto Press, 2010.
22. London: Routledge, 2004.
23. *Marx* (Oxford: Oneworld, 2004).
24. London: Granta Books, 2005.
25. London: Profile Books, 2010.
26. London: Bookmarks, 2009; Chicago: Haymarket Books, 2010.

recent studies by Michael Lebowitz and István Mészáros. In 2010 Mészáros published a powerful critique of the structural limitations of bourgeois thought. *Social Structure and Forms of Consciousness*[27] explores the theoretical ramifications of Marx's claim, as outlined in the tenth of his theses on Feuerbach, that "the standpoint of the old materialism is civil society; the standpoint of the new is human society, or social humanity". Mészáros's book shows how bourgeois thought is fundamentally limited by its naturalisation of the historical standpoint of civil society, and how this limitation can be overcome from a perspective rooted in the standpoint of workers' struggles against capitalism. For these struggles provide a point of departure from which to conceptualise capitalism both as a system of exploitation and as a historical mode of production. Mészáros thus provides a powerful restatement of the classical Marxist strategic orientation towards workers' struggles. Similarly, in 2003 Lebowitz published a substantially revised edition of his 1992 book *Beyond Capital: Marx's Political Economy of the Working Class.*[28] As its subtitle suggests, Lebowitz focuses on the under-explored subjective side of Marx's critique of capitalism with a view to defending his orientation towards the working class. Winner of the 2004 Isaac and Tamara Deutsher Memorial Prize, Lebowitz expanded the themes of *Beyond Capital* in his *Following Marx: Method, Critique and Crisis.*[29]

Idiosyncratically, *Following Marx* combines detailed methodological chapters with rich concrete applications of the method to contemporary debates and processes. Clearly a powerful contribution to a strand of Hegelian Marxism which owes much to his reading of the *Grundrisse*, this book complements Marcello Musto's edited collection *Karl Marx's Grundrisse.*[30] Combining comprehensive essays on each of the *Grundrisse's* main themes with others detailing Marx's intellectual biography over the period in which it was written, and finally a selection of essays exploring its reception, the breadth and depth of scholarship represented in this collection is evidence of the continued vitality of work on Marx within the academy.

A similar story can be told of Gavin Kitching and Nigel Pleasants' edited collection *Marx and Wittgenstein: Knowledge, Morality and Politics.*[31] Against a widespread conception of vast differences between

27. New York: Monthly Review Press, 2010.
28. London: Palgrave, 2003.
29. Leiden: Brill, 2009.
30. London: Routledge, 2008.
31. London: Routledge, 2002.

these two thinkers, the editors not only point to the commonalities and differences between the two but also argue that each can mutually enrich the other though their contributions to a conception of social practice that is at once material and mental. These philosophical concerns are shared by another important contributor to recent Anglophone literature on Marx: Bertell Ollman. As with Lebowitz's attempt to escape the one-dimensional reduction of Marx to political economy, Ollman's powerful defence of dialectical modes of thought, *Dance of the Dialectic: Steps in Marx's Method,*[32] explores not merely Marx's conceptions of capitalism and communism, but more importantly the way that he understood the unity of the two through his dialectical conception of the emergent nature of communism within capitalism.

By contrast, David Leopold's scholarly reconstruction of Marx's early thought, *The Young Karl Marx,*[33] concludes with the claim that Marx's refusal to outline blueprints for a new order was a major failing of his system, and that it is dangerous to imagine the new society in embryo within the old. Leopold's study centrally concerns Marx's conception of the state: its emergence; its modern form; and its future replacement. Marx, he suggests, was stronger on the first and second of these themes than he was on the third. In a very different rereading of Marx's early writings – tellingly not referenced in Leopold's text – Stathis Kouvelakis reconstructed Marx's early intellectual biography in a way that emphasised his relationship to the work of Heinrich Heine at the expense of other youthful influences. In *Philosophy and Revolution: From Kant to Marx,*[34] Kouvelakis argues that by contrast with the elitism of the Young Hegelians, "Heine's and Marx's road was altogether different, for they never lost sight of the red thread that bound democracy to the revolution". This vision of socialism from below, while being at odds with Leopold's demand for blueprints, complements the works by Draper, Harman, Lebowitz, Mészáros, Nimtz, and Ollman *et al.*

The contemporary political implications of this type of perspective are explored in Paul Le Blanc's *Marx, Lenin, and the Revolutionary Experience.*[35] This study opens with a defence of the relevance of Marx's critique of capitalism to modern conditions – a more controversial position when it was published than it would become a year or two

32. Urbana: University of Illinois Press, 2003.
33. Cambridge: Cambridge University Press, 2007.
34. London: Verso, 2003.
35. London: Routledge, 2006.

later – before moving on to ask sharp questions about the political side of Marxism. At a more theoretical level, Alex Callinicos' *Imperialism and Global Political Economy*[36] articulates a Marxist explanation of contemporary imperialism from within the conceptual architecture of Marx's *Capital*. Callinicos extends Marx's method of rising from the abstract to the concrete through a series of different determinations to integrate an account of the relations within the system of states into Marx's critique of political economy.

If Callinicos examined the relevance of Marx's work to our understanding of imperialism, Thomas Patterson's *Karl Marx, Anthropologist*[37] makes a powerful case for the importance of Marx to the study of anthropology. He shows how Marx made a fundamental contribution to our understanding the historical nature of human essence, and how this underpinned the theoretically and practically informed empirical research carried out by himself and others. This, in turn, informed his conceptualisation of capitalism as a mode of production which created the conditions for human self-actualisation. Against oft-repeated caricatures of this vision of history, Kevin Anderson, in a superb close reading of Marx's mature writings, *Marx at the Margins*,[38] demolishes the claims that Marx embraced a teleological and unilinear model of history. Through a discussion of Marx's commentary on issues of race, nation, and ethnicity in non-Western societies, he shows how Marx avoided abstract universals by exploring "the specific ways in which the universalising powers of capital and class were manifesting themselves in particular societies or social groups".

I am very aware that these notes have only touched upon the scope and quality of contemporary Marx scholarship in the Anglophone world. Nevertheless, I think that even this brief snapshot points to the vitality of this research. The powerful studies surveyed above suggest that Marx's ideas are, if anything, even more relevant today than they were in the nineteenth century. Marx made fundamental contributions to our understanding of environmental as well as economic crises; his work provides the necessary conceptual infrastructure upon which to build an adequate conception of contemporary imperialism; and it illuminates the structural limits of bourgeois thought generally and of bourgeois conceptions of politics more specifically. Moreover, Marx drew attention to those collective forms

36. Cambridge: Polity, 2009.
37. Oxford: Berg, 2009.
38. Chicago: University of Chicago Press, 2010.

of struggle within capitalism which provide the strategic basis for a real democratic alternative to capitalism, and he provided a wealth of tactical resources that point towards a politics that might realise the potential of these struggles. Whatever the undoubted limits of his thought, the recent Anglophone literature on Marx provides a wealth of evidence to suggest that it would be a grave mistake for contemporary radicals to dismiss his legacy.

Marx in France

Jean-Numa Ducange

It is no longer possible to keep up with all the French newspapers and magazines proclaiming a "return to Marx" – from *Courrier international* to *Point*. The 2005 biography of Karl Marx by Jacques Attali (a high official, close to the current government) was so successful that it was put out in a cheap edition for a mass audience.[1] More recently, Edgar Morin, by his own account no friend of Marxism, published a series of essays on the subject.[2] We are thus certainly re-encountering Marx, and this interest precedes the current economic crisis. But we should not read too much into it. What most of these presentations evoke is Marx the prophet of globalization, the extraordinary economist who called attention to the contradictions of capitalism before they were widely recognized. For a fairly broad public, it is above all this particular Marx who has "come back," occasioning multiple reprints of *Capital* and its key passages, as well as more heterodox works such as Paul Mattick's *Marx and Keynes* – brought out in translation by one of France's top publishing houses.[3]

For other approaches (political, philosophical, even "sociological"), the situation is quite different. Compared to the conjuncture of the 1960s (the last period to have known a lively interest in Marx, in a context we can recall), the current turn has its own distinctive character. To be sure, several prestigious scholastic competitions have included some of Marx's works in their canon, prompting the republication of many texts. The entrance examination for the sciences has thus incorporated *The 18th Brumaire of Louis Bonaparte* under the heading "Thinking about History," and the first volume of *Capital* (in German) has recently been made a requirement for the advanced degree in philosophy (the *agrégation*). All this reflects a certain presence of Marx in academic institutions, marginal compared to other thinkers,

1. J. Attali, *Karl Marx ou l'esprit du monde* (Paris: Fayard, 2005).
2. E. Morin, *Pour et contre Marx* (Paris: Éditions du temps présent, 2010).
3. P. Mattick, *Marx et Keynes* (Paris: Gallimard, 2010).

Socialism and Democracy, Vol.24, No.3, November 2010, pp.169–174
ISSN 0885-4300 print/ISSN 1745-2635 online
DOI: 10.1080/08854300.2010.513622

but significant in light of the "great nightmare of the 1980s,"[4] when he had been proclaimed dead and buried. The publication of primers in Marxism by the Presses Universitaires de France (PUF) is indicative of the new trend.[5]

A custom of permanent reference to Marx and Marxism is kept alive moreover in a sector of the French left that identifies with certain particular political traditions. Leaving aside major social struggles, the combined impact of the Trotskyist-based far left and the Left Front (an alliance between the Communist Party and a left split-off of the Socialist Party), which together account for about 10% of the vote in national elections, helps keep up a certain "classist" vocabulary stemming from Marxism which is stronger in France than in other countries. The obsession of certain Socialist Party leaders with a "Bad-Godesberg à la française,"[6] as against the supposed dinosaur Marxism (*"archéo-marxisme"*) of a big part of the left, says a lot about this custom.

Still, one cannot situate an intellectual position merely with reference to some possible political counterpart. In this respect, the phrase "a thousand Marxisms" of philosopher André Tosel conveys well the explosion of readings and interpretations of Marx in France. Several journals reflect this diversity. Especially important is the team around the journal *Actuel Marx* (published since 1987), which, every three years since 1996, has organized a worldwide conference of Marx specialists at the University of Nanterre.[7] Other journals, less directly academic and more directly linked to radical leftist political currents,[8] have recently devoted special issues to Marx and his reception in France and in the world.[9] Several seminars, often led by the same persons as these journals, pursue ambitious projects on Marx's work.[10]

4. The title of F. Cusset's book, *Le grand cauchemar des années 1980* (Paris: La Découverte, 2009).
5. See e.g. M. Löwy, G. Duménil, E. Renault, *Lire Marx* (Paris: PUF, 2009).
6. The reference here is to the 1959 congress of Germany's Social Democratic Party at which it explicitly renounced Marxism.
7. http://actuelmarx.u-paris10.fr
8. On these differences, see E. Barot, "Le communisme n'est pas une Idée (Court état du marxisme en France)," *Contretemps*, n°7 nouvelle série (2010).
9. See *Contretemps*, "Marx hors limites: Une pensée devenue monde," ancienne série n°20 (2007); *La Pensée*, "Connaître Marx," n°360 (2009).
10. For example, the interdisciplinary seminar "Marx in the 19th Century," linked to the Center on the History of Systems of Modern Thought (Philosophy Department, Université de Paris 1), whose leaders include Jean Salem, Isabelle Garo and Stathis Kouvelakis, confronts Marx's texts and Marxist traditions every week of

Alongside these journals and seminars exists a myriad of small partisan or activist publishers, with diverse sensibilities but mostly committed to (re)publishing Marx or analyses of his texts, often around a theme of current interest. Examples include: from La Fabrique, texts of the young Marx on the theft of wood, edited by Daniel Bensaïd (1946–2010), and articles and correspondence on the Paris Commune;[11] from Amsterdam publishers, a commentary by Pierre Macherey (a former student of Althusser) on the Theses on Feuerbach;[12] and from Demopolis, new translations of extracts from *Capital* directed at a broad public.[13] We should also mention the Syllepse collection "mille marxismes" which links little-known or forgotten texts of the Marxist tradition (Bukharin, Rubin) with innovative essays, sometimes by foreign authors. In this respect, the recent publication of works by Fredric Jameson and other Marxists of the Anglophone world (e.g., David Harvey) helps lead certain circles of the intellectual left back to Marx's texts.

There are divergences among these journals, seminars, and publishers, reflecting more or less the political sensibilities of the "left of the left" yet helping to create intellectual spaces where Marx is at the heart of political and theoretical debate. To understand how this disparate ensemble bears more precisely on the knowledge of Marx's own texts, the question of "which Marx" one can read in French is decisive. Without repeating what has been developed elsewhere,[14] we must stress that there is a major hiatus between the profusion of contributions and references to Marx and the availability and quality of his texts. For example, even as the theories of Toni Negri resonate widely on the radical left, the text of the *Grundrisse* – on which Negri has published a long commentary – has become unobtainable despite the fact that it existed earlier in two competing editions.

To address this major problem, Éditions Sociales (formerly linked to the Communist Party) launched GEME (Grande Édition Marx

---

the academic year without dissociating philological rigor from theoretical and political engagement: www.marxau21.fr. A collection of works based on this seminar is forthcoming from the publishing house La ville brûle.

11. D. Bensaïd, *Les dépossédés : Karl Marx, les voleurs de bois et le droit des pauvres* (Paris: La Fabrique, 2007), K. Marx and F. Engels, *Inventer l'inconnu: Textes et correspondance autour de la Commune* (Paris: La Fabrique, 2008).
12. P. Macherey, *Marx "1845": Les "thèses" sur Feuerbach* (Paris: Éditions Amsterdam, 2008).
13. K. Marx, *Qu'est-ce que le capitalisme?* (Paris: Demopolis, 2010).
14. J.-N. Ducange "Editer Marx et Engels en France: mission impossible?", *Revue Internationale des Livres et des Idées,* n° 16 (2010).

Engels), whose goal is to offer the Francophone public a systematic edition of the works of Marx and Engels by publishing new translations based on the *Marx Engels Gesamtausgabe* and putting online the old translations within the framework of a vast program of computerization supported principally by the Maison des sciences de l'Homme of Burgundy and the Fondation Gabriel Péri. So far, only one GEME volume has appeared,[15] but several have been announced for 2010–11.[16] Meanwhile, the main edition of Marx remains the one directed by Maximilien Rubel (1905–1996) and published by Gallimard – an unfinished edition that has been criticized both for its editorial choices and for its translations. This edition dissociates Engels from Marx, viewing Engels as the father of Marx*ism* and hence as being implicated in later corruptions of the Marxian agenda.[17] Overall, however, the availability of certain titles from the backlog of Éditions Sociales (up to now the publishers of the greatest number of texts), along with the timely reprints by other publishers that we have noted, constitute a notable ensemble – though nonetheless not up to the level of other languages (there is at this time no French equivalent of the *Collected Works*).

New translations reflecting in part the focus of present-day reconsiderations – the new translation of the *1844 Manuscripts* as well as the commentaries on them – point toward further inquiry into the young Marx and the concept of alienation, extending a tradition begun by the Frankfurt School.[18] The concept of ideology is again at the heart of certain projects[19] while the writings of Althusser are again being questioned.[20] The philosopher Lucien Sève, an erstwhile critic of Althusser, revisits his rapport with Marx and his political trajectory in a series of volumes, *Marx avec nous?*, of which the most recent addresses more specifically the anthropological dimension of the Marxian agenda.[21] We should also note here the revival of interest in alternatives to Marxism in the name of Marx, including several studies on late-19th-century reformism and revisionism.[22] Historians are revisiting

15. K. Marx, *Critique du programme de Gotha* (Paris: Éditions sociales, 2008).
16. See www.gabrielperi.fr
17. See Ducange, "Editer Marx et Engels."
18. K. Marx, *Manuscrits économico-philosophiques de 1844* (Paris: Vrin, 2007); E. Renault (ed.), *Lire les manuscrits de 1844* (Paris: PUF, 2008).
19. I. Garo, *L'idéologie ou la pensée embarquée* (Paris: La Fabrique, 2009).
20. See esp. J.-C. Bourdin, *Althusser, une lecture de Marx* (Paris: PUF, 2008).
21. L. Sève, *L'Homme?* (Paris: La Dispute, 2009).
22. E. Jousse, *Réviser le marxisme? D'Edouard Bernstein à Albert Thomas* (Paris: L'Harmattan, 2007).

Marx's contribution, as shown by the translation of several unpublished works of Eric Hobsbawm under the title *Marx et l'histoire*.[23] Critical assessments of topics long of interest to Marxist historians, such as the history of the labor movement and the French Revolution, are appearing.[24] We should also mention studies on the publishing institutions (both political and non-political), which have framed the construction of Marxism in France, as well as the attention given to the translators and presenters of Marx in France from the beginnings. In a period of widespread rejection of capitalism, popularizations are being reprinted.[25]

The examples given here are by no means exhaustive. To be complete, we would also have to detail Marxist inspiration in the works of contemporary sociologists (S. Bouquin,[26] S. Béroud) and the debates with those inspired by P. Bourdieu; we would have to remind ourselves of how a certain approach to political ecology is inspired by Karl Marx; we would have to call attention to the cross-fertilization of Marxism and the sciences; and so on. It is a rich array of work whose multiple dimensions, whatever their uncertainties, nonetheless clash sharply with the virulent anti-Marxism of the 1980s which had made the reading of Marx almost impossible.

Research on Marx thus promises to continue. His republished economic writings, especially *Capital*, will certainly inspire reflection and will open up new intellectual space in university economics departments, which are currently dominated by a quasi-hegemonic neoliberalism. As for the political crisis, it may prompt a return to Marx's writings on the 1848–1871 sequence. The supposed "Bonapartism" of President Nicolas Sarkozy has already encouraged journalists to refer to the opening sentences of the *18th Brumaire*, while at a deeper level there have been essays trying to decode contemporary political reality in the light of Marxian analyses.[27] In 2011, the observances and demonstrations planned around the Commune of 1871 should not neglect *The Civil War in France* and the readings it has

23. E. Hobsbawm, *Marx et l'Histoire* (Paris: Demopolis, 2008).
24. C. Mazauric, *L'histoire de la Révolution française et la pensée marxiste* (Paris: PUF, 2009).
25. See the collection "Réception des marxismes," forthcoming in *Cahiers d'histoire: Revue d'histoire critique* (2010-11); also the reprint of C. Cafiero, *Abrégé du capital de Karl Marx* (Paris: Le Chien rouge, 2008) or the texts of P. Lafargue, *Paresse et revolution* (Paris: Tallandier, 2009).
26. S. Bouquin (ed.), *Résistances au travail* (Paris: Syllepse, 2008).
27. For a reappropriation of Marx for today via R. Luxemburg, see D. Muhlman, *Réconcilier marxisme et démocratie* (Paris: Seuil, 2010). Cf. E. Barot, *Marx et les deux visages de la Révolution* (Paris: La ville brûle, 2010).

given rise to. Finally we should note that post-colonial studies and gender studies – relatively new in France, and often stimulated by translations from English – have inserted themselves into the relatively narrow space between the long-standing presence of Marxism and the changing economic and political situation. All this leads us to think that the debates around Marx are far from over.

Translated by Victor Wallis

Marx in Germany

Jan Hoff

In 2008–09 the student organisation of *Die Linke* (The Left), the *Sozialistisch-Demokratischer Studierendenverband* (SDS – Socialist Democratic Students League) launched a nationwide campaign for starting *Capital* reading-groups. In recent years there were some media reports that sales of *Capital vol. I* surged because of the current economic crisis, rising from several hundred in 2007 to a few thousand in 2008. This comes on top of a long tradition of high-quality research in Germany on Marx's critique of political economy.

The theoretical underpinnings of recent German Marx-research have been closely examined by Ingo Elbe,[1] and have been put in the context of global Marx-research by Jan Hoff.[2] A core topic of the German debate on *Capital* is value theory, especially an interpretation called *monetäre Werttheorie* (monetary theory of value). Many German Marx researchers agree that Marx's theory of value can be understood as a critique of pre-monetary theories of value. Accordingly, they assume that there is a necessary and specific interconnection between Marx's concept of value, his definition of abstract labor, and his theory of money. Examples of the *monetäre Werttheorie*-reading of Marx can be traced back to the 1970s, but this interpretation also prevails in more recent studies.[3] Among the younger generation of scholars, this understanding of the Marxian theory of value is hardly contested.

The various interpretations of Marx's theory of value that were launched by researchers like Hans-Georg Backhaus and Helmut

---

1. See below for more details.
2. Jan Hoff, *Marx global. Zur Entwicklung des internationalen Marx-Diskurses seit 1965* (Berlin: Akademie Verlag, 2009).
3. Michael Heinrich, *Die Wissenschaft vom Wert. Die Marxsche Kritik der politischen Ökonomie zwischen wissenschaftlicher Revolution und klassischer Tradition* (Münster: Verlag Westfälisches Dampfboot, 1999); Michael Heinrich, *Kritik der politischen Ökonomie. Eine Einführung* (Stuttgart: Schmetterling Verlag, 2004); Jan Hoff, *Kritik der klassischen politischen Ökonomie. Zur Rezeption der werttheoretischen Ansätze ökonomischer Klassiker durch Karl Marx* (Köln: Papyrossa Verlag, 2004).

Socialism and Democracy, Vol.24, No.3, November 2010, pp.175–180
ISSN 0885-4300 print/ISSN 1745-2635 online
DOI: 10.1080/08854300.2010.513623

Reichelt in the 1960s and 1970s or by Michael Heinrich in the 1990s form the starting point for the younger scholars' approach to Marx. The link between the categories of value, commodity, and money is relevant to the interpretation of Marx's theory of commodity money. During the 1990s, Heinrich had put forward a critical view of Marx's theory of money as a commodity. Ingo Stützle, a disciple of Heinrich, has more recently drawn attention to this problem.[4] According to Stützle, Marx clearly views money as a commodity in his critique of political economy. Marx states in *Capital*: "We have seen that the money-form is merely the reflection thrown upon one single commodity by the relations between all the other commodities. That money is a commodity is therefore only a discovery for those who proceed from its finished shape to analyse it afterwards. The process of exchange gives to the commodity which it has converted into money not its value but its specific value-form."[5] The *monetäre Werttheorie*-reading of the relation between value and money is supported by Stützle, who argues that Marx's theory of commodity money clashes with the empirical reality of present-day capitalism, on the grounds that with the imposition of the Bretton Woods system and its fixed exchange-rates, money ceased to be a commodity. Stützle finally pleads for a deeper understanding of Marx's method in order to cope with these problems. The discussion on the problem of commodity money was afterwards again taken up in a book by Dieter Wolf, Stephan Krüger, and Ansgar Knolle-Grothusen, who defend Marx's theory of commodity money against Heinrich and Stützle.[6]

An important aspect of the German debate (in both its Western and its Eastern versions) has been the close philological examination of the Marxian texts. In this context, the MEGA[2] (the second edition of the *Marx-Engels Gesamtausgabe* [complete writings]) is of special relevance, as it includes Marx's excerpts, notes, and marginal notes, which enable us to reconstruct the complete development of his political economy. For instance, the current German debate on value theory takes into account not only the theoretical distinctions between the different versions of chapter one of *Capital I*, but also a text called *Ergänzungen und Veränderungen zum ersten Band des "Kapital"* (Supplements and

4. Ingo Stützle, "Die Frage nach der konstitutiven Relevanz der Geldware in Marx' Kritik der politischen Ökonomie," in Jan Hoff, Alexis Petrioli, Ingo Stützle, Frieder Otto Wolf (eds), *Das Kapital neu lesen – Beiträge zur radikalen Philosophie* (Münster: Verlag Westfälisches Dampfboot, 2006), pp. 254–286.
5. Marx, *Capital I*, trans. Ben Fowkes (New York: Vintage Books, 1977), p. 184f.
6. Dieter Wolf, Stephan Krüger, Ansgar Knolle-Grothusen, *Geldware, Geld und Währung. Grundlagen zur Lösung des Problems der Geldware* (Hamburg: Argument Verlag, 2008).

revisions to the first volume of *Capital*).[7] Marx wrote this text in 1871–72 as a basis for the reworking of his value theory (and especially his value-form analysis) for the second German edition of *Capital*. This essential Marxian text can be read as an insightful and self-clarifying commentary on his own theory of value. It was first published in German in 1987 and is still not translated into English.

Publication of the *Marx-Engels Werke* (MEW) edition has also been resumed, at least partly due to the recent growth of interest in Marx and Marxism. Moreover, some single editions of Marx's writings have also sold well. The most important journals of Marx studies in Germany, *Beiträge zur Marx-Engels-Forschung: Neue Folge* and *Marx-Engels-Jahrbuch,* serve as discussion forums mainly for MEGA^2-related research. The articles in both journals encompass such topics as the Marx-Engels-relation, the category of "capital in general," the theory of the falling rate of profit, the "beginning" of Marx's dialectical presentation, and Marx's reception of his sources.

The most recent trend of Marx research in Germany focuses on the reception of Marx's theory since the 1960s. Ingo Elbe[8] explains how Marx was referred to in West German debates on the critique of political economy (especially regarding Marx's value theory and his conception of the object), on state theory, and on the theory of revolution. According to Elbe, three major tendencies can be distinguished in the reception and discussion of Marx's theory. First is "traditional" Marxism, which Elbe specifically criticizes. This trend turned Marx's thought into a *Weltanschauung* and a theory of the evolution of nature and society. A second trend, Western Marxism, originated with Lukács and Korsch in the 1920s. Western Marxism is characterized by Elbe as a critical-revolutionary theory of social praxis. The third trend is the West German "*neue Marx-Lektüre*" (new reading of Marx) that emerged in the 1960s and 1970s, and which is still predominant today among West German Marx scholars. According to Elbe, this trend is characterized by the questions it raises regarding Marx's critique of political economy. It turns to Marx's theory of economic forms, his theory of fetishism and mystification. It therefore focuses on Marx's theory of the forms that represent abstract labor and on those critical dimensions of Marx's thought that point to epistemological questions. It takes Marx's method of exposition into account,

7. MEGA^2 II.6, edited by J. Jungnickel, W. Focke, R. Hecker, B. Lietz (Berlin/GDR: Dietz Verlag, 1987), pp. 1–54.
8. Ingo Elbe, *Marx im Westen. Die neue Marx-Lektüre in der Bundesrepublik seit 1965* (Berlin: Akademie Verlag, 2008).

and examines how the various economic forms are interconnected within the totality of economic categories. This new reading of Marx identifies his approach as a distinctive and unique theory differing in its method, object, and epistemology both from pre-Marxian classical political economy and from "modern" post-Marxian economics.

During the 1990s Michael Heinrich published a major study of Marx's relation to classical political economy.[9] He argued that Marx had underestimated the theoretical gap between himself and the classics, because Marx did not recognize that his critique of political economy was located on a different "theoretical field," which went beyond the classics not only in its theoretical insights but also in its underlying premises. Astonishingly, Heinrich's thesis on Marx's relation to the classics was either neglected (by most of his colleagues) or instantly accepted as an axiom (by his disciples), but has never been put to the serious and intensive discussion it deserves.

Another book by Heinrich[10] seeks to introduce the critique of political economy to young readers. It is written from the standpoint of the "*neue Marx-Lektüre.*" Like Elbe and others, Heinrich sharply distinguishes Marx's theory from the traditionalist "*Weltanschauungs*-Marxism." A more recent monograph by Heinrich[11] comments on the beginning of *Capital I*, focusing on the paradoxical character of Marx's 1867 value-form analysis and drawing on the self-clarification manuscript mentioned above.

Another new reading of Marx, especially of *Capital I*, has been put forward by the philosopher Christian Iber.[12] Despite his role as one of Germany's best-known Hegel experts, Iber does not interpret *Capital* from the standpoint of the *Hegelmarxismus* (Hegelian Marxism) manifested in the works of Hans-Jürgen Krahl and others. For Iber, the Marxian project consists of the critique of the whole field of political economy. The theoretical background he shares with Heinrich and many other German researchers is shaped by the idea of a fundamental distinction between Marx and Marxism – between viewing Marx as a

9. Michael Heinrich, *Die Wissenschaft vom Wert. Die Marxsche Kritik der politischen Ökonomie zwischen wissenschaftlicher Revolution und klassischer Tradition* (Münster: Verlag Westfälisches Dampfboot, 1999).
10. Michael Heinrich, *Kritik der politischen Ökonomie. Eine Einführung* (Stuttgart: Schmetterling Verlag, 2004).
11. Michael Heinrich, *Wie das Marxsche Kapital lesen?* (Stuttgart: Schmetterling Verlag, 2008).
12. Christian Iber, *Grundzüge der Marxschen Kapitalismustheorie* (Berlin: Parerga-Verlag, 2005).

scientist and philosopher and viewing him as founder of the Marxist *Weltanschauung*.

Helmut Reichelt, who belonged to the first generation of the "*neue Marx-Lektüre*" (a product of the student revolt of the 1960s), was a disciple of Horkheimer and Adorno. In a recent book[13] he has summarized his research of the last decades. In his view, the initial aim of the "*neue Marx-Lektüre*" was to reconstruct Marxian method. The main topic of Reichelt's more recent work was the problem of the specific "objectivity" of value, which has to be considered in the light of a peculiar theory of "validity."

Other authors have also contributed to the interpretation of the Marxian critique of political economy. Dieter Wolf, who is highly critical of Reichelt's theory of "validity," has examined the problem of contradiction within dialectics.[14] Nadja Rakowitz has criticized Engels' reading of the beginning of *Capital* (as has Christopher Arthur in the English-speaking debate),[15] and Gerhard Stapelfeldt has underlined the differences between Marx and the classical political economists.[16] Both Wolfgang Fritz Haug[17] and Michael Berger[18] have offered introductions to *Capital*. Sven Ellmers' book represents a new interpretation of Marx's theory of class.[19]

Some young Marx interpreters address political questions in a rather indirect way - by pointing to Marx's critique of certain forms of socialist theory and practice. In a recent monograph, Hendrik Wallat points out that Marx aimed at criticizing certain anti-individualist traits of 19th-century socialism.[20] The author of the critique of political economy rejected both Etatism and Anarchism. Finally, Marx criticized the (unconscious) "socialist" perpetuation of certain

13. Helmut Reichelt, *Neue Marx-Lektüre. Zur Kritik sozialwissenschaftlicher Logik* (Hamburg: VSA-Verlag, 2008).
14. Dieter Wolf, *Der dialektische Widerspruch im* Kapital (Hamburg: VSA-Verlag, 2002).
15. Nadja Rakowitz, *Einfache Warenproduktion. Ideal und Ideologie* (Freiburg: Ca Ira, 2000); Christopher Arthur, "Engels as Interpreter of Marx's Economics," in C. Arthur (ed.), *Engels Today: A Centenary Appreciation* (New York: St. Martin's Press, 1996), pp. 173–209.
16. Gerhard Stapelfeldt, *Der Liberalismus. Die Gesellschaftstheorien von Smith, Ricardo und Marx* (Freiburg: Ca Ira, 2006).
17. Wolfgang Fritz Haug, *Neue Vorlesungen zur Einführung ins „Kapital"* (Hamburg: Argument, 2006).
18. Michael Berger, *Karl Marx: „Das Kapital." Eine Einführung*, Ullstein, München (2003).
19. Sven Ellmers, *Die formanalytische Klassentheorie von Karl Marx. Ein Beitrag zur „neuen Marx-Lektüre"* (Duisburg: Universitätsverlag Rhein-Ruhr, 2007).
20. Hendrik Wallat, *Das Bewusstsein der Krise. Marx, Nietzsche und die Emanzipation des Nichtidentischen in der politischen Theorie* (Bielefeld: Transcript, 2009), p. 359ff.

forms and principles attached to bourgeois society. So Wallat also addresses some features of a socialist society according to Marx, even though he avoids focusing primarily on present-day political movements.

The Berlin historian Wolfgang Wippermann has recently studied the history of Marxist thought.[21] Wippermann puts forward the idea of Karl Marx's "four lives." Marx's first life was his actual lifetime, which was mainly shaped by his intensive work on *Capital* and by his activity as a political revolutionary. After his death in 1883 his ideas continued to exist as a kind of "second life," because they were taken up and partly modified by the working-class movement of both the Second and the Third Internationals. This development is seen by Wippermann in a specifically critical light, i.e. as a deformation of Marx's original theory. However, Marx also led a "third life" within the theoretical approaches of "dissident" Marxist theorists like Korsch, Lukács, and Gramsci. In Wippermann's opinion, the more recent renaissance of Marx's theories could represent a "fourth life," because Marx deserves to be read again in the present – not only as an economist, but also as a philosopher and a historian. Wippermann stresses the role of Marx's ideas within the recent discussions on globalization, but he also points to the relevance of Marx's views on topics such as Bonapartism, "Asiatic Despotism," or critique of religion.

All in all it is clear that the recent German debate on Marx (and especially on Marx's *Capital*) has both strengths and weaknesses. However, it might be inappropriate to speak of a "Marx renaissance," inasmuch as Marx's writings have always been studied seriously. Within this tradition of German Marx research, the younger scholars offer a perspective for the future. I hope that German discussions on Marx will be more thoroughly incorporated in the international Marx debate.

---

21. Wolfgang Wippermann, *Der Wiedergänger. Die vier Leben des Karl Marx* (Wien: Kremayr & Scheriau, 2008).

Marx in Italy

Gianfranco Ragona

Over the last decade, after the *Marx-Engels Gesamtaugabe* (the historical-critical edition of the complete works of Marx and of Engels) was taken up again (MEGA2), the true "Marx Renaissance" that has swept across many countries of Europe and the world also reached Italy. A key moment was the 2004 International Symposium on Marx in Naples, whose proceedings were published by Manifestolibri.[1] Three years later, the same publishing house, among the most active in this field, produced the volume *Da Marx a Marx?* (From Marx to Marx?), fruit of a symposium occasioned by the publication of a very substantial history: *Storia dei marxismi in Italia* (History of Italian Marxisms). This work, by Cristina Corradi,[2] helped extend the Marx-Renaissance into a Marxism-Renaissance, by critically examining some earlier works of Italian Marxism, including those of Lucio Colletti, Galvano Della Volpe, Cesare Luporini, Piero Sraffa, and Claudio Napoleoni. The seventieth anniversary (in 2007) of Antonio Gramsci's death prompted a further wave of meetings and editorial initiatives, helping to re-launch the work of Italy's most important 20th-century Marxist.

However, these discussions lack the support of a complete Italian edition of Marx and Engels' works. The task begun in 1972 by Editori Riuniti – modelled upon the German edition *Marx-Engels Werke* and initially planned to consist of 50 volumes – was halted in 1990, with 18 volumes still unpublished. At the start of the new century, a group from Milan University led by Mario Cingoli picked up the baton, drawing on the philological investigations underlying the MEGA2. The result was the decision to continue the edition from

1. Marcello Musto (ed.), *Sulle tracce di un fantasma. L'opera di Karl Marx tra filologia e filosofia* (On the tracks of a Spectre: The oeuvre of Karl Marx between philology and philosophy) (Rome: manifestolibri, 2005).
2. C. Corradi, *Storia dei marxismi in Italia* (Rome: manifestolibri, 2005); *Da Marx a Marx? Un bilancio dei marxismi italiani del Novecento*, ed. Riccardo Bellofiore (Rome: manifestolibri, 2007).

Socialism and Democracy, Vol.24, No.3, November 2010, pp.181–186
ISSN 0885-4300 print/ISSN 1745-2635 online
DOI: 10.1080/08854300.2010.513626

where it had been interrupted, and in 2008, volume XXII came out[3] and others are at the planning stage.

This Marxian renaissance has been largely ignored by the various political formations that still refer (though in a residual and too often ritualistic manner) to Marx and to "Marxism," as the proceedings of their most recent Congresses show. The Communist Re-foundation Party (*Rifondazione comunista*), the Party of the Italian Communists (*Partito dei comunisti italiani*), the Critical Left (*Sinistra critica*), and other lesser formations all lack the ability to build a cultural policy commensurate with their official declarations about the need for a new theory updated to the 21st century. They have neither the commitment to study nor the courage to make proposals that could translate the aspiration toward socialism underlying Marx's work – as both scientist and revolutionary – into concrete programs. Sporadically, cultural associations or study centers affiliated with existing parties try to rekindle the need for reflection,[4] but these attempts get little attention from the party leaders, who are concerned first and foremost with their own survival and with that of their organisations.

Thus, recent discussion has remained confined mostly to university buildings, conference halls, or the offices of some courageous publishing house. Despite this, the number of publications over the past half-decade has been prodigious. Of these, some have been of considerable interest, capable of stimulating further debate and of indicating new avenues for research, especially in philosophy and economics. Here I can only mention them briefly, making a drastic and subjective selection.[5]

In 2004, Finelli published a study under the eloquent title *Un parricidio mancato* (A failed parricide), in which he deals with the relationship between Hegel and the young Marx, and brings to fruition

3. K. Marx and F. Engels, *Opere complete. XXII. Luglio 1870-ottobre 1871*, edited by Marco Vanzulli (Naples & Rome: La Città del Sole/Editori Riuniti, 2008), pp. XIII–945.
4. The Livio Maitan Study Center in Rome, for example, promoted the book *Pensare con Marx. Ripensare Marx. Teorie per il nostro tempo*, edited by Cinzia Arruzza (Rome: Edizioni Alegre, 2008).
5. Recent works include: Stefano Petrucciani, *Marx* (Rome: Carocci, 2009); Diego Fusaro, *Bentornato Marx. Rinascita di un pensiero rivoluzionario* (Milan: Bompiani, 2009); *Lessico marxiano*, eds. Antonio Negri, Christian Marazzi, Sandro Mezzadra, Paolo Virno *et al.* (Rome: manifestolibri, 2008); and two recent works by the philosopher Costanzo Preve: *Marx inattuale. eredità e prospettiva* (Turin: Bollati Boringhieri, 2004), and *Ripensare Marx. Filosofia, idealismo, materialismo* (Potenza: Ermes, 2007).

reflections and studies he had developed over the preceding years.[6] He reaches a conclusion in which the centrality of *Capital* is silhouetted in a light that is anything but economic. He shows the substantially subaltern role of the young Marx, incapable of truly emancipating himself from his Maestro to make the step from idealism to materialism, which in the eyes of many later observers represented the authentic cipher of "Marxism of the founder." He then looks at the controversial theory of subjectivity: for Hegel the subject is fully constituted in the relationship with otherness, whereas for the young Marx it maintains a primordial organicistic nature. Thus, reflecting the materialistic conception of history (but still capable of making a decisive contribution to historical understanding of the evolution of human societies), the subject that Marx accepts at this level of elaboration leaves the individual dimension of the human being entirely out of the picture. This gives rise, in Finelli's view, to a fruitful paradox: that Marx's very indifference toward the history of the individual enabled him to reach a scientific theory of capital, "the true subject of modernity," which in its movement ignores and crushes individual subjects.[7] After the defeat of 1848, the attempt at "parricide" would thus make possible a mature approach to Hegel, helping Marx to abandon his previous "metaphysics of the subject."[8] The Marx who is critical of political economy thus gains access to a different scientific model, hinging upon the criterion of truth typical of German idealism from Fichte to Hegel, but cleansed of every metaphysical residue. Finelli defines that model in terms of the "epistemological circle of the presupposition-position": just as, for Hegel, the truth of the concept is lodged in a dialectical process that entails subsuming the whole of reality beneath it, likewise capital, as the main subject of modernity, is a real abstraction since it appropriates to itself all of its external presuppositions, transforming them into its own products. Lastly, Finelli appears to suggest, the fact that Marx dropped his early and idealistic "communism without individuals"[9] was again and sinisterly to resonate in 20th-century political Marxism.

Further developments, at different levels of interest, originality and depth, have also surrounded the thorny question of the link

---

6. R. Finelli, *Un parricidio mancato. Hegel e il giovane Marx* (Turin: Bollati Boringhieri, 2004). On the young Marx, cfr. also Mario Cingoli, *Il giovane Marx. I. (1842-1843)* (Milan: Unicopli, 2005).
7. Finelli, *Un parricidio mancato,* pp. 12–13.
8. *Ibid.,* p. 304.
9. *Ibid.,* p. 305.

with Hegelian doctrine,[10] as well as with themes of liberty and the relationship between organicism and individualism in Marx's philosophy. Ernesto Screpanti, for example, starting from some leads in North American analytical Marxism, has published a research article *in search of* a "libertarian communism," a formula that appears to offer a radical statement of substantive democracy. However, it appears debatable whether this perspective need be based on Marx's works: to achieve this goal, Marx's thought is not only split – following Althusser – between the young idealist and the social scientist, but is further subdivided. And indeed, Screpanti is clear on his method, although he does not eliminate all perplexities: he aims to found a completely new theory of liberation by making a "selective reconstruction," based on the conviction that only the "scientific core" of the Marx critical of political economy is still vital, and that for this reason all "components that are in contrast with it" should be removed from his philosophy:[11] the idealism, determinism, philosophy of history, and references to morals contained in his pre-scientific works, to which though, when necessary, Screpanti himself has recourse for some of his arguments.

Again with a philosophical approach, but paying attention to the political consequences, that is, to those inherent in the action they may trigger in the world, Luca Basso has sustained the thesis of the absolute distance of Marx from any organicistic temptation. Preferring the term "singularity" rather than "individuality" and using arguments taken from the early works, up to the *Grundrisse*, he tries to show that, from the Marxian perspective, there is neither holism nor any type of atomistic individualism, rather an attempt at "co-implication" of the various elements. He stresses that Marxian thought did not proceed in a linear manner, but that neither the enrichments nor the changes of perspective, which the author clearly sees, lead to justification of the well-known hypothesis of an epistemological break. On the contrary, Basso traces a thread of continuity through those works: the fundamental trend toward realisation of the individual in the community.[12]

Among the most stimulating analyses offered by Italian scholars, the perspective of the economist Bellofiore is noteworthy. He centers the

10. On this theme, Roberto Fineschi has made important contributions at the philological and interpretative levels, of which see in particular, *Marx e Hegel. Contributi a una rilettura* (Rome: Carocci, 2006).
11. E. Screpanti, *Comunismo libertario. Marx, Engels e l'economia politica della liberazione* (Rome: manifestolibri, 2007), p. 161.
12. L. Basso, *Socialità e isolamento: la singolarità in Marx* (Rome: Carocci, 2008).

debate on Marx around the theme of living labor, thus the notion of exploitation – a word that objectively has ethical connotations but that Marx never uses in a moral or worse moralistic sense. Bellofiore retrieves Marx's intellectual contribution as overall social science, placing the accent on the thesis of the "*monetary* constitution of the capitalistic command over *living* labor, and of the class struggle first and foremost *in the heart of production*."[13] The process of valorizing capital, in this light, does not belong exclusively to the sphere of production, because living labor is observed in both phases that involve the market: first the acquisition of labor, then the creation of surplus value. Undoubtedly, though, the way in which capitalists are enabled to use the special good that is labor is central and decisive: an important observation, because it is at this level that the capitalistic command over the work process comes into play, and the possibility of valorizing it depends in the last analysis on the class struggle and on the degree of co-operation achieved, that is, on the participation or subalternity of the workers. In this proposed interpretation, we finally see the living body of Marx, which had peeped out again and again from the whirlpool of initiatives, from the thousands of pages of commentary, from the tables of symposia on the author of the *Communist Manifesto*, but only as a dinner guest carved out of stone: the political Marx.

The so-called "political Marx," today certainly neglected, cannot be set against the economist, the philosopher or the sociologist. But it is equally true that many of the elements stressed in the Italian debate cannot be left out of any serious analysis: the contradictory, and fundamentally unfinished, nature of a reflection that was nevertheless extraordinary in terms of its depth and range; the significance of his economic formulations; his problematic relationship with the philosophy of his time. But the ethical and political dimension actually appears to be the decisive element of that critical philosophy, fundamentally guided and unified by his aspiration toward emancipation of those exploited under capitalism. If politics is removed from it, Marx would risk being reduced, at best, to the subject of continual speculations of a sort of "scholastic Marxism," in the worst case into one of the dignified, but dead, classics: dead some time after 1883 perhaps, but undoubtedly buried.

The French "Marxologist" Maximilien Rubel declared, a few years before his death, that ideas can only change other ideas; but he added, "when ideas change, they bear witness to the existence of new men.

13. R. Bellofiore, "Quelli del lavoro vivo," in Bellofiore (ed), *Da Marx a Marx?* (note 2), p. 199.

Through a critical and serious reading of Marx, it is possible today to get a real idea of today's world, and this is the first condition for being able to transform it."[14] Fifteen years later, the road to change still appears a long and a steep one: but in Italy some nevertheless appear to intend to follow it doggedly.

14. Entretien avec Maximilien Rubel [1994], in *Maximilien Rubel. Pour redécouvrir Marx*, ed. Miguel Abensour and Louis Janover (Paris: Sens & Tonka, 2008), p. 138.

Marx in Russia

Vesa Oittinen

Russia is, for easily understandable reasons, in a special position when we speak about post-1989–91 receptions of Marx. During the Soviet period, Marx was one of the chief icons of the official state ideology – Marxism-Leninism – and although the role of Lenin was in practice stressed much more than that of Marx, the fact remains that almost every Soviet citizen had adopted something from Marx and his main ideas. In this sense, most members of Russia's present-day political and scientific élite are "ex-Marxists". Such a figure as Aleksandr Jakovlev (1923–2005), "the godfather of perestroika", whom Gorbachev made the Politburo member responsible for Marxist-Leninist ideology in 1987, but who only a few years later converted into a zealous adherent of neo-liberalist economic politics, is in no way an exception among the older or middle-aged generation of present Russian leadership. Indeed, the way the seemingly all-powerful Marxist-Leninist ideology quietly evaporated after the breakdown of the Soviet Union, as if it had never existed, was one of the most striking features of the political change leading to the birth of a new Russia.

The prevailing interpretation in the West of the Soviet Union's intellectual climate is that of a rather simple dichotomy: on one side, ideological lip service to Marx and Lenin, and, on the other, critical dissidents. Soviet reality, however, was much more complicated. Non-Marxist thought was to a certain degree allowed: a good example is the case of Aleksej Losev, an adherent of *fin-de-siècle* Russian religious idealism, who after a short sentence in a labor camp in the 1930s could for the rest of his life work almost uninterruptedly on the history of ancient aesthetics. By contrast, those who took Marx seriously – i.e. non-ideologically – encountered many difficulties. The most important "critical" Marxist of the late Soviet period, Eval'd Il'enkov, committed suicide in 1974 after having been harassed for decades by Party officials. Il'enkov had been the central figure of the "Marx renaissance" in Soviet philosophy of the 1960s, a phenomenon which paralleled

Socialism and Democracy, Vol.24, No.3, November 2010, pp.187–192
ISSN 0885-4300 print/ISSN 1745-2635 online
DOI: 10.1080/08854300.2010.513628

the rediscovery of Marx in the West at the same time, but obviously was not much influenced by it.

Other names in this current include Merab Mamardashvili, who in 1968 published in the main philosophical journal of the country, *Voprosy Filosofii*, a much-debated article on the analysis of consciousness in the works of Marx, and Aleksandr Zinov'ev, whose dissertation[1] on the method of rising from the abstract to the concrete in Marx's *Capital*[2] was written as early as 1954, only one year after Stalin's death. Although this work circulated only in some hectographed copies, it had a big impact, and it paved the way for perhaps the most important publication of this early Soviet "Marx renaissance", Il'enkov's *Dialectics of the Abstract and the Concrete in Marx's "Capital"* (1960).[3] This book, which won the esteemed Chernyshevski Prize, was quite an event and nurtured hopes of a renewal of Marxist thought in the Soviet Union. These expectations did not, however, come true. The advent of Brezhnev regime at the end of the 1960s – a period later to be called the "era of stagnation" – created an atmosphere hostile to critical and innovative thinking and led to a reinforcement of ideological control of society. The Soviet philosophers who in the first half of the 1960s were still keenly interested in Marx, withdrew into private and non-official spheres. Mamardashvili, although he later had good contacts with such Western Marxists as Althusser, developed his own, highly idiosyncratic philosophy, while Zinov'ev concentrated on formal logic and soon emigrated. This frustration and disappointment regarding the possibilities of Marxism characterized the Soviet 1970s and 1980s. Gorbachev could justly lament, at the beginning of *perestroika*, that Marxist social theory had not been developed at all in the Soviet Union during the last decades. Above all, Marxism had not been used in the analysis of the Soviet society itself, and so it was easy for the "reformers" of the Yeltsin era to discard Marx as a completely unsuitable thinker for modern societies.

Although the renunciation of Marx in the new Russia in the early 1990s was nearly total – typically, the hundreds of chairs of Marxism-

1. That is, the so-called "kandidatskaja dissertatsija", which roughly corresponds to the PhD thesis in the West.
2. A.A. Zinov'ev, *Voskhozhdenie ot abstraktnogo k konkretnomu (na materiale "Kapitala" K. Marksa)*, "avtoreferat", Moscow 1954; published in book form by the Institute of Philosophy of the Russian Academy of Sciences in 2002.
3. E.V. Il'enkov, *Dialektika abstraktnogo i konkretnogo v "Kapitale" Marksa*, Moscow 1960; a new edition, containing the passages removed from the first version by the publisher, appeared in 1997 (Moscow: ROSSPEN, 464 pp.)

Leninism in the universities were almost overnight re-baptized as chairs of "culturology" so that the professors could remain in their jobs - there soon emerged, nonetheless, some strains of independent and critical Marx research.[4] Above all, the MEGA publishing project was saved from catastrophe, and it continued in a new form under the changed circumstances.[5] But although several distinguished Russian Marx scholars - such as Georgij Bagaturija and Irina Antonova - continue their work in the new MEGA project, their influence on the general academic or intellectual atmosphere is very restricted.

The same can be said of such Marx scholars as Viktor Vazjulin of Moscow Lomonosov University, who has patiently built up an entire school of Marx interpretation, the so-called "logico-historical school". At first sight, Vazjulin seems to continue the tradition of Il'enkov in stressing the importance of studying the method of Marx's *Capital*, but he quite ambitiously sees in the "logic" of Marx's *chef-d'oeuvre* a key to the whole of world history. The Vazjulin school does not have many supporters in Russia itself, but it flourishes in the University of Crete, where some of Vazjulin's previous Greek students now teach.[6] Another noteworthy Marx scholar in present-day Russia is Andrej Ballaev, who in 2004 published a collection of "Marxological" essays, *Chitaja Marksa* (Reading Marx).[7] The book consists of analyses of the works of the young Marx, especially of Marx's reception of Stirner in the mid-1840s, and of the concept of ideology in Marx. According to Ballaev, Stirner exerted more influence upon Marx than generally assumed.

A more substantial attempt to renew Marx scholarship is that of the group around the Moscow economics professor Aleksandr Buzgalin. Since the demise of the Soviet Union, Buzgalin has been an active protagonist of leftist politics and globalization critique. He is one of the founders of the journal *Alternativy*, published since 1991. The movement around the journal is one of the most serious modern Left projects

4. See, for example, Alex Levant, *The Soviet Union in Ruins* (Saarbrücken: VDM Verlag Dr. Müller, 2008), a report on how fragments from the Soviet past and attempts to build new forms of Marxism merge in present-day Russia.
5. For details about the reorganization of the MEGA publishing project, see e.g. Jürgen Rojahn, *Publishing Marx and Engels after 1989: The Fate of the MEGA*, www.iisg.nl/imes/documents/mega-e98.pdf.
6. For more information, see the homepage of the "Vazjulinians" at www.ilhs.tuc.gr/en/index.htm. Vazjulin's main works are *Logika "Kapitala" Karla Marksa* (Moscow: izd. MGU 1968; 2nd ed. 2002) and *Logika istorii* (Moscow: izd. MGU 1988; rev. ed. 2005). Among his Greek pupils, who have published mostly in Greek, are Dimitrios Patelis and P. Pavlidis.
7. A. Ballaev, *Chitaja Marksa* (Moscow: Praksis, 2004).

in present-day Russia, in sharp contrast to the Communist Party of Russia led by Gennadij Zjuganov, which in fact is not at all a Marxist but rather a "social-patriotic" movement.[8] In recent years, the Alternativy group has begun to speak of itself as representing the "Post-Soviet School of Critical Marxism"[9] and to see its task as the adaptation of Marx's theory and methodology and the application of Marxian analysis of capitalism in present circumstances characterized by the restoration of capitalism in Russia and the new type of global problems.[10] Although the Buzgalin group may be the most important single phenomenon in the kaleidoscope of post-Soviet Russian Marxism, some of its theoretical stances have been criticized as too abstract or even as declamatory formulations typical of the old Soviet frame of mind.[11] The Buzgalin group is not the only Marx-oriented association in Russia today. Supporters of the theoretical legacy of Evald Il'enkov are a further movement worth noting; they organize annual "Il'enkov Readings" where often more than a hundred papers are presented.[12]

8. This is not the place to analyze the ideology of the Zjuganov party (Communist Party of the Russian Federation, CPRF) in depth, so suffice it to say that it in fact has replaced the Marxism-Leninism of the old CPSU with a geopolitical worldview not unlike Samuel Huntington's theories of the clash of civilizations. In this context, socialism is no longer seen as a universal alternative to capitalism, but rather as a solution suitable especially for Russia's geopolitical circumstances. Correspondingly, the Bolshevik leaders and Lenin are not viewed as protagonists of an international workers' and socialist movement, but instead as "great figures" of the Russian past. It is obvious that such a "foreigner" as Marx has difficulty finding a place in the nationalist pantheon of the Zjuganovites. Some researches have compared the CPRF with such populist movements as the Argentine Peronists. For a more detailed analysis of the CPRF ideology, see e.g. my article, "Ein populistischer Zwitter. Rußlands KP zwischen Leninismus und Staatspatriotismus", in: *Blätter für deutsche und internationale Politik* 8/1995, 946–56.
9. A German translation of their manifesto has been published by the Rosa Luxemburg Foundation: A. V. Buzgalin, A. I. Kolganov, *Postsowjetischer Marxismus in Russland: Antworten auf die Herausforderungen des XXI. Jahrhunderts. Thesen zur Formierung einer wissenschaftlichen Schule,* trans. Günter Mayer, Michael Dewey, Ingrid Mayer, and Gerhard Rüdiger (Berlin: Rosa Luxemburg Foundation, 2007).
10. The themes are further developed in several books edited by A. V. Buzgalin, the most recent of which are *Marksizm: Alternativy XX veka (debaty postsovetskoj shkoly kriticheskogo marksizma)* (Moscow: URSS ed., 2009), and (together with A. I. Kolganov), *Predely kapitala: metodologija i ontologija* (Moscow: Kul'turnaja revoljutsija, 2009).
11. For a thoroughgoing analysis of the authors of the Buzgalin/Kolgunov group, see Günter Mayer and Wolfgang Küttler, "Postsowjetische Marxisten in Russland", in: *UTOPIE Kreativ*, 201/202, July-August 2007, 740–63. As far as I know, the Buzgalin group members have not reacted to the critique of Mayer and Küttler.
12. See e.g. the Il'enkov web page hosted by Prof. Andrei Maidanskij, at: www.caute.net.ru/ilyenkov/eng/index.htm. One of the most prominent Il'enkovians is Prof. Sergei Mareev of Moscow, who recently published a book *Iz istorii sovetskogo*

One of the most interesting post-Soviet Marxists in Russia at the moment is Vadim Mezhuev (b. 1933), a theoretician of culture, who has some contacts to the Buzgalin group but works at the Institute of Philosophy of the Russian Academy of Sciences. In 2007, he published a polemical book *Marks protiv marksizma* (Marx against Marxism), in which he reproached Soviet science and philosophy as not recognizing at all what kind of thinker Marx really was. Step by step, Mezhuev attempted to deconstruct ideological clichés of Soviet interpretations, such as the hardened thesis that Marx should in all his analyses have followed the scheme of four or possibly five economic formations. According to Mezhuev, Marx's concept of socialism has nothing to do with the "Real Socialism" of the Soviet era, but refers to the "realm of freedom" beyond the economic formation (i.e. material production) and consists thus of wealth from which the "restricted bourgeois form" has been removed, as Marx famously wrote in the *Grundrisse*. Mezhuev seems to think that a Marxist theory of culture could be created on the basis of this interpretation.[13]

Another important publication trying to deconstruct the Soviet-era interpretation of Marx is Teodor Ojzerman's *Marksizm i utopizm* (2003). Ojzerman, born in 1914 but still active, was in the Soviet period a noted expert in Marx's philosophy. His books on the subject, especially *Formirovanie filosofii marksizma* (Moscow 1963, 2nd ed. 1977)[14] were probably the best analyses of Marx's philosophical thought that the Soviet literature could offer. They were, however, burdened with the usual ideological clichés, and so Ojzerman decided after the demise of the USSR to publish a critique of Soviet Marxism which at the same time was a self-criticism. Ojzerman's analysis of the over-ideologized Soviet picture of Marx is in many ways similar to Mezhuev's, but is more systematic, going scrupulously through all

---

marksizma. Lukach – Vygotskij – Il'enkov (Moscow: Kul'turnaja revoljutsija 2008) trying to show that there existed in the Soviet period a subterranean current of creative Marxism in philosophy. Lately, there have been disputes among the Il'enkovians and it seems that they are splitting into two camps.

13. Vadim Mezhuev, *Marks protiv marksizma* (Moscow: Kul'turnaja revoljutsija, 2007). Of course, Mezhuev's attempt to distinguish between alienated production in the sphere of the "economic formation" and non-alienated cultural production becomes problematic if applied too strictly, and leads to a kind of Kantian dualism where the "realm of freedom" slides into the transcendent. I have analyzed Mezhuev's conception in a review in *Voprosy Filosofii* 3/2009, 176–79, and the philosophical journal *Logos* is preparing a thematic issue on Mezhuev and his interpretation of Marx.
14. German translation: *Die Entstehung der marxistischen Philosophie* (Berlin: Dietz, 1965), English translation: *The Making of the Marxist Philosophy* (Moscow: Progress, 1981).

the claims of both "Diamat" and "Histmat" [dialectical and historical materialism] to interpret Marx's ideas (such as the famous metaphor of "base and superstructure") and comparing them with the authentic formulations of Marx. Interestingly enough, the Marx which remains after all ideological additions have been stripped, is for Ojzerman essentially the Marx of *Grundrisse,* whose humanistic message did not consist in any prophecies of a future communist society, but in the idea of Man as the "main productive force".[15] Both Ojzerman and Mezhuev thus see the foundations of a future Marxist humanism in the *Grundrisse,* which in itself is already a remarkable shift in the many-faceted history of Russian and Soviet interpretations of Marx.

Although the new receptions of Marx in Russia are still fragmentary and disparate, it is beyond doubt that Russia has the potential to become one of the leading centers of a new Marx research and interpretations of Marxism. This supposes, however, an ability to cope in a critical manner with the immense heritage of Soviet Marxism – that is, a "deconstruction" of the Diamat and Histmat traditions.

15. T.I. Ojzerman, *Marksizm i utopizm* (Moscow: Progress, 2003), pp. 193, 595. Marx speaks of Man as the *Hauptproduktivkraft* e.g. in *Grundrisse* (Berlin: Dietz, 1972), p. 325.

Marx in China

Daping Hu

The latest global conditions are changing people's attitudes toward Marxism. Chinese and others are in the same boat; *Capital* and its manuscripts become the focus. But then, as an existing socialist country, China faces difficulty in formulating its Marxist discourses, because its reform and opening-up practice of the last 30 years has produced critical diversities of social structure and ideology.

What is happening in China today might be called re-Marxization, i.e., adding a new dimension to Marxist theories. If we consider Chinese reception of Marx as the Sinicization of Marxism, then re-Marxization goes in a different direction, which is the incorporation of China into the global capitalist system after construction of the market economy since the mid-1990s. Re-Marxization means that many Chinese Marxist scholars are beginning to reconsider Marx's critique of modern capitalism in a different way under the condition of market and globalization. In comparison with dominant ideology, it means: (1) there will be an emphasis on socialism with Chinese characteristics; (2) Marxism will be studied more as the critique of capitalism than as a guide to socialism; (3) if the process by which Marxism became the dominant ideology was the Marxization of old China, then re-Marxization demonstrates theoretically a new phase of Chinese modernization. Here I will review some characteristics of this new trend.

First, both Western and Chinese scholars have been puzzled by the theory of socialism with Chinese characteristics. In recent international representations of China, we find conflicting arguments. For example, Harvey views China – based on its recent economic and social performance – as neoliberalism "with Chinese characteristics,"[1] while Arrighi saw the Chinese path to opulence ("Smithian growth") as a universal economic model from a long historical perspective.[2] Similar differences exist among Chinese scholars. Most Chinese have

1. David Harvey, *A Brief History of Neoliberalism* (New York: Oxford UP 2005).
2. Giovanni Arrighi, *Adam Smith in Beijing* (London: Verso 2007).

Socialism and Democracy, Vol.24, No.3, November 2010, pp.193–197
ISSN 0885-4300 print/ISSN 1745-2635 online
DOI: 10.1080/08854300.2010.513621

acknowledged that there is no single and homogeneous China. On the one hand, there is an obvious gap between practice (the market) and theory (socialism). And on the other, there are two different Marxist discourses: ideological and non-ideological (or academic). More important, we can't usually distinguish one from the other. Under such conditions, as a new trend, re-Marxization is just one possible future for Chinese Marxist theories.

Second, its origins and formations. As we know, there have always been two different paths of Marxian studies in China. One is of that of professional Marxist researchers who focus on the meta-theories of Marx, reading original texts and constructing the Principal System (official textbook) and its Chinese form (developed by Chinese revolutionary leaders as the Sinicization of Marxism). The other is that of scholars from diverse fields who use Marxism as a method. Re-Marxization has the same dual aspect, although both dimensions reflect the changing post-Cultural Revolution reality. While all kinds of long-term socialist goals (such as egalitarianism) were never abandoned, reform with the direct goal of economic development has inevitably brought some significant social and ideological problems centering on inequality. In the official narrative, this is the consequence of concentrating on economic and neglecting social and ideological development, that is, "predominance of efficiency over equality." Against this background, mainstream morality and theory (including some Marxist discourse, especially in economics) advocate the market economy. But social problems in China have become more serious. Re-Marxization has therefore emerged as an official hope distinct from Sinicization. This new trend seeks to reframe world history as the basis of China's market-oriented modernization.

We find a serious theoretical problem here. If Marxism calls for a market economy, then what kind of relation can exist between its role in critiquing capitalism and its role as the guide to socialism? This question became the starting-point for reinterpretation of Marx in the field of meta-theoretical research. Of course, Chinese Marxists, unlike some Western scholars, do not regard China today as a capitalist society. Most of them try to create a new discourse using such concepts as textology (textual critique), fetishism, Western Marxism, and the critique of modernity. In the mid-1990s, the slogan of "Back to Marx" was popular in the Chinese academy. Under this slogan – which means an authentic Marx different from its popular images, especially the one constructed by standard textbooks – many scholars began to criticize the Principal Textbook which was initiated under Stalin. What could be the authentic Marx? Most scholars regard Marxism as a critique of modernity. Certainly, Chinese scholars replace capitalism with modernity. In so doing, they evade the ideological problem posed by the official consensus on the nature of the Chinese economy (as being at once market-based and socialist). By the same token, they consider the theory of fetishism as the center of Marxism (in line with Western Marxism following Lukács's *History and Class Consciousness*).

Zhang Yibing (of Nanjing University) is one of the philosophers who interpret Marxism along the subjective path. He insists that Marxian historical dialectics has its subjective dimension, whose aim is to criticize the supposed naturalness of the modern capitalist economy.[3] He criticizes economic determinism and develops textological perspectives. Finally, he regards the latest form of Marxism as historical phenomenology or historical epistemology, aimed at criticizing capitalist logic and its consequences.[4] A research team based on Zhang's program has played a key role in China; its recent achievement is the six-volume *History of Understanding Capitalism*.[5] Wu Xiaoming (of Fudan University) is the most important of the philosophers who try to interpret Marx in relation to Western philosophical tradition. He sees Marx's major contribution as his critique of this tradition's internal logic. Therefore, he develops Marx's critique of modernity in ways similar to Heidegger. The Fudan group is one of the most influential groups for Marxist studies in China today. Other key research includes the construction of cultural philosophy based on Western Marxism.

All efforts at reconstructing Marx's perspective try to use it to address social problems of China today. Bourgeoisification (positivization or neoliberalization) of economics and sociology received official support ten years ago. Something important has changed since then. Many scholars recognize that it is necessary to rediscover the Marxist base for social research, and some of them have tried to develop Marx's theory to reveal contradictions of current Chinese society based on capital production. For example, the sociological research team in Tsinghua University (including Sun Liping and Shen Yuan, *et al.*) is trying to develop a Marxist sociological perspective similar to Michael Burawoy's. Scholars in Shanghai represented by Wang Xiaoming have applied this in several topic areas, such as the

3. Zhang Yibing, *The Subjective Dimension of Marxian Historical Dialectics* (Nanjing: Nanjing University Press 2002).
4. Zhang Yibing, *Back to Marx: Philosophical Discourse in the Context of Economics* (Nanjing: Jiangsu People's Publishing House 1999).
5. Zhang Yibing (ed.), *The History of Understanding Capitalism* (Nanjing: Jiangsu People's Publishing House 2009).

changes of working-class lifestyle in Shanghai, the modern metropolis, and popular culture. Some of their books and papers have profiled the new ideology in China today.[6] A more complex trend is the so-called Chinese New Left, which consists of various scholars and popular thinkers. Although as a theoretical movement it is not strictly Marxist, it has affected the reception of Marx since 2000. Wang Hui, Cui Zhiyuan, and Zuo Dapei are outstanding representatives.

Although there is no dialogue among the above trends, all of them are obviously changing Chinese attitudes to Marxism, and building a new theoretical basis for the re-reception and re-understanding of Marx.

Third, potential long-term effects of re-Marxization on theories and reality. The new trend not only embodies a reception of Marx different from the official one; it also opens many dimensions of Marxism for the Chinese people and is improving relations between Chinese Marxists and their Western colleagues, such as the international New Left, New Social Movements, etc. Today, most Chinese Marxist scholars have accepted Marx as the prophet and critic of capitalist globalization and crisis (from economic to political and ecological). They are not going "beyond" Marx's theory; they still view Marxism as the most powerful theoretical instrument to analyze modern economic development and its limits. They see the logic of *Capital* and the *Grundrisse* as more important than their political conclusions. They find Marxism's greatest promise in discovering the nature of current capitalist globalization and in confronting neoliberalism. At the new starting-point, we can imagine that Chinese Marxists will share more and more concerns and interests with their Western colleagues, and will develop a more distinctive local Marxist discourse than they had before.

Finally, difficulties and problems. As we know, the bases for reinterpretation and reconstruction of critical theory are (empirically) the facts of capitalist globalization and (theoretically) *Capital* and the *Grundrisse*. There is no distance between Chinese and Western scholars in the first aspect, but the Chinese will face some special problems in the second aspect. The most important thing is that neoliberal economics has dominated the interpretation of *Capital* supported by Chinese market practice. If *Capital* is reread as the framework for building a market economy, then Chinese Marxist theories will lose their basic function of finding the real new world by criticizing the old

6. Wang Xiaoming, *In the New Ideological Aura* (Nanjing: Jiangsu People's Publishing House 2002).

one. Were this the case, Chinese Marxism would be limited to configuring a "spiritual civilization";[7] but this is virtually impossible. Gaining a deeper historical and a broader global perspective for the reception of Marx in China today is just one aspect of the whole question; the point is still to change the logic of capital.

7. "Spiritual civilization" is the simplified formulation of the aim to build a socialist society that is culturally and ideologically advanced, which was raised by CPC after 1949. The CPC has always held that material progress will suffer delays and setbacks unless it promotes cultural and ethical progress as well, and China can never succeed in revolution and construction if it relies on material conditions alone. But, when market economy becomes the basis of Chinese society, this aim is challenged.

Marx in South Korea

Seongjin Jeong

Marxist scholarship is currently reviving in Korea[1] after about two decades' retreat since the 1990s. The recent opening of a graduate school specializing in Marxist studies[2] is a reflection of this. Korea has a long history of socialist thought and politics, starting from its colonial period (1910–45), but several factors have played a role in the current renaissance of Marxism. First, the completion of the cycle of two oscillating variants of capitalism, Keynesian-statist and neoliberal, with its traumatic results, above all, the East Asian Crisis in 1997 and subsequent deepening of social polarization, was enough to fracture the neoliberal-Keynesian consensus around TINA (the view that "there is no alternative" to capitalism) and reawaken the search for alternatives. Second, the fading away of Stalinism, which had historically framed the development of Marxist scholarship and politics in Korea, paved the way for a new start after the time lag.

Marx's works were first introduced to Korea during the colonial period. They were mainly imported from Japan by radical Korean intellectuals, who received and utilized them as the theoretical weapons for the national liberation struggle. However, it was extremely difficult for Koreans to study Marx's works in this period, because the colonial rulers forbade the free discussion and publication of radical literature. Among the few Marxist academic works then published, Baik Nam-Un's book on the economic history of Korea[3] was notable, though it was written in Japanese and was merely a mechanical application of Stalin's five-stage scheme of historical development to the Korean case.

---

1. I am thankful to Marcello Musto for his encouragement and help writing this paper. In this paper, the expression Korea is used to indicate either South Korea (Republic of Korea) or the Korean peninsula as a whole. However, North Korea (Democratic People's Republic of Korea) is always indicated as North Korea. The titles of Korean-language and Japanese-language works are given here in English.
2. Department of Political Economy at Gyeongsang National University, http://marxism.gnu.ac.kr
3. Baik Nam-Un, *Korean Socio-Economic History* (Tokyo: Kaizosa, 1933).

Socialism and Democracy, Vol.24, No.3, November 2010, pp.198–204
ISSN 0885-4300 print/ISSN 1745-2635 online
DOI: 10.1080/08854300.2010.513627

As soon as Korea was liberated from Japanese rule in 1945, socialist publications exploded in Seoul and Pyongyang. Hundreds of socialist books, journals, and newspapers poured out, including first official Korean editions of *The Communist Manifesto* and *Capital*.[4] However, the first short "Spring of Marxism" was brutally repressed in South Korea with the establishment of the anti-communist government of Rhee Syngman in 1948. In the meantime, the North Korean regime allowed Marxist scholarship to the extent that it was of use for its rule, and published the first complete Korean edition of Marx's *Capital* during 1956–59 as well as *Marx Engels Collected Works [MECW]* during 1961–65.[5] However, serious Marxist scholarship phased out in North Korea with the rise of *Juche*, the extreme version of national communism. After the Korean War, not just socialist politics but also academic studies on Marx were severely repressed in South Korea under the anti-communist dictatorships of Rhee Syngman (1948–60), Park Chung Hee (1961–79), and Chun Doo Hwan (1980–87). Even just carrying Marx's books was punished by more than two years in prison. Progressive scholars who wanted to study Marxism in this period had no way but to do so under such rubrics as dependency theory, the Frankfurt School, or alienation in "early Marx."

Marxism flourished in Korea after the Kwangju People's Uprising in 1980 and the Great Democratic Struggles of 1987. The Anti-Communist Law could not prevent the sudden and explosive growth of publication of Marxist literature which began in the mid-1980s. The government's arrest and acquittal of Kim Tae-Gyeong, president of the publisher of the first volume of *Capital* in 1987[6] was the turning point. About 70 Korean versions of various works of Marx and Engels were published during 1987–1991.[7] Reflecting the rise of anti-systemic movements in this period, Marxist books tended to concentrate on issues of revolutionary praxis rather than academic topics. Also, the academic quality of the publications and translations was not good; the first complete South Korean edition of *Capital* was not even based on the German original.[8]

---

4. At this time, only Volume 1 and 2 of *Capital* were translated from the Japanese edition.
5. The publication of the North Korean edition of *MECW* seems to have been discontinued after only 10 volumes were translated from the Russian edition.
6. Karl Marx, *Capital*, Vol.1, trans. Kim Young-Min (Seoul: IhRonGwaShilCheon, 1987).
7. Chung Moon-Gil, *Contours of Marxology in Korea* (Seoul: MunHakGwaJiSungSa, 2004).
8. Karl Marx, *Capital*, 3 vols, trans. Kim Soohaeng (Seoul: BiBong Publisher, 1989–90). However, a direct translation, by Kang Shin-Joon, published by IhRonGwaShilCheon (1987–90), was completed soon thereafter.

The most unfortunate aspect of this second "Spring of Marxism,"[9] though seldom recognized by contemporary Korean progressives, was that what South Korean radicals rediscovered was actually some versions of Stalinism rather than classical Marxist tradition. Indeed, many Korean progressives rushed to embrace various official communist parties' textbooks as "orthodox" Marxism during the 1980s, after they disowned their earlier intellectual influences, such as the Frankfurt School or dependency theory. "Rediscovery of Marxism" reached its high point during late 1980s when the two variants of Stalinism, PD (the People's Democracy tendency, which regarded the USSR as model socialism) and NL (the National Liberation tendency, which followed Kim Il-Sung's *Juche*), debated furiously around the characterization of Korean society and related revolutionary strategies. While PD conceived Korea as embodying neo-colonial state monopoly capitalism, requiring an anti-imperial and anti-monopoly-capital people's democratic revolution, NL argued for the anti-imperial and anti-semi-feudal people's democratic revolution to overthrow a colonial semi-feudal Korea. Yoon So-Young, a leading theoretician of PD, summarized the position of PD as the formula of "strengthening monopoly *cum* deepening dependency."[10] However, it was obvious from the start that both tendencies shared fatal theoretical defects, such as economic determinism, catastrophism and stagism. As the extreme detachedness of both versions of Stalinism became clear with the development of Korean capitalism, the terrain of the debate itself could not but implode even before the collapse of Stalinist regimes in 1989.

Because most Korean progressives of the 1980s had viewed the Stalinist regimes as the actualization of Marxism, regardless of their degeneration, it was natural that they threw away not just Stalinism but also Marxist tradition as a whole after their disintegration. The second "Spring of Marxism" was as short-lived as the first one. It mutated into various kinds of reformism via post-Marxism. The conversions of Yi Jin-Kyung[11] and Lee Byung-Cheon, prominent theorists of PD during 1980s, to Deleuzian postmodernism were only typical examples. In this period of disillusionment and confusion, *Theory*, a quarterly Marxist journal, launched by a "united front" of a dozen Marxist scholars, stretching from Althusserians to Trotskyists, played

9. If the first "Spring" for Marxism was 1945–48, the second was 1987–91.

10. Lee Byung-Cheon and Yoon So-Young, "Trends and Tasks of Post-war Studies in Economics in Korea," *Current Stage and Prospects of Humanities and Social Sciences in Korea* (Seoul: YeokSaBiPyungSa, 1988).

11. Yi Jin-Kyung was also a leading theoretician of PD. See his *Theory of Social Formations and Methodology of Social Sciences* (Seoul: AhChim, 1987).

a significant role in checking the wholesale drift to Post-Marxism during the 1990s, as did the publication of complete Korean editions of *Ausgewählte Werke in sechs Bänden* (Berlin: Dietz Verlag, 1970-72)[12] and the *Grundrisse*.[13] The rehabilitation of Trotsky was also one of the small positive spin-offs of the demise of Stalinist regimes for Korean progressives. However, the main trend was irresistibly submission to postmodernism, post-Marxism and TINA ("There Is No Alternative [to capitalism]"), and immersion in the so-called immaterial world of globalization.

The East Asian Crisis of 1997 was a moment of awakening for Korean progressives to the forgotten contradictions of capitalism, emphasized by Marx. Deepening social polarization and inequality under the neoliberal assault on working people after the crisis provided fertile ground for the "return to Marx." The Democratic Labor Party, which openly called for democratic socialism, won parliamentary seats in 2003. Although reformists still dominated the progressive parties, some even joining the neoliberal governments of Kim Dae-Jung (1998–2002) and Roh Mu-hyun (2003–07), serious attempts at Marxist renewal were made after the crisis. These included the launching of *Radical Review*, a successor of *Theory*, in 1999 and inauguration of *Marxcommunale*, a biennial anti-capitalist conference, in 2003.

The changed mood of Korean radicals could be sensed when Yi Jin-Kyung returned to Marx after a decade-long odyssey to postmodernism.[14] However, as is evident in his concepts like "mechanical surplus value," Yi chose to keep the postmodernist baggage. Eventually, Yi identified himself with Communalism or Autonomism.[15] Yoon So-Young, who had retreated to Althusserian philosophy during 1990s, resumed publishing a series of books on Marx, around the work of his GwaCheon Research Center. Yoon tried to extend Marx's critique of political economy by incorporating the profit-rate economics of Gérard Duménil and the historical sociology of Giovanni Arrighi and applying them to the analysis of alterglobalization movements and the current global financial crisis.[16] Jeong Seongjin also tried to

12. Kim Se-Kyun ed, *Selected Works of Karl Marx and Friedrich Engels*, 6 vols (Seoul: Park-JongChull Publisher, 1991–97). Kim also published a book on Marxist analysis of Korean labor politics, *Democracy and Workers and Peoples' Politics in Korea* (Seoul: HyunJangEhSeoMiRaeReul, 1997).
13. Karl Marx, *Grundrisse*, trans. Kim Ho-Gyun (Seoul: BaikEui, 2000).
14. Yi Jin-Kyung, *Capital beyond Capital* (Seoul: EeWho, 2006); *Future Marxism* (Seoul: GreeBee, 2006).
15. Ko Byung-Kwon *et al.*, *Communalist Manifesto* (Seoul: GyoYangIn, 2007).

contribute to the return to Marx in Korea in his two books on Trotsky's political economy and empirical Marxian analysis of the Korean economy.[17]

Among various disciplines of Marxist scholarship, economics has been traditionally strong in Korea. Korean Marxist economists played a crucial role in founding the Korean Social and Economic Association (KSESA), equivalent to the Union for Radical Political Economics, in 1987, though they lost the hegemony to Keynesian heterodox economists after 1991. The favorite area of Korean Marxist economists has been Marx's value theory.[18] Some of them published their works in prominent international journals. Lee Chai-on's "Single-System Interpretation" of Marx's transformation theory and Rieu Dong-Min's intervention in the debates on the Okishio Theorem are notable.[19] They also tried to apply Marxian value theory to understanding the information technology revolution. For example, Kang Nam-hun's attempt to define the value of "information goods" as the socially necessary labor to produce a "version" rather than its copy, ignited a big controversy,[20] where Chai Man-Soo intervened and argued that there is no substance of value in "information goods" and their price is just a monopoly price.[21]

Marx's crisis theory has been the central research topic for Korean Marxists especially after the East Asian Crisis in 1997. Notable among them is Kim Soohaeng, who tried to develop Ben Fine's interpretation of Marx's law of the falling tendency of the rate of profit by linking it with some Japanese Marxist crisis

---

16. Yoon So-Young, *Marx's Capital* (Seoul: GongGam, 2009); *Generalized Marxism and Alternative Left* (Seoul: GongGam, 2008); *2007–2009 Financial Crisis* (Seoul: GongGam, 2009).
17. Jeong Seongjin, *Marx and Trotsky* (Seoul: Hanul, 2006); *Marx and the Korean Economy* (Seoul: ChaikGalPhi, 2005).
18. For example, refer to Korea Social and Economic Studies Association, ed., *Studies in Theories of Value* (Seoul: PulBit, 1995).
19. Lee Chai-on fully developed his "Single System Interpretation" in his *New Discovery of Marxian Political Economy* (Kwangju: Chonnam National University Press, 2008). Rieu Dong-Min, "Has the Okishio Theorem been Refuted?" *Metroeconomica*, Vol. 60, No. 1 (2009).
20. Kang Nam-hun, *Political Economy of the Information Revolution* (Seoul: MunHwa-GwaHakSa, 2002); Kang Nam-hun *et al.*, eds, *Debates on the Value of Information Goods* (Osan: Hanshin University Press, 2007).
21. Chai Man-Soo is one of few remaining Stalinists in Korea and upholds the thesis of state monopoly capitalism. As late as 2006 Chai published a Korean equivalent of the CPSU's textbook on political economy: *Workers' Introduction to Economics* (Seoul: Workers' Institute of Social Science, 2006).

theories.[22] However, against Kim and Fine's falling-profit-rate approach to crisis, Kim Seong-Gu recently argued that the current crisis should be understood through Marx's theory of cyclical overproduction.[23]

Compared to economics, Marxism has been much more marginalized in other areas of social science and humanities. The effects of the postmodern fad after the demise of communism were especially virulent and are yet to be overcome. Even after the ebb of postmodernism, most progressive philosophers or literary critics leaned toward Autonomism instead of classical Marxism. Indeed, Autonomism-related ideas seem to win some currency in Korea after 2000.[24] For example, Park Seung-Ho attempted to reconstruct Marxist theories of modern capitalism around the concept of commodity fetishism, drawing upon the Open Marxism of John Holloway.[25]

Despite the significant advances since its rediscovery in 1987, Marxist scholarship in Korea still leaves a lot to be desired. First of all, there has not yet been any serious attempt to publish the complete Korean edition of *MECW*. Considering the disproportionate strength of Marxist scholarship in economics in Korea, it is a shame that the complete Korean edition of *Theories of Surplus Value* has yet to be published. It has something to do with the fact that Marxism in Korea is disappointingly underdeveloped in its basics, such as Marxology, compared to its application and politics. Marx has always been read politically or tendentiously and in liaison with Marxism, Lenin, etc. In this respect, Chung Moon-Gil's meticulous philological works on the historiography of *MECW* and Yahng Hee-Seok's judicious study on the relation between Hegel's dialectic and Marx's method in *Capital* are precious exceptions.[26]

---

22. Kim Soohaeng, *Economic Crisis and Panic in Capitalist Society* (Seoul: Seoul National University Press, 2006). Kim had taught Marx's *Capital* at Seoul National University, the top university in Korea, and supervised a dozen PhD students specializing in Marxist economics.
23. Kim Seong-Gu, "A Criticism on the Theory of Falling Rate of Profit from a Methodological Perspective," *MARXISM 21*, Vol. 7, No. 1 (2010).
24. Joe Jeong-Hwan is a leading theoretician of Autonomism in Korea. See his *Autonomia* (Seoul: GalMuRi, 2003).
25. Park Seung-Ho, *Critical Reconstruction of Theories of Modern Capitalism of the Left* (Seoul: Hanul, 2004).
26. Chung Moon-Gil, *Nibelung's Treasure* (Seoul: MunHakGwaJiSungSa, 2008); Yahng Hee-Seok, "Hegel and the Labor Theory of Value," *MARXISM 21*, Vol. 2, No. 2 (2005).

Considering the recent growth of counter-hegemonic institutional capacities for Marxism in Korea, such as the launching of several Marxist journals[27] as well as radical left political organizations, it is not mere wishful thinking to suggest that the third "Spring of Marxism" is just around the corner. Of course, for this to happen, progressive social movements and solidarity, which have been somewhat weakened under the recent neoliberal assaults of the Lee Myung-bak government, need to be rebuilt. Marxist scholarship in Korea needs to share in this task if it hopes to benefit from it.

27. Among them, *MARXISM 21*, launched in 2004, *Revolutionary Socialist*, launched in 2008, *Studies in Workers' Social Science*, launched in 2008, and *Marx 21*, launched in 2009, are important.

Marx in Japan

Hiroshi Uchida

Marx scholarship in Japan dates from the beginning of the 20th century. The *Communist Manifesto* was translated into Japanese in 1904 by Shusui Kotoku and Toshihiko Sakai, in the context of a socialist movement arising in the early years of Japanese industrialization. By the time of the Fifteen Year War period (1931–45), when government censorship became very strict, most of the works of Marx and Engels had been translated into Japanese, while Marx scholars debated whether Japanese capitalism was modern or was still half-feudal.

Japanese capitalism miraculously revived and developed in the post-war period (1955–73). Marxian economists debated whether the "dual structure" of the economy – a few big businesses and a huge sector of small or middle-scale workshops – would restrain or accelerate economic development. High technology largely spared Japan the effects of the oil shocks of 1973 and 1979, while the US and European economies were suffering from "stagflation." The Toyota system as a symbol of Japanese economic leadership interested Marx scholars in comparison with Fordism. Since the Japan bubble of the 1990s, however, Japanese society has been trying to move from an econo-centric way of life to a post-econo-centric society.

Japanese Marx scholarship encompasses a vast field of topics, including basic philological and theoretical studies, showing Marx in the light of history of political economy, philosophy, and the socialist movement, studying Marx's life, and developing his economic theory to encompass present-day capitalism. The financial crisis of 2008 occasioned many public meetings and university conferences on Marx. *Capital* is being widely reread. There has been a general flourishing of Marx scholarship since the 1990s.

The newspaper *Asahi shimbun*[1] reports a Marx revival in Japan. Many books on Marx have appeared, including Tatsuru Uchida and

1. August 23, 2010

Socialism and Democracy, Vol.24, No.3, November 2010, pp.205–211
ISSN 0885-4300 print/ISSN 1745-2635 online
DOI: 10.1080/08854300.2010.529729

Yasuhiro Ishikawa's *Let Us Read Marx, Young People*[2] and a new translation by Hiroshi Hasegawa of the *Economic-Philosophical Manuscripts of 1844.*[3] The complete *Marx-Engels Werke* have already been translated into Japanese and published by Otsukishoten, and *Selected Works of Marx and Engels* has recently been published by Chikumashobo.

Japanese Marx scholarship has probably been influenced by the tradition of philological scrutiny applied to Chinese classical literature. Such an approach has been applied to the *Economic-Philosophical Manuscripts of 1844,* in particular, to analyzing the sequence of Marx's reflections on political economy (where he drew on James Mill) and on Hegel's philosophy.[4]

The late Wataru Hiromatsu's pioneering 1974 edition of *The German Ideology* in the original German text and Japanese translation has been reprinted.[5] It has prompted a reconsideration of the *MEGA2* version of that text, based on the principle that a key prerequisite to editing manuscripts is to put their contents in the correct writing order. In 2002, Masato Kobayashi published a Japanese revised version grounded in this approach.[6] Four years earlier, Tadashi Shibuya had already published an edition[7] (acknowledged by Kobayashi in his Afterword) based on photocopies of the manuscripts at the International Institute for Social History in Amsterdam.

Japanese Marx scholars have contributed greatly to the *MEGA2* edition of *Capital.* Izumi Omura's *The New* MEGA *and the Genesis of Marx's* Capital[8] is a typical philological work. Omura introduces the significance of the *MEGA2,* details philologically the way *Capital* was composed, clarifies the writing order of the 1861–63 manuscripts,

---

2. Tatsuru Uchida and Yasuhiro Ishikawa, *Let Us Read Marx, Young People* (Tokyo: Kamogawashuppan, 2010). All Japanese titles are given here in English.
3. Karl Marx, *Economic-Philosophical Manuscripts of 1844,* trans. Hiroshi Hasegawa (Tokyo: Kobunsha, 2010).
4. See Ryuji Yamanaka, *The Paris Manuscripts* (Tokyo: Ochanomizushobo, 2006); also the review article by Hiroshi Uchida, *Associe,* No.17 (2006), which proves that Yamanaka's edition is philologically and theoretically correct, rejecting the *MEGA2* version.
5. *The German Ideology* (Tokyo: Kawadeshoboshinsha, 2006). In 1965 as a graduate student at Tokyo University, Hiromatsu had published a provocative article, "The Editorial Problems of *The German Ideology,*" in *Materialism Studies,* in which he condemned Adoratskii's edition of *The German Ideology* as "forgery." He gave a detailed critique of the then prevailing version and proposed a new edition. Most Marx scholars in Japan kept a shocked silence; only a few responded positively.
6. *The German Ideology* (Tokyo: Iwanamishoten, 2002).
7. *The German Ideology* (Tokyo: Shinnihonshuppan, 1998).
8. Izumi Omura, *The New* MEGA *and the Genesis of Marx's* Capital (Tokyo: Hassakusha, 1998).

and critically researches Engels' edition of *Capital I* and *III*.[9] A similar publication is Keizo Hayasawa's *The Genesis of Volume II of* Capital *and the New* MEGA.[10] This book draws on Engels' letters to show how Engels edited the 1884–85 manuscripts for Volume II.

Akihiro Matoba's *New Translation of the Communist Manifesto*[11] is significant because it is based on the original London 1848 (Burghard) edition, without the name of the author. It includes a long introduction and many valuable documents, making it an exceptional contribution to worldwide Marx scholarship.

Japanese Marx scholarship is not limited to philological research; it also addresses theoretical issues. The tragic outcome of the Soviet model of "socialism" compels us to reconsider the nature of transitional post-capitalist society. Minoru Tabata's *Marx and Association: Rereading Marx*[12] is a response to this imperative. Tabata shifts the focus from "socialism" or "communism" to Marx's frequently invoked concept of "association" (*Assoziation*; *Verein freier Menschen*). He finds that Japanese translations of the German *Marx-Engels Werke* gave "association" 20 different meanings. The translators were unaware that Marx's image of post-capitalist society centered on the idea of "association" because they did their work under the influence of Soviet political authority.

Tabata finds that Marx first used the word "association" in order to redefine the 1789 Declaration of the Rights of Man on the basis of Rousseau's theory of association as body politic. This raises the issue of the relationship between democracy and association. Marx and Engels, in *The German Ideology*, discuss the association of individuals, pointing out that in bourgeois society association takes the antagonistic forms of selfish competition and bureaucratic rule – both of which appear as "illusory association."

Real forms of association are evolving. For instance, the Japanese Constitution (Art. 21) guarantees "freedom of association" – long a goal of workers' struggles. People also unite across borders. Marx emphasizes that as factory workers are brought together and trained to increase capitalist profit, they gradually acquire "general intellect"

9. Omura also helped edit the MEGA2 version of *Capital II* (Berlin: Akademie Verlag, 2008). The 1868–81 manuscripts for Volume II, as published in *MEGA2*, have also been studied by Teinosuke Otani and Kenji Mori.
10. Keizo Hayasawa, *The Genesis of Volume II of* Capital *and the New* MEGA (Sendai: Tohoku University Press, 2004).
11. *New Translation of the Communist Manifesto*, trans. Akihiro Matoba (Tokyo: Sakuhinsha, 2010).
12. Minoru Tabata, *Marx and Association: Rereading Marx* (Tokyo: Shinsensha, 1994).

and become aware that the productive power of capital belongs to them. They then begin to associate mutually. In the 1840s Marx had not yet developed the concept of association, but when he considered financial credit in the 1864–65 manuscripts for *Capital III*, he identified the important concept of cooperative society (*Genossenschaft*) as a possible transitional form toward post-capitalist society. The critical point is how the associated people, who want to be free individuals, manage to control and adjust between production, exchange, distribution and consumption.

As is well-known among Marx scholars, Marx conceived the transition from capitalist to post-capitalist society in three stages: (i) *individual* private *property*, (ii) *capitalist* private *property*, and (iii) re-establishment (*Wiederherstellung*) of *individual property*, based on (a) cooperation among free workers and (b) co-possession (*Mitbesitz*)[13] of means of production produced by land and labor, i.e., the "associated" (post-capitalist) mode of production. Through (iii), Marx anticipates the society of "free individuals" mentioned in the *Grundrisse*. Tabata's research on Marx's idea of association is theoretical, but the concept has practical implications.

Marx for the 21st Century, edited by Hiroshi Uchida, has been published in English with an introduction by Terrell Carver.[14] It summarizes Marx studies in Japan since 1990, examining the relevance of Marx scholarship from a 21st-century perspective. Topics discussed include modernity, political economy, Marx's theory of history, Marx and Keynes, distributive justice, the environmental crisis, the concept of civil society, and Japanese cultural eclecticism, as well as a number of philological explorations. Of particular interest is the chapter in which Kunihiko Uemura takes issue with the frequent characterization

13. The late Motonobu Hironishi's book, *The Mistranslation of Marx's* Capital (Tokyo: Seiyusha, 1966), now re-published (Tokyo: Kobushishobo, 2002), is an extraordinarily important contribution to exact comprehension of Marx's legal terminologies. It uncovers many misunderstandings and mistranslations of Marx texts in Japan, which may also be found in other countries. Hironishi distinguishes, based on his precise knowledge of property law, between *Gesamtbesitz* (collective possession), *Mitbesitz* (co-possession) and *Gemeinbesitz* (possession in common); Marx himself was ambivalent regarding the three terms in Germanic law. Hironishi argues that re-establishment of individual property is nothing but the individual sharing of corporate stock under terms of equality between manager and worker.
14. Hiroshi Uchida (ed.), *Marx for the 21st Century* (London: Routledge, 2006). Chapter authors include Kunihiko Uemura, Makoto Itoh, Hiroshi Uchida, Masanori Sasaki, Daisuke Arie, Hideaki Kudo, Makoto Nishibe, Hiroshi Mizuta, Shoken Mawatari, Akitoshi Suzuki, Makoto Noguchi, Akihiro Matoba, Koichi Takakusagi, and Tadashi Shibuya.

of Marx (in post-colonial debates) as narrowly modernist and Eurocentric, noting that Marx may even have forecast contemporary Chinese development. Also noteworthy are Makoto Ito's reflections on the experience of central planning and the possible relevance of Piero Sraffa's ideas to the development of China's "socialist market economy."

Among Japanese works published in English, Takahisa Oishi's *The Unknown Marx*[15] is a detailed study of the *Economic-Philosophical Manuscripts of 1844*. Oishi rejects the traditional misunderstanding of Marx's thought that prevails even now. He focuses on Marx's early critique of national (political) economy in contrast with Ricardo and Proudhon, arguing that the totality of Marx's thought had been established in the 1840s. We may note, however, that even in *The Poverty of Philosophy* (1847) Marx had not yet fully elaborated his theory of capital accumulation.

Yutaka Nagahara's uniquely titled book, *We, or the Defective Existences,*[16] is an attempt to philosophize the late Kozo Uno's principles of economics. "Defective existences" refers to people who are deprived, through commoditization, of human nature and of nature itself. Uno posits the *unnaturalness* (*muri* in Japanese) of the commoditization of labor power. Nagahara further argues that commoditization has shaped not only labor power, but also woman as producer of future labor power, and finally earth itself as an instrument of production. Nagahara's core problematic is the methodological relationship of Uno to Marx. Uno utilizes Marx's "descending method" - mentioned in the "1857 Introduction" to the *Grundrisse* - for abstracting in two contexts: (1) nationality of capitalism (English capitalism being the classical model for Marx), and (2) distinction of logical stages - from commodity to money, and from money to capital. The latter distinction determines the starting point of what Marx called (in the same "1857 Introduction") the "ascending method," which finds capitalist reproduction of commodity implicit in commodity. Thus, Nagahara tries to develop Uno's method as a "circular system of description."

Norihiko Hiyama's *Philosophy of Abstract Human Labor*[17] is a defense of the late Wataru Hiromatsu's value theory as expressed in his book, *The Philosophy of Marx's* Capital.[18] The Uno school and the

15. Takahisa Oishi, *The Unknown Marx* (London: Macmillan, 2001).
16. Yutaka Nagahara, *We, or the Defective Existences* (Tokyo: Seidosha, 2008).
17. Norihiko Hiyama, *Philosophy of Abstract Human Labor* (Tokyo: Ochanomizushobo, 2006).
18. Wataru Hiromatsu, *The Philosophy of Marx's* Capital (Tokyo: Keisoshobo, 1987).

Hiromatsu school have been debating what is the appropriate value theory. Kozo Uno argued that money is generated by the *exchange relationship* between commodity owners who each want to satisfy their respective desires through the consumption of use-values. Contrarily, Hiromatsu insisted that money originates not in the *exchange process*, but rather as a *value form*. His argument presumes (i) commodity agents whose consciousness is reified, so that they cannot recognize their own interests, and (ii) a transcendental cognitive subject that observes the situation of the commodity agents and takes the role of settling the *aporia* (difficulty) that affects them.

Marx carefully points out that the valuation of a given commodity in terms of other commodities can never be definitive, because value is *abstract generality* (it cannot be expressed completely with *concrete individuals*). Hiyama, by contrast, thinks that value can be fully expressed with the concrete. The impossibility of such complete expression had already been noted by Aristotle; in order to settle Aristotle's *aporia*, Kant limits the sphere of transcendental reason, rejecting the notion that it can be fully grounded by empirical data. Though Hiromatsu's transcendental subject is expected to overcome that impossibility, it is just a replacement of the *aporia*.[19]

Marx's Theory of the Genesis of Money[20] by the late Samezo Kuruma is the English translation of a work whose Japanese title was *Theory of the Value-Form & Theory of the Exchange Process.*[21] In this exceptionally incisive work, Kuruma pays careful attention to Marx's crucial sentence, "The difficulty lies not in comprehending that money is a commodity, but in discovering *how, why,* and *through what* a commodity is money." Probing the theoretical implications, Kuruma traces the genealogy of money systematically, starting from simple commodity, via value-form, via fetish character of commodity, to exchange-process. In this perspective, Marx's *how* refers to Section 3 of Chapter I of *Capital I, why* to section 4, and *through what* to Chapter 2, respectively.

Overall, Japanese Marx studies have made many important contributions. The present survey suggests three observations. The first concerns *The German Ideology*. Somehow disputes over *The German Ideology* have focused disproportionately on philological editorial issues,

---

19. See the review of Hiyama's book by Hiroshi Uchida, *Associe*, No. 19 (2007).
20. Samezo Kuruma, *Marx's Theory of the Genesis of Money* (Denver: Outskirts Press, 2009).
21. Samezo Kuruma, *Theory of the Value-Form & Theory of the Exchange Process* (Tokyo: Iwanamishoten, 1957).

disregarding the deeper question of why Marx referred to that work (in his 1859 preface to the *Critique of Political Economy*) as establishing the theoretical basis for his materialist view of history. The reason may lie in the way in which he there depicted – citing changes in production methods – the historical stages leading from primitive society up to capitalism via three intermediate social formations. His next task would be to lay bare the evolution of capitalism itself.

The second point relates to the study of present-day capitalism. There is a pressing need to investigate the nature and impact of new forms of capitalist organization, including those arising from digital technology and bio-engineering.

The third point is practical. Most of the discoveries of Japanese Marx scholarship have remained unknown overseas, because the Japanese language is essentially local. If the works are to contribute to worldwide Marx study, they must be quickly translated into other languages, or else Japanese Marx scholars will have to write their articles and books directly in English.

Notes on Contributors

Kevin B. Anderson, University of California (USA), author of *Lenin, Hegel, and Western Marxism* (University of Illinois Press, 1995) and of *Marx at the Margins* (University of Chicago Press, 2010). <kanderson@soc.ucsb.edu>

Paul Blackledge, Leeds Metropolitan University (England), author of *Reflections on the Marxist Theory of History* (Manchester University Press, 2006) and of *Marxism and Ethics* (SUNY Press, forthcoming 2011). <P.Blackledge@leedsmet.ac.uk>

Armando Boito, Universidade Estadual de Campinas (Brazil), author of *Política neoliberal e sindicalismo no Brasil* (Xamã, 2002) and of *Estado, política e classes sociais* (Unesp, 2007). <armando.boito@gmail.com>

Terrell Carver, University of Bristol (England), author of *The Postmodern Marx* (Manchester University Press, 1998) and of "*The German Ideology* Never Took Place," in *History of Political Thought*, vol. 31, no. 1 (2010). <tfcarver@earthlink.net>

Paresh Chattopadhyay, University of Quebec (Canada), author of *The Marxian Category of Capital and the Soviet Experience* (Praeger, 1994). <paresh.chattopadhyay@internet.uqam.ca>

George Comninel, York University (Canada), author of *Rethinking the French Revolution: Marxism and the Revisionist Challenge* (Verso, 1987) and "Historical Materialist Sociology and Revolutions," in G. Delanty and E. Isin (eds), *Handbook of Historical Sociology* (Sage, 2003). <comninel@yorku.ca>

Jean-Numa Ducange, University of Rouen (France), editor of Karl Marx, *Le 18 Brumaire de Louis Bonaparte* (Livre de poche, 2007) and Karl Marx, *Critique du programme de Gotha* (Éditions sociales, 2008). <jean-numa.ducange@univ-rouen.fr>

Jan Hoff, Ph.D at Freie Universität Berlin (Germany), author of *Karl Marx und die „ricardianischen Sozialisten"* (PapyRossa, 2008) and of *Marx global. Zur Entwicklung des internationalen Marx-Diskurses seit 1965* (Akademie, 2009). <JMHoff@web.de>

Daping Hu, Nanjing University (China), co-author of *the History and Logic of Western Marxist Philosophy* (Nanjing University Press, 2002) and author of *Back to Engels* (Jiangsu People Publishing House, 2010). <hudacn@nju.edu.cn>

Socialism and Democracy, Vol.24, No.3, November 2010, pp.212–213

ISSN 0885-4300 print/ISSN 1745-2635 online

DOI: 10.1080/08854300.2010.518416

Seongjin Jeong, Gyeongsang National University (South Korea), co-editor of *Marxist Perspectives on South Korea in the Global Economy* (Ashgate, 2007) and co-author of *Ideas of Alter-Globalization Movements* (Hanul, 2010) [in Korean]. <seongjin@gnu.ac.kr>

Michael A. Lebowitz, emeritus, Simon Fraser University (Canada), author of *Beyond Capital: Marx's Political Economy of the Working Class* (Palgrave-Macmillan, 2003) and of *The Socialist Alternative: Real Human Development* (Monthly Review Press, 2010). <mlebowit@sfu.ca>

Luiz Eduardo Motta, Federal University of Rio de Janeiro (Brazil), author of "Poulantzas e o Direito," in *Dados*, vol. 53, no. 1 (2010). <luizpmotta@ig.com.br>

Marcello Musto, York University (Canada), editor of *Karl Marx's Grundrisse: Foundations of the Critique of Political Economy 150 Years Later* (Routledge, 2008) and of *The Marx Revival: Essays on the Critique of Contemporary Society* (Palgrave, forthcoming 2011). <www.marcellomusto.com>

Vesa Oittinen, University of Helsinki (Finland), author of *Spinozistische Dialektik* (Peter Lang, 1994) and editor of *Max Weber and Russia* (Aleksanteri Institute, 2010). <vesa.oittinen@helsinki.fi>

Gianfranco Ragona, Turin University (Italy), author of *Maximilien Rubel (1905–1996). Etica, marxologia e critica del marxismo* (FrancoAngeli, 2003) and of *Gustav Landauer. Anarchico, ebreo, tedesco* (Editori Riuniti University Press, 2010). <gianfranco.ragona@unito.it>

Francisco T. Sobrino, Editorial Board of *Herramienta* (Argentina). <fsobrino@dysyn.com>

Hiroshi Uchida, emeritus, Senshu University (Japan), author of *Marx's Grundrisse and Hegel's Logic* (Routledge, 1988) and editor of *Marx for the 21st Century* (Routledge, 2005). <bqe03244@nifty.com>

Victor Wallis, Berklee College of Music (USA), editor of *Socialism and Democracy* and author of "Workers' Control and Revolution," in D. Azzellini and I. Ness (eds), *Ours to Master and Own: Workers Councils from the Commune to the Present* (Haymarket Books, 2011). <zendive@aol.com>

Rick Wolff, New School University (USA), co-author (with Stephen Resnick) of *New Departures in Marxian Theory* (Routledge, 2006), and author of *Capitalism Hits the Fan* (Interlink Books, 2010). <www.rdwolff.com>